Without You,
There Is No Us

Without You, There Is No Us

*MY TIME WITH THE SONS OF
NORTH KOREA'S ELITE*

Suki Kim

CROWN PUBLISHERS
New York

Published in the United States by Crown Publishers, an imprint of the Crown Publishing Group, a division of Random House LLC, a Penguin Random House Company, New York.

www.crownpublishing.com

CROWN and the Crown colophon are registered trademarks of Random House LLC.

Library of Congress Cataloging-in-Publication Data
Kim, Suki, 1970–
Without you, there is no us : my time with the sons
of North Korea's elite / Suki Kim.—First edition.
pages cm
1. Kim, Suki, 1970–   2. English teachers—Korea (North)—
Biography.   3. Korea (North)—Politics and government—
2011–   4. Korea (North)—Social conditions—21st century.
5. Elite (Social sciences)—Korea (North)   6. Education—
Government policy—Korea (North)   I. Title.
PE64.K45A3 2014
818'.603—dc23
[B]   2014012730

ISBN 978-0-307-72065-8
eBook ISBN 978-0-307-72067-2

Printed in the United States of America

Map by Mapping Specialists
Jacket design by Na Kim

Photo on page 3: Sunchon Airport, Pyongyang, 2002. The airport greeter holds a "Sun of the 21st Century" sign to commemorate Kim Jong-il's sixtieth birthday.

Photo on page 155: Students at PUST taking their final exam in December 2011.

10 9 8 7 6 5 4 3

First Edition

FOR MY MOTHER
AND MY SISTER

Without You, There Is No Us

Prologue

TIME THERE SEEMED TO PASS DIFFERENTLY. WHEN YOU ARE shut off from the world, every day is exactly the same as the one before. This sameness has a way of wearing down your soul until you become nothing but a breathing, toiling, consuming thing that awakes to the sun and sleeps at the dawning of the dark. The emptiness runs deep, deeper with each slowing day, and you become increasingly invisible and inconsequential. That's how I felt at times, a tiny insect circling itself, only to continue, and continue. There, in that relentless vacuum, nothing moved. No news came in or out. No phone calls to or from anyone. No emails, no letters, no ideas not prescribed by the regime. Thirty missionaries disguised as teachers and 270 male North Korean students and me, the sole writer disguised as a missionary disguised as a teacher. Locked in that prison disguised as a campus in an empty Pyongyang suburb, heavily guarded around the clock, all we had was one another.

PART ONE

Anti-Atlantis

1

AT 12:45 P.M. ON MONDAY, DECEMBER 19, 2011, THERE WAS A knock at my door. My heart sank. I knew who would be there. I ignored it and continued shoving my clothes into the suitcase. The knock came again. She knew that I was inside, and she was not going to go away. Finally I stopped what I was doing and opened the door. There stood Martha, a lanky twenty-four-year-old British girl with glasses, with whom I had been sharing teaching duties. "You must come to the meeting right now," she said. I sighed, feeling the weight of the past six months there among thirty Christian missionaries, now gathered in secret for the pre-Christmas prayer meeting. Then she whispered, "He's dead," pointing at the ceiling. I thought that she meant God, and I was momentarily confused. I have never read the Bible, and my family is largely atheist. Then she said, "*him,*" and I realized she meant the main God in this world: Kim Jong-il.

Was it fate that my North Korean experience began with his birthday and ended with his death? It was February 2002 when I first glimpsed the forbidden city of Pyongyang as part of a Korean-American delegation visiting for Kim Jong-il's sixtieth birthday celebrations. It was only a few months after 9/11, and George W. Bush had just christened that country part of an "axis of evil," so it was an inauspicious time for a single American woman to cross its border with a group of strangers.

Over the next nine years, with each implausible crossing of its immutable border, I became further intoxicated by this unknown and unknowable place. This isolated nation existed under an entirely different system from the rest of the world, so different that when I arrived in 2011, I found myself in "Juche Year 100." The Democratic People's Republic of Korea (DPRK) follows a different calendar system, which counts time from the birth of their original Great Leader, Kim Il-sung, who died in 1994; *Juche*, which roughly means "self-reliance," is at the core of North Korea's foundational philosophy. Almost every book I ever saw there was written by or about the Great Leader. The state-run media, including the newspaper *Rodong Sinmun* and Chosun Central TV, reported almost exclusively on the Great Leader. Almost every film, every song, every monument heralded the miraculous achievements of the Great Leader, the role passed down through three generations, from Kim Il-sung and Kim Jong-il to Kim Jong-un, who was twenty-nine when he assumed power in 2012 and became the world's youngest head of state. It has been reported that every home in the country is fitted with a speaker through which government propaganda can be broadcast, and that more than thirty-five thousand statues of the Great Leaders are scattered across the country.

But while the regime dabbles with nuclear weapons, provoking repeated United Nations sanctions, the people of North Korea suffer. The 1990s famine (known as the Arduous March) killed millions, as much as a tenth of the entire population, and even now the World Food Program reports that 80 percent of North Koreans experience food shortages and hunger. It is estimated that forced labor, executions, and concentration camps have claimed over a million lives since 1948. According to the latest UN report, the DPRK maintains some twenty gulags holding some 120,000 political prisoners (Human Rights Watch estimates 200,000). These numbers are inevitably approximate since nothing there is verifiable. Almost no North Koreans are allowed out—defectors risk execution—and almost no foreigners are allowed in except those on packaged tours, most holding European passports, and they get to see only what is allowed. In this global age of information, where secrets have become an anachronism, North Korea stands apart.

My obsession with this troubling country—because it indeed became an obsession—was based on more than just journalistic interest. The first time I entered North Korea, I was not sure what a "delegate" was and did not know much at all about the pro–Kim Jong-il group I was traveling with. This makes me sound either extremely irreverent or extremely young, but I was neither. My ignorance was willful. Since getting a visa into the country was so difficult, I thought it was best not to appear too inquisitive. But there was something else, too: a part of me, a very insistent voice inside, did not want to know those details. For those of us who grew up in 1970s South Korea, anything to do with North Korea is accompanied by a certain foreboding. And for those of us whose family members were abducted into North Korea, this fear runs still deeper. If I had known as much as I do now, more than a decade later, I doubt I would have made that first, fateful trip. But I did get on a flight from JFK, on Korean Air, one of the world's most modern and luxurious airlines, and then almost twenty hours later, via Seoul and then Beijing, boarded North Korea's state-owned Air Koryo, where the only reading material was a magazine about the Great Leader. And I would cross that same border into Pyongyang repeatedly for the next nine years.

Every story has its origin in a time that came before. My obsession had its roots in the year 1945, decades before I was even born. It was then, when the five-thousand-year-old kingdom of Korea was divided by the Allies who liberated it from Japan, that everything went wrong. And since then everything has continued to be wrong, and nothing, not even the three-year-long war that began in 1950, has made much difference.

Or maybe my obsession became inevitable when I was a child growing up in South Korea. The years I lived there remain unnervingly still, pristinely intact in my mind. As I get older, the memory of those years grows bigger, each nook casting a longer shadow. Such is the condition of a first-generation immigrant for whom everything is separated into *now* and *then*, into *before the move* and *after*. The ocean that separates the adoptive home and the old country also divides time.

I was just thirteen when we came to America. The early eighties in South Korea was a time of political unrest and economic upheaval, and my father's businesses—from the shipping company and mining ventures to the hotels—collapsed rapidly. Bankruptcy in South Korea was punishable by a hefty jail term, and we fled our home in the dead of night. Like many new immigrants to America, my family was now poor and kept moving—from Queens to Jersey City to the Bronx to Fort Lee. I grasped few of the vast changes that seemed to have occurred overnight in my physical surroundings. I knew that I was no longer in Korea, and yet it was beyond my comprehension that this loss of home was permanent. Another foreign concept that took time to absorb was that I was now *Asian*, a term that I had heard mentioned only in a social studies class. Back home, yellow was the color of the forsythia that bloomed every spring along the fence that separated our estate from the houses down the hill; I certainly never thought of my skin as being the same shade. Those years were also marked by silence. My mother tongue was suddenly gone, replaced by unfamiliar sounds called English. It seemed a miracle when I took the SAT and made it to college.

After graduation, I spent a couple of years in London, searching for something I could never quite name, then returned to New York to a series of part-time jobs and a rent-stabilized apartment in the East Village, where I spent my twenties. But I never felt at home there either and kept subletting my apartment and taking off, often on meager writing fellowships that required me to live in some remote place, whether it be a hundred-year-old cabin in New Hampshire or an empty room facing a desert hill in Wyoming. There were no cell phones then, and I was always calling my parents collect. I remember getting off a Greyhound bus one afternoon and standing in a phone booth outside a coffee shop in Taos, New Mexico, and my father, on the line from New Jersey, ending the call with: "If you keep moving like this, one day you'll be too far away to come back."

During those itinerant years, I once found myself on the Ligurian coast of Italy, which sounded better than it felt. It was a place whose awe-inspiring beauty so oddly failed to touch me that for years afterward I would look for an opportunity to drop the word *Liguria* in conversations, such as "I wore this dress often that autumn I was living in Liguria" or "I never finished that novel I was working on in Liguria," as if to remind myself that I had spent nearly two months there.

Some experiences are like that. You live through them, and

yet you aren't quite there. Korea was the opposite. My first thirteen years remained real for me like nothing since. When you
lose your home at a young age, you spend your life looking for
its replacement. Over the years, I have never considered any
apartment more than temporary. Each one remains spare, with
bare walls and no personal touches—as though I might need to
grab everything in a few seconds and run. People often ask me
where my things are. The question always brings me back to
South Korea; in my mind, I finally return. I put down my suitcase at the base of the incredibly long flight of steps I have never
forgotten and look up at my childhood home, towering above.

Strangely, in 2002, when I visited Pyongyang for the first
time, I felt more at home than I had since I left Seoul as a child.
There was a sense of recognition. The past was all right there
before me: generations of Koreans separated by division; decades of longing, loss, hurt, regret, guilt. I identified with it in
a way that I could never shake off. I thought that if only I could
understand the place, then I could find a way to help put the
fragments back together. Like most Koreans, whether from the
North or South, I dreamed, perhaps irrationally, of reunification. I returned repeatedly until 2011.

I am often asked, "Which Korea do you come from? North
or South?" It is a nonsensical question. The chance of me or
any Korean out and about in the world being from the North
is almost nil. Virtually no one gets out of North Korea. It is a
locked nation. Locked away from South Korea, from the rest of
the world, from those of us whose families got trapped there. It
is the sort of a lock for which there is no "open sesame," and the
world seems to have forgotten why it was sealed tight to begin
with and who threw away the key.

My Korea is the South—the industrial, overachieving, better half that spewed out Hyundai and Samsung and in the six

decades since the bloody war has established itself as the fifteenth richest country in the world. But the South is never just the South. Its very existence conjures up the unmentionable North, which, with its habitual nuclear threats and the antics of its bizarre dictator, casts a shadow far beyond its own peninsula. In recent years, North Korea has steadily become a siren for the hankering mind, making outsiders wait and guess and then wait some more, indefinitely.

Both my parents hail from families separated by the partition. And it is really the unrequited heartbreak of those separations—a heartbreak that lasts generations—that brought me North. If this were the sort of story that invites readers to nod with empathy and walk away both satisfied and educated, I would say that I traveled full circle. But in truth my journey was barely half a circle, a sad one that could never be completed, because those who were at the center of the harrowing history are almost certainly long dead, or old and dying, and time is running out before their stories are lost in the dust of the past.

The Korean War lasted three years, with millions either dead or separated. It never really ended but instead paused in the 1953 armistice exactly where it began, with Koreas on both sides of the 38th parallel. Historians often refer to it as the "forgotten war," but no Korean considers it forgotten. Theirs is not a culture of forgetting. The war is everywhere in today's Koreas.

There is, for example, the story of my father's young female cousins, nursing students aged seventeen and eighteen, who disappeared during the war. Decades later, in the 1970s, their mother, my father's aunt, received a letter from North Korea via Japan, the only contact her daughters ever made with her, and from that moment on, she was summoned to the Korean Central Intelligence Agency every few months on suspicion of espionage until she finally left South Korea for good and died in San Antonio, Texas. The girls were never heard from again. And there was my uncle, my mother's brother, who was just seventeen when he was abducted by North Korean soldiers at the start of the war, in June 1950. He was never seen again. He might or might not have been taken to Pyongyang, and it was this suspended state of not knowing that drove my mother's mother nearly crazy, and my mother, and to some degree me, who inherited their sorrow.

Stories such as these abound in South Korea, and probably North Korea, if its people were allowed to tell them. Separation haunts the affected long after the actual incident. It is a perpetual act of violation. You know that the missing are there, just a few hours away, but you cannot see them or write to them or call them. It could be your mother trapped on the other side of the border. It could be your lover whom you will long for the rest of your life. It could be your child whom you cannot get to, although he calls out your name and cries himself to sleep every night. From Seoul, Pyongyang looms like a shadow, about 120 miles away, so close but impossible to touch. Decades of such longing sicken a nation. The loss is remembered, and re-membered, like an illness, a heartbreak from which there is no healing, and you are left to wonder what happened to the life you were supposed to have together. For those of us raised by mothers and fathers who experienced such trauma firsthand, it is impossible not to continue this remembering.

I FIRST BECAME aware of the Pyongyang University of Science and Technology (PUST) by chance. In February 2008, I was assigned by *Harper's* magazine to follow the New York Philharmonic to Pyongyang, where they were to perform in a concert.

About a hundred foreign correspondents rushed to be a part of it. Not being a real journalist—at least I did not consider myself one—I dreaded the prospect of covering the DPRK alongside so many veterans, until I realized how little they knew of North Korea, and how little they managed to find out. A cable news anchor hosted a special in which she watched the concert on TV with an "average" North Korean family that had been selected by the government. She then asked "random" North Koreans, also selected by the regime, questions such as "Do you think America is your sworn enemy?" and taught one interviewee the word *friend*, which the woman dutifully repeated.

As a prelude to the media extravaganza in Pyongyang, I attended a party in Beijing. (Though Pyongyang is only a couple of hours' drive from Seoul, you have to go through China to enter it.) The party was held at the U.S. embassy in honor of the Philharmonic's patrons. They were a colorful bunch—ranging from the founder of Compaq computers to a PR guru for the NFL to a Japanese countess from Venice, Italy. The women were dressed in furs. Twenty-five of them had donated $50,000 each for the novelty of such a trip, and they were visibly excited. One of them told me giddily that she had never even been to South Korea, but here she was going to the North! Another told me that he really enjoyed going to "backward" places, and there were no more "backward" places left except for North Korea. A few others urged that I must, absolutely must, meet a certain Mrs. Gund, who turned out to be a Korean Brazilian woman around my age whose husband had at one time appeared on the *Forbes* list of the wealthiest men in the world.

It was Mrs. Gund who mentioned that an international university was being set up in Pyongyang, and that the faculty would all be foreigners. It seemed improbable, but when you follow North Korea, you become used to unlikely scenarios. I asked for more information, and she shrugged and told me to email a certain President Kim, the head of the entire operation.

President Kim turned out to be James Kim, an evangelical Christian Korean-American, and a quick Internet search brought up interviews with him about a similar college he had set up in the early 1990s in Yanji, China, called Yanbian University of Science and Technology (YUST). In one of the interviews, Kim said that he had raised $10 million from evangelical churches worldwide to construct the school in Pyongyang. When asked whether any of the money had made its way to the DPRK's regime, he claimed to have brought all the building materials and equipment in from China. Running the school would be quite expensive, with heating costs alone estimated to be at least $1,500 per day. In response to a question about who would fund its operations, he demurred and referred to the "bank of heaven."

Although the school was still under construction, I immediately submitted an application to teach there, and for the next couple of years, I exchanged emails about it with various people in China, South Korea, and the United States. I knew little except that they were spokespeople for President Kim, who, according to my principal contact, Joan, was very busy traveling. Joan, who was based at the YUST campus, wrote long, digressive emails about the Yanji flowers blooming in the spring and the busy schedule she was keeping in the grace of the Lord overseeing the "project."

For the first year of our correspondence, the project seemed vague at best. Once, I was contacted by a Korean-American librarian from a university in Illinois, who invited me to a fundraising event for PUST at a church in Evanston. About fifty or so Asian students—mostly Korean-American or Korean—were there, and for about an hour they prayed and cried. Strange as it was, the event seemed to legitimize the existence of the school.

Finally, in December 2009, a call came from President Kim's Seoul office, telling me to get ready to go to Pyongyang in a few months. No one ever questioned me about my faith, and I did not volunteer any information. I received almost no instructions. What should I bring? How would I be able to keep in touch with those at home? Such questions went unanswered.

Then came the boat incident. On March 26, 2010, the South Korean Navy ship *Cheonan* sank off the country's west coast, and forty-six sailors died. An international investigation revealed that the ship had been blown up by a North Korean submarine torpedo. Inter-Korean relations chilled, and the door that seemed to have opened a crack shut. I doubted that the school would be operating anytime soon, or that anyone would be able to get a visa. The project was on pause again.

At the end of that year, however, PUST finally opened. Somehow my application had been lost, they said, and they had assembled the teaching staff for the first semester from those at their YUST branch. Be ready to come in the spring, Joan wrote.

Then silence again until April 2011, when an email with the subject line "Purchase List" appeared in my in-box. My visa, once approved for "entry," had to be stamped by as many as thirty-five government agencies within North Korea to be approved for "release." President Kim had asked that the process be expedited or waived altogether for the PUST teachers, and they were waiting for a new law to pass for this to happen. "A new law? That could take months, even years!" I said via Skype, but Joan assured me that in North Korea such a thing could happen in a matter of days and told me to start packing.

Joan said that I would need a refrigerator, as well as toilet paper and butter. Was there no way of getting those things there? I wondered. You bring everything to Pyongyang, I was told. I wired money to Joan so that she could purchase a refrigerator and have it shipped from China, but I was not sure whether a block of frozen butter would survive the long-haul flights from New York to Pyongyang. There were so many things, it turned out, that I could not do without. You would think that, being a writer, I would have put books at the top of my list, but in fact, books were the last things on my mind. The things I packed were more basic: an extra pair of glasses, disposable contact lenses, sanitary napkins, ibuprofen, vitamins and antibiotics of all kinds, plus as many protein bars as I could jam in my suitcases.

Visas to North Korea are almost always issued on the eve of the visitor's entry date, and plane tickets from Beijing to Pyongyang can only be purchased with a visa in hand. This meant that I had to leave for Asia immediately and be on call—which is how I found myself stuck in Seoul for the next seven weeks waiting for my visa, which had been blocked at the last minute. The wait came with no excuse or explanation. In any negotiation, North Korea has absolute power regarding who does what, and at what price, because there is always a price.

THAT SUMMER, MONSOON came early. In that part of Asia, rain begins one day and does not stop for a month straight. This usually happens in July, but it had begun by mid-June that year, and I was miserable. I had already been waiting more than a month for North Korea to approve my visa when the rain began. I would be awoken at dawn by the pelting sound against the windowpane, my hair soaked from humidity. Despite air-conditioning, I was perpetually sweaty and sluggish, which only added to my feelings of helplessness. The year had started badly and was turning worse. I had recently been through a horrible breakup that came on the heels of nine blighting years.

Seoul was not easy either. My sister, who had always been my emotional rock, had moved back there from New York. She was not well, and my morning ritual consisted of cutting up organic Asian pears and melons for her after soaking them in organic vegetable wash. We were worried about bacteria because her immune system was compromised, and this state of worry was jarring to me since I was the perennial younger sister and had never taken care of her before. In the afternoon, I would accompany her to doctors for checkups, blood tests, or physical therapy. Or I would take her two girls, aged seven and eleven, to band practice and to get their chicken pox shots, the things that moms in all parts of the world do, although I did not fit in among the South Korean moms and was always reminded of the fact that I had never become a mother myself.

I should have been keeping tabs on the breaking news about North Korea, which inevitably concerned the heir apparent Kim Jong-un, whom the foreign media referred to as either "Precious Leader" or "Supreme Leader," but instead I took solace in writing emails to an old lover in Brooklyn with whom I had just reconnected. I knew that I was not ready for another relationship, but I wanted to love him that summer. Nothing distracts a wounded soul during trying circumstances like new love, even the recycled kind, and every night as I willed myself to sleep in that thick, heavy Seoul monsoon, I would remind myself that I had this lover back home, and all I had to do was finish the trip safely so I could get back to him. He did not love me and was perpetually busy, so he wasn't good about answering my needlessly beseeching emails. But he did respond when he felt like it. That summer, in the flooded city of Seoul, his emails were like glimpses of the sun.

Waiting for news of my visa, I often thought about those who had gone missing, my mother's brother and my father's cousins. How their mothers must have waited, and waited, not moving houses after the war for as long as possible so that their sons and daughters could be sure of finding their way back home. Every day, the mothers must have hoped that this would be the day. They must have looked up expectantly each time a doorbell rang. *Perhaps that is my child. Please let it be my child. Yes, it has to be.* Because it is nonsensical, the idea that you would never see your baby again. Because in *our* world nothing is ever lost without a trace.

That summer was also about many other kinds of waiting. I waited for the day when I would stop hurting over my failed engagement. I waited for the man in Brooklyn to email me back with some sign of affection because at that point in my life, I was especially susceptible to kindness. Most of all, I waited for my sister's treatments to be over, so that she wouldn't be in pain. In the midst of all this, I waited to hear about the visa to North Korea, which I believed in the depths of my heart was my way out of whatever I was feeling.

Then in late June, a phone call came. My visa had been cleared and I would be teaching in the summer semester. The orientation would take place in Beijing in three days' time, and by the first of July we would leave for North Korea.

2

For a place shrouded in rumors of violence, Pyong-yang always appears surprisingly gentle, at least at first. This visit, my fourth, was no different. The horizon was empty except for a handful of old airplanes, perched on the tarmac like ancient flies. The surrounding farmland looked as though it belonged in a story about someplace where nothing bad ever happened and the villagers meant you no harm. Against the stark stillness stood a lone airport terminal topped with a giant portrait of Kim Il-sung. In the distance a group of huddled men waited to guide each delegation.

Whenever I come upon the tattered phrase "deafening silence," I recall that initial impression, that quiet wonder upon finally beholding the object of so much fascination. Finding that this modern-day Atlantis, or anti-Atlantis, really exists after all, you want an explanation, an apology, some clarity. Yet there it is, just a tiny airport on the outskirts of a capital city, nothing more or less.

The silence is strange, since wherever else you are in Pyong-yang, your senses are never left in peace. Inevitably music blasts from a speaker nearby. Sometimes it is a love song, sometimes a marching tune, but the topic is always the same. Virtually every building is adorned with a slogan, every TV screen with the same image, the way advertising billboards fill the horizon in Western societies, but in North Korea there is only one product: the Great Leader. Yet beneath such noise is terrifying silence. Everything has been so hushed for decades that if you press your ear to the stillness, you can almost hear the muted cries.

The customs official took my American passport, glanced at it, and asked if I spoke Korean. The North Koreans I had met in the past always seemed proud to be Korean. Despite the war between us that had loomed more than half a century, when Koreans find themselves around Westerners, it is always us against them. When I answered him in Korean, he smiled and let me pass. Immediately we had to give up our passports and cell phones to the minder who was waiting for us. The small airport looked a lot brighter than I remembered, and the baggage carousels were actually moving this time. (The first time I flew into Pyongyang in 2002, soon after the famine, bags had simply been thrown on the floor, and the bathroom was a pitch-dark hole with no toilet paper.)

My fellow teachers and I followed the minder to a bus that had been sent by PUST. About ten minutes beyond downtown Pyongyang, after crossing Chungsong (Loyalty) Bridge and the Taedong River, we took an exit onto a narrow road with farmland on either side. This led to a gate bearing the school's name, with a tiny gatehouse on its left, beyond which the campus came into view. The place was so secluded that it might have been a sanitarium. There was a lot of concrete, and the dull heaviness of the buildings imbued the place with a sense of the forlorn. To the left was a slim, tall stone monument that reached higher than the nearby five-story building topped with massive letters spelling out LONG LIVE GENERAL KIM JONG-IL, THE SUN OF THE 21ST CENTURY! The building contained classrooms, and it was connected by an enclosed walkway to the cafeteria building, which was connected to a health clinic and bathhouse, which were in turn connected to the dormitories, so that the buildings and the walkway formed a sort of horseshoe. The walkways had windows on either side, and it struck me then that there was no privacy here, that anyone's movements were visible. The only structure not connected to the rest was an austere gray building to our right, which stood on its own.

It would not be true to say that a sense of dread came over me the first time I beheld the set of buildings in that isolated compound that was soon to be my refuge and prison. I simply felt nothing, much the way I felt nothing the first time I saw New York at the age of thirteen. That first glimpse comes with no history, no warning. The school was just a school. The students whose faces would fill that 248-acre space with meaning for me were still nowhere to be seen. Instead, I was preoccupied with the logistics of the place. Who approved it and why, and who was here, both to teach and to be taught?

The next morning, my alarm clock went off at 5 a.m., and for a moment I was lost. This happens in any new city, but when that city is Pyongyang, it takes an extra moment to get your bearings. The teachers' dormitories were made up of cookie-cutter, modern two-bedroom apartments, each about five hundred square feet. From the entrance, there were two rooms to the right, both with queen-sized beds, an open kitchen with a dining table, a small living area with a leather couch, a TV, an intercampus phone, almost floor-to-ceiling windows, and a modern bathroom. I had mine all to myself, and it was nicer than almost any dorm room I had lived in.

The first thing I saw when I looked out my fifth-floor window was a plain green stretch of land and two buildings just beyond the campus. One of the buildings was a drab yellow, with a blue roof, and looked a bit like a New England–style barn; the other was a concrete building barricaded by a stone wall. During my entire stay I would never find out what they were, as I learned not to ask many questions.

Fighting off pangs of loneliness and fear, I got up and switched on the kettle, which I had bought in Beijing, and looked for coffee in my suitcase. Over there, coffee will feel like currency, someone had told me, and this was true. I am not loyal to any brand, but in my dormitory at PUST, my Breakfast Blend coffee from Trader Joe's felt like a true luxury, the mark of capitalism, a reminder of the outside world. I added a few drops of the long-lasting milk I had brought with me, which had a pungent, synthetic taste I would never get used to. So I stood there, with my first morning coffee in Pyongyang, looking out at the bleak, unknowable buildings. I felt as far away from everything I knew as if I had been erased overnight.

I had been told that breakfast was between 6:30 and 7:30 in the cafeteria, and when I stepped outside, I could see the cylindrical stone monument towering into the sky in the distance. On either side of the path were tiny orange and pink flowers that looked as generic as the buildings. I saw no one and slowly walked toward the cafeteria, passing three identical-looking student dormitories on my right. The walk took about five minutes, and I would do this three times a day for a month for that summer semester, and more months in the fall, although I did not know then that I would be able to last that long. On my way I saw the Pyongyang skyline, so hazy that I could barely make it out. And on the horizon was a lone smoke stack belching thin, occasional smoke, the only sign of life in that still landscape.

. . .

IT WAS THE kind of a cafeteria you might see anywhere. Past the heavy glass door was a huge hall packed with tables. There was a self-service food station, where students and teachers lined up separately. Breakfast was porridge and boiled eggs. I took a metal tray and was beginning to help myself when I heard my name being shouted from one of the tables.

"Hello, how nice we meet again!" said a man brightly. From his accent, I could tell that he was North Korean. Who could I possibly bump into here? I took a deep breath and turned around, facing a round tanned face and smiling eyes. They all have smiling eyes, the minders, but Mr. Ri stood out. During the New York Philharmonic coverage in 2008, he had been assigned to the foreign journalists, although he shadowed me most of the time as I was the sole Korean-speaking journalist among them and was thus seen as more of a threat. He had been particularly friendly and had spoken to me in casual Korean, talking about his wife, for whom he was trying to quit smoking.

The men I had met there in the past liked cigarettes. American cigarettes, in particular, were a novelty. They would swear that the United States was their number one enemy, and yet carrying a pack of Marlboro Lights seemed to be a sign of privilege and class. Visitors to North Korea often bring cigarettes and whiskey for their minders as a kind of hedge against their eternal watchfulness. I had brought a few cartons on that trip, too, and when I gave them out, whoever was on the receiving end inevitably asked if they were purchased in China or America. They said that there were many fake Marlboro Lights in China.

On the Philharmonic trip, Mr. Ri and I had chatted so effortlessly that at times it was confusing to make sense of our relationship, since his job was to report on me, and my job as a magazine correspondent, reporting on the event, was not all that different. It is remarkable how quickly camaraderie develops when tensions are high.

The thirty-six hours in Pyongyang on that trip were a whirlwind. It turned out that that was the whole point. It was a PR event carefully orchestrated by the DPRK regime, with the American orchestra providing the incidental music. There was nothing any of us could write about except what we were allowed to see, which was a concert like any other, a few staged welcome performances, and the usual tourist sites. It was a lesson in control and manipulation. The real audience was not those in the concert hall but the journalists whose role was to deliver a sanitized version of North Korea to the outside world, and what shocked me was how easily seduced they were. Both CNN and the *New York Times* reported that the performance drew tears from the audience, and soon the major newspapers around the world followed with stories about this successful experiment in cultural diplomacy. Lorin Maazel, then the conductor of the Philharmonic, declared that seventy million Koreans would thank him forever. I witnessed no crying in the audience—all handpicked members of the Party elite—nor did any of the correspondents I spoke to after the performance. The tears I recall from that trip were a different kind.

Although it was my second time visiting North Korea, I burst into tears while saying goodbye to my minder. I was not a journalist on assignment in that moment. Instead I was thinking of my grandmother and my uncle, and my great-aunt and her daughters, and of the millions of Korean lives erased and forgotten. Right there, on the tarmac, before boarding the chartered flight with everyone in our mission, I told Mr. Ri that

I was sick of this division, and that I would probably never see him again because the people of his country were not allowed to leave or even have contact with the rest of the world, that his country was so isolated that even I, a fellow Korean, could only visit it as part of the American delegation, shadowing the American orchestra, and that it broke my heart to see how bad things really were there. I said all this standing on that tarmac, my face covered with tears, the floodgates open after thirty-six hours of enforced silence. This, in hindsight, was thoughtless of me. I was about to climb onto that flight and return to the free world, but he was stuck there, and the other minders saw this encounter. But, surprisingly, tears ran down his face too, along with the faces of two other minders nearby. They said nothing, just cried and cried.

My first reaction to seeing Mr. Ri here, three years later, was that of relief. He had not been punished for crying with me at the airport. He was okay! Then I felt afraid. He had met me as a journalist, so what would he make of the fact that I stood before him as a missionary teacher? It was a mystery to me why I had been allowed in. Joan and President Kim knew that I was a writer, although they thought of me as a novelist, which they must not have considered a threat. But they had only to Google me to find out that I had in fact published a fair number of articles and op-eds about North Korea. The most recent piece had been a feature essay on defection, a taboo topic. But President Kim had also been very interested in the Fulbright organization—which had given me a fellowship—and asked me to arrange a meeting between him and the Seoul division's director, which I did. And I had been referred to him by the powerful Mrs. Gund. Whatever the reason, I had passed their vetting.

Mr. Ri called me over to join him where he was sitting with another man. He looked genuinely happy to see me again, and I also gave him a bright hello.

"How have you been? What brought you here?" he asked.

I played along. "Oh, life . . . I've been teaching since I last met you. First in America, then in Seoul, now Pyongyang." This was mostly true—I taught creative writing. He seemed satisfied with this answer and urged me to eat. The cloudy porridge, or watery boiled rice, tasted like it looked. If Mr. Ri recalled our tears from three years ago, he said nothing. To ease the moment, I acted jolly. The minders liked to talk in circles, to tease and be teased.

"Do I look older?" I asked him. "I guess you can see the full-blown old maid in me now."

"No, still fine. Barely fine. Just hanging in there!" he said. We both laughed, but it felt hollow and did nothing to dispel my feelings of paranoia.

This seemed to be the staff area. Nearby a group of about thirty young women in khaki army uniforms sat hunched over their metal trays. Mr. Ri explained that they were guards to keep us safe. It was hard to believe that these women in their early twenties had been sent to stand guard at PUST, where the students were all male. I felt protective of them, so far from home, so vulnerable, so outnumbered by men. Who were they guarding? The teachers or the students? Or were they more like prison guards, there to make sure we did not escape? For the entire time I was there, I would see them patrolling the campus. I tried to speak to them a few times, but they never replied.

From outside the cafeteria, I heard the sound of a marching song, hollered in unison, and as soon as it ended, dozens of young men poured in. Then more came in, and more, until the cafeteria filled with hundreds of them. They were in their late teens and early twenties, dressed in white or blue dress shirts, black pants, and ties. My first impression was that they looked like an army. The armistice agreement had been signed more than half a century ago, and the rest of the world had moved on. Even most South Koreans had moved on; although there is mandatory military service for all men there, they do not live in a constant state of threat. Here, however, it was as though someone had put his giant thumb on the pause button in 1953, and even the students were ready for battle.

Once inside, they quickly gathered their metal spoons and chopsticks and took seats at tables for four. I knew that I was allowed to sit with them from the next day on, and the thought of getting to know young North Koreans made me feel more hopeful about my time there. When I asked one of the teachers how they would feel about sitting with me, she said that there would not be any problem—they were all eager to practice their English. Already I could see that they were just as curious about me; some stared throughout their meal. When I tried returning their gaze, however, they quickly looked away.

3

As it happened, the first day of class—the day when a group of mostly American teachers took on the education of 270 North Korean young men—fell on July Fourth, but no one seemed to notice the irony. There was no red, white, and blue here. No barbecues and fireworks. Never having taught English as a second language before, I felt nervous as well as excited. Remembering the dress code, I put on a light blue button-down shirt, a calf-length gray skirt, and a pair of low heels. I had been warned that women generally did not wear pants in North Korea, and I could not remember ever having seen them on previous trips to Pyongyang.

At 7:15 a.m., I stood outside my dormitory facing the five-story structure where classes were held, known as the IT (Information Technology) building. To its left was the monument I had seen when we first drove in. Students called it the Forever Tower because the words OUR GREAT LEADER IS FOREVER WITH US were carved into one side, top to bottom. It resembled the Tower of Immortality in Pyongyang, which bears the same message, and I wondered how many such towers there were around the country. As I approached the IT building, I could hear music booming from a speaker in the foyer. I would soon get used to the blasting intrusion of recorded music, but on that first day, it struck me as ominous, and intensified the feeling of being watched. I could hear the lyric, "I want to walk endlessly, my beloved Pyongyang night. Please don't advance, beautiful Pyongyang night." It was one of their most popular songs, a student would tell me later—an ode to Pyongyang.

As I entered the main door, a female guard nodded from a booth. The walls along the staircase displayed the portraits of Kim Il-sung and Kim Jong-il, along with such exhortations as "Keep your feet firmly on the ground of your motherland and keep your eyes on the world!" and "Let's think in our way and create in our way!" The narrow hallway on the second floor was lined with teachers' offices, ending in an area decorated with three scrolls reading: LEADER LUCK, GENERAL LUCK, CAPTAIN LUCK. In Korea, if you are born from good parents, it is said that you have "parent luck." If you marry well, you have "husband luck." So according to the scrolls, this nation was lucky in three things, Kim Jong-il, the General; his dead father, the Leader; and his young son, the Captain. This was the first mention of the heir apparent, Kim Jong-un, I had come across in all my visits to Pyongyang.

At the end of the hall were four freshman classrooms, which served as homerooms. There were one hundred freshmen, one hundred sophomores, and about seventy graduate students. Because the school had been open for less than a year, there was not yet a junior or senior class—all the undergraduates had transferred from other universities and started anew as freshmen. According to a memo from President Kim's office, there were seventy-five foreign teachers and staff. However, I counted only thirty or so teachers, about half of them Caucasian and the other half of Korean origin, from countries around the world. (None were South Korean, mainly because of visa issues.) Of the thirty teachers, about half spoke at least some Korean, but the rest did not.

The freshmen were divided into four groups according to their proficiency in English, Class 1 being the strongest and Class 4 the weakest. I was assigned to teach Reading and Writing to Classes 2 and 4 (another set of teachers handled Speaking and Listening) for an hour and a half each in the morning. The afternoons were reserved for office hours and group activities.

Our textbook, *New Horizon College English 1*, had been used in China at YUST and was approved by the "counterparts." These so-called counterparts were the North Korean teaching staff who oversaw our lessons. Everything, from books to lesson plans, had to be approved by them before we could share it with students. If any extra material was to be used in class, we were required to submit it a few days before the lesson for approval. All through that summer, I was never quite sure who the counterparts were or where they were, and even after I returned in the fall and taught English to a few of them, the mention of the word *counterpart* never failed to make me nervous.

Beth, a thirtysomething British woman who served as the dean of the English department and signed her group emails "In Him," assigned me a teaching assistant. Katie, my TA, was a recent Cornell graduate who had just spent a year at YUST teaching the children of the teachers. Her help in preparing lessons would prove valuable, especially since I was often secretly occupied taking notes for my book. We were given a rough schedule of the textbook chapters we were expected to cover each week and a list of afternoon activities designed by a group of teachers, including Beth.

But there was an even more important set of expectations

that had been communicated haphazardly, in group emails and staff meetings, during Skype sessions with Joan, and in the hotel lounge in Beijing.

Though we never had the promised orientation, at least not a formal one, I had somehow accumulated a long list of scribbled notes warning me about what I could and couldn't do, or could and couldn't say.

- Boil water before drinking, just to be safe, but in order to boil something in your room, you will need to buy a gas tank and have it installed. Or bring a water purifier. Recently there was a paratyphoid problem in the Rang Rang district, where the school is located, due to its poor water sanitation.

- Dress for class as if you were going to a work meeting: a skirt and jacket for women, slacks and a jacket for men. Nothing too fancy. Avoid a lot of ornamentation on clothing, e.g., jackets that have sequins. Around the campus, dress respectably. No shorts or T-shirts with flip-flops; those are acceptable only in the dorm. Jeans are forbidden. Kim Jong-il does not like blue jeans because he associates them with America.

- When you step outside the campus—which won't happen except for occasional shopping or sightseeing trips—be careful about the way you look and what you say. Do not approach or start a conversation with anybody. If you must, there should be a good reason. A minder and a driver will always accompany you. Any pictures or video footage must be reviewed by your minder. If you take a picture of the outside, it could be a problem.

- All trips require permission beforehand. If you visit any monuments on trips or eat at foreigners-only restaurants, you will have to pay for the minder and the driver. You will need to pay for the gas. Euros, Chinese renminbi, and U.S. dollars will be accepted, but the North Korean won is used only at Potonggang Department Store or at Tongil Market. Soon those trips will be curtailed, since the school is setting up a little shop on campus.

- There is a health clinic on campus, as well as the Friendship Hospital for foreigners in downtown Pyongyang, which is used by the diplomatic community, but bring any medication you might need.

- You are responsible for bringing a laptop for your own use. For music, bring an iPod rather than CDs, which are feared since they could be passed to people. If you leave your laptop in your office over the weekend, they might inspect it, so do not leave things unattended.

- Bring more than one flashlight and plenty of batteries because the campus is not lit at night and electricity is spotty.

- Bring cash; you will not be able to use ATMs or credit cards.

- When you talk to students, be very careful about the topic of conversation. Steer away from political issues, things that are too personal, or anything about the outside world. Do not try to be clever about initiating certain topics of discussion, and do not be overenthusiastic in talking about your own culture.

- Do not bow your head or fold your hands or close your eyes to pray at meals. Pray with your eyes open. Do not say anything about religion and do not use religious titles to address each other. If a student comes to you and asks for a Bible, you should be very polite and say that you cannot do that. There is always a chance that these requests are made in order to test you. One faculty member was tricked by a minder and then asked to leave.

- Never hint that there is something wrong with their country.

- You will be able to use the Internet in your room, and the telephone and fax machine in President Kim's office if there is an emergency, but communication will be monitored. Be careful which sites you visit on the Internet, and when you write home, speak positively about what is going on and do not discuss politics.

- No foreign magazines or books will be allowed into Pyong-yang except those declared and preapproved; physical books are more of a problem than e-books since they could be passed around.

- Be careful with your terminology: Great Leader, Dear Leader, Precious Leader. Those names have to be carefully used, or better yet, just stay away from discussing them at all. Be careful about how to handle images too. For example, Air Koryo offers in-flight magazines. You take one to your office and it has a picture of Kim Jong-il, and let's say you end up sitting on it by mistake. Then you are in big trouble, because the photo is like the person. It is the same with the portrait of Kim Il-sung on the pins every North Korean wears. These men are regarded as deities, at least officially. Make sure you do not throw away, fold, tear, or damage any visual representation of them. Do not point at such images either. It would be considered an act of disrespect and you would be punished.

- If someone comes up and asks about politics, just answer "I don't know," or say, "Oh, is that so?" End of conversation.

- Reunification is a sensitive topic. Just stay away from it.

- Do not say *Bukhan* (North Korea) or *Namhan* (South Korea). *Chosun* (the name for the last Korean kingdom) is what North Korea calls itself.

- Do not speak Korean and always use English. Remember, many people around you will know English and understand what you are saying, so be careful what you say.

- Do not get into long conversations with the guards or minders.

- Do not make comparisons. For example, do not say their food is different from yours because that could be construed as critical.

- Eating with locals on outings is prohibited.

- Be careful with gifts. You must not give one thing to one person; you have to give it to everyone. Otherwise, it could be considered a bribe.

- Living in Pyongyang is like living in a fishbowl. Everything you say and do will be watched. Even your dorm room might not be secure. They could go through your things. If you keep a journal and if you say something in it that is not complimentary, please do not leave it in your room. Even in your room, whatever you say could be recorded. Just get in a habit of not saying everything that is on your mind, not criticizing the government and things of that sort, so you won't slip.

- When you come out of Pyongyang, avoid all interviews with press. Make sure you know whom you share things with afterward. Do not give press any information about PUST.

It was astonishing how quickly I would adapt to these rules, which seemed so absurd when I first wrote them down. Now, at 8 a.m., as I entered the classroom, I hoped I would remember to avoid all the forbidden topics. I took a deep breath and found myself standing in front of twenty-six young men, all of them neatly dressed and sitting up very straight.

Even now, writing in Manhattan, my heart beats faster recalling that initial meeting. Oddly enough, the first word that came to my mind was *beauty*. Something about that first moment in the classroom felt so clean and serene, and it was as though everything went silent, and there I was stepping onto a field of white, untrodden snow. They were young, and I remember them as beautiful, although on this point I cannot be certain as I soon began to delight in looking at them like they were my children, and can no longer recall a time when I didn't.

.   .   .

THE NIGHT BEFORE, Katie had come to my room to help me with the lesson plan. "I've got blisters from wearing heels," she said, throwing off her dress shoes and plopping onto my sofa. Then she squinted her eyes, rubbing the sole of her foot with the brusqueness of a much younger girl. "Wow, you've got TV!" she exclaimed and pressed the remote, but when she saw that it tuned into only a few Chinese channels and CNN Asia, she quickly lost interest and turned it off. Her room did not have a TV, she said, not that she ever watched much TV. In China, where she had taught at YUST, she usually went to bed by 8 p.m. after reading the Bible, and her focus would be much the same here. There were Bible studies most evenings, and Sunday services in the third-floor meeting room at the teachers' dormitory—all permitted by the counterparts. Since the school had been built and would be maintained with money from the evangelical Christian community, the missionaries could practice their religion as long as they kept it from the students and didn't proselytize. Missionaries were not paid salaries from the school but were individually funded by their churches back home.

"I never waited to come here my whole life or anything like all those other people . . . I'm just twenty-three," she shrugged. There was nothing in the rules about whispering, but now that the conversation had turned to religion, we lowered our voices. We also turned the TV back on, hoping it would muffle our voices if we were being recorded. She explained that some of the YUST faculty had been waiting to come to PUST for as long as a decade, but most were South Korean nationals and not allowed a visa. North Korea was the evangelical Christian Holy Grail, the hardest place to crack in the whole world, and converting its people would guarantee the missionaries a spot in heaven. Katie's path to PUST had been easier. She had a job waiting at a Christian NGO in the Middle East, but it did not start until September. "Joan asked if I wanted to come here for the summer, so I said okay," she told me, "because the Lord has his ways!" She spoke with the ease of one for whom the future was brimming with possibilities. She added that she might apply to law school at the end of the year although she wasn't quite sure, and she cocked her head just slightly as she lingered on the word *might*.

For a moment, I felt a pang of envy. I remembered those few drifting years after college, taking off alone with a backpack to explore the world. I thought I was playing a dare with life then, challenging my limits, but I was scared most of the time and wept for no clear reason in dingy hostel rooms across Europe and Central America. But the years had worked their magic, and that scared girl I had been in that remote place in time had dissolved into infinite invisible threads, so thin and delicate that I could almost touch her and then lose her the next minute. Now, almost two decades later, it felt as though she had reappeared, still uncertain, still afraid.

Katie began telling me her life story with youthful exuberance, taking for granted that I would be interested, which in fact I was. It was in college that her American father met her mother, an exchange student from South Korea. They now lived in Maryland, where he worked as an engineer. He was worried, she said with a laugh, that she might catch the eye of some high-level Workers' Party guy. But she told him that the worst thing that could happen to her would be getting kicked out, and her mother said, "What do you mean, the worst thing? That would be the best thing! The worst thing would be if they were to detain you!"

I empathized with her father and worried for her sake. Katie was tall, about five foot nine, and enigmatically beautiful, with chestnut, shoulder-length hair, a creamy complexion, and hazel eyes that sometimes appeared green. Her father thought that North Korean men might whisk her off in the middle of the night, and I felt nervous about her taking off to the Middle East alone. When I voiced this concern, she suddenly became quiet.

"I stay away from men," she said. It wasn't always easy being half Korean, she told me. She did not know much Korean, but she knew the word *twiggy,* a derogatory term for people of mixed parentage. In college, she had a Korean-American boyfriend she loved. She knew that, as the eldest son of the eldest line of his family clan, he could not marry a woman of mixed blood, and she told him this worried her. But he said that by the time they married, his grandparents would be dead and it wouldn't matter. Still, the relationship ended badly, leaving her heartbroken. Soon afterward, she found refuge in God. She had been raised Christian, but until then she did not have true faith. She swore then that she would never entrust her heart to anyone except Him. God would not disappoint her the way men had.

It occurred to me then that everyone's threshold for pain is different. For some, the end of a romance is devastating enough to make them turn to religion for refuge. For others, it is simply a cautionary tale, something to keep in mind for future loves. Like Katie, I could not shake off the hurt of a bad relationship, and instead sat brooding with that pain for years. Yet, now that I found myself so far from home, it was hard to understand why I had stayed unhappy for so long. Sometimes the longer you are inside a prison, the harder it is to fathom what is possible beyond its walls.

That night, however, we had a job to do. The first lesson was on letter writing, and Katie and I decided that we would ask the students to write to us about anything they wanted and would use the letters to gauge their proficiency in English. We wanted to keep it simple, because Beth had warned us that many of the students did not know even the basics of how a letter is written, and that we must explain it to them. After all, it was not clear how functional North Korea's postal system was. There did not seem to be any mailboxes, and letters took a long time to be delivered; besides, when you suspect that the contents will be monitored, letters lose their meaning.

What if you forget me? I had asked my lover from the JFK airport before heading off. At the other end of the phone, he remained silent. I imagined he did not know how he would feel months later, or perhaps my question struck him as childlike. Ever since I was thirteen years old, whenever I went away, I had always feared that I would be forgotten. Since we were dealing with North Korea, there was no guarantee as to when I would return, and he did not want to make any promises. Even if we swore by them, they would have been just words. But I was a writer. I believed in words, even if they only masked the uncertainty of time passing.

From this side of the border, however, there was no way of reaching out to him. In a few days, I was told, the school would connect Internet service to the faculty dormitory, and I would be able to email him. But I already knew from the rules that whoever was in charge would be able to see everything on screen. I had set up a new email address specifically for my stay there, as recommended by Joan, so that there would be as little as possible for them to monitor.

I imagined the lovers of the past who ended up on either side of the border after the war. Neither letters nor phone calls since. I imagined them waiting, waiting for a sign of their beloved. I had never experienced the desperate longing of a mother for her child—the loss and yearning my grandmother and my great-aunt must have felt. But I understood the longing of lovers, and I imagined them waiting for the border to open, the days turning into weeks and then years, which then became the rest of their lives. I imagined the longing of not just one person but of an entire nation. The idea of it put the concept of a long-distance relationship to shame. The eternal wait must have become a test of loyalty. Who could stay faithful to their beloved the longest? Love did not conquer all. Lovers were punished for loving—the forced separation bled their hearts. I imagined these pent-up feelings percolating in the air and hushed in the soil of the Korean peninsula, this diseased nation split in two.

THAT FIRST MORNING, as I looked out at their alert faces, a boy rose from his seat, and all the others followed. They then shouted out, in unison, in English, "Good morning, Professor!" I scanned the room once and said, "Good morning, gentlemen!" I am not sure why I addressed them as "gentlemen." It was not a word I would have used with a group of American college students. Perhaps it was the way these particular boys looked in that particular moment, so immaculate and orderly that I was reminded of the way my father often used the word *gentleman* to describe any foreign male he admired. It was one of those English words that had infiltrated the Korean language, where it came to denote a sort of dashing modern man.

The boys burst out laughing. Some looked embarrassed and kept giggling. And so the first lesson began—more of a get-to-know-you session than a real lesson. I told them to ask anything they wanted to know about me and Katie. One by one, they stood up from their seats to ask questions.

"How many siblings do you have?"

"When is your birthday?"

"What is your favorite color?"

One boy asked, "Did you enjoy the flowers outside this morning on your walk to class?" These must have been the tiny orange and pink flowers I had seen, and Katie was quick to ask, "Did you plant them?" They nodded, smiling shyly.

Suddenly I remembered a similar moment just a few years before at a private university in the Midwest where I taught creative writing to undergraduates. On the first day of class, I had told the students to ask me anything. I hoped they would want to know about the secret to writing well, and I was prepared to welcome them by saying that there was no secret and that we each had to find our own voice. Instead, they had only one question: "Did our university approach you for this job or did you have to apply for it?" The message was clear. They wanted to know if I was worth their tuition. That moment had been like a splash of cold water, and I never liked to reflect upon it afterward. I wondered what made young people of a similar age think so differently.

The young men in my first period belonged to Class 4, which meant their English was expected to be the weakest, yet I had no problem understanding them. Still, the next group, Class 2, spoke markedly better English, and their questions were more sophisticated. One asked Katie, "You look Asian. Are you Korean?" Katie told them that her mother was Korean and her father was American. The class nodded, although I could not tell if her answer made sense to them.

Then a tall boy stood up to ask me if I suffered from motion sickness. The last time he had flown, he told me, he found it quite shaky. I asked him where he had flown, and he mumbled that it was domestic. I had never heard of domestic routes in North Korea until then but thought it best not to probe further. He must have been one of the select few who had experienced plane travel.

I asked the students to pick a topic of their choice and write a letter in English to me or Katie. On the board, I showed them the way a formal letter is written—the date, address "Dear so-and-so," followed by a comma, some sample sentences, "Sincerely," and so forth. It seemed strange to be teaching something so basic to college students, and yet, as I faced the blackboard with a piece of chalk between my fingers, I had only to tilt my face thirty degrees upward and I would be staring straight at the portraits of Kim Il-sung and Kim Jong-il—one dead and the other hanging on for his dear, great life. And when I faced the boys, my eyes rested on two very similar slogans on the wall behind them: "Our Party sent our students to college to read a lot of books and study hard," attributed to Kim Il-sung, and "Our Party wants our students to study hard," by Kim Jong-il. Every student, at all times, wore a pin bearing the tiny image of Kim Il-sung's face on a red background on the left-hand side of his chest, presumably because it was closer to the heart.

I told them that the letter was not only a convenient short writing exercise, but also a way for me to get to know them better, and that it would not be graded. Hearing this, they seemed both relieved and disappointed. I could not tell if they wanted to be graded or not. In those first few days, the students nodded so eagerly at everything I said that I was never sure if they had understood anything at all. When they handed in their letters, I saw that most of them had copied my sample word for word, starting with "Dear so-and-so," and signing the letters "Sincerely, Suki."

They wrote about their families, their ardent desire to better their English, and their love of sports, mainly basketball and soccer, although one student did write of his passion for golf and how he played it often. I learned that many of their fathers were doctors and scientists. One student wrote that his family had moved to Mansudae Avenue just a few weeks ago, thanks to the Great Leader, and another mentioned his nice home on Unification Street. From this, I gathered that Mansudae Avenue and Unification Street were coveted addresses. Another wrote about a family outing to Okryu-gwan, Pyongyang's best restaurant, about yoga being his favorite pastime, and about how he hated candy. A third student wrote that his friend was born in Beijing because his father had been a diplomat.

It was clear that these were not the North Koreans I was used to seeing depicted in the media. I had spent months interviewing defectors in Chinese border towns as well as in Seoul, and nothing in their testimony could have prepared me for these young men. Most of the defectors were impoverished farmers from the northern edge of the country, bordering China, very far from Pyongyang. My students, however, came from the upper echelon of the DPRK. Many of them had transferred from either Kim Il-sung University or Kim Chaek University of Technology—the equivalent of Harvard or MIT. They missed the prestige of their old schools and their friends there. Some of them seemed reluctant to serve as guinea pigs in their government's brand-new experiment where the teachers were all foreigners and the lessons were conducted in English.

Interestingly, almost none of the students brought up the Great Leader in the first letter, as if there was a tacit understanding not to go there. Yet one student wrote:

*The Juche ideology is the most correct and unique one. It illumi-
nates the way of the world's revolution. The Great Leader applied
the Juche ideology to the whole sphere of revolution and construction. As he led our revolution correctly, our country was able to
grow from a poor country to a powerful and prosperous nation.
Nowadays, his idea is admired as the best in the world.*

About five minutes before the end of the second period, I
saw the face of Beth, the dean, who was at the window, looking nervous and motioning me to come outside. My heart sank.
Had I already done something wrong? Said something inappropriate, somehow been reported by a student from the first
class? Each group had a monitor, who ordered the rest of the
class to rise and call out "good morning" when I walked in and
gave me a roll book, in which I was required to briefly note what
I taught each day. I would eventually learn that there was also a
vice monitor and secretary, whose identities were not revealed,
and Dr. Joseph, a Korean-American missionary in his fifties and
our liaison with the counterparts, had told us that any of these
students or others might report on us or record the class with
an MP3 player. The counterparts, he said, would read the students' reports or listen to the recordings and would sometimes
observe our classes. I became nervous that I had come this far
only to be thrown out.

My worries were unfounded. There had been a room change
at the last minute, and I had walked into the wrong class. Instead of Class 2, I had just taught Class 1. The mix-up caused
a great stir, and Beth was not sure whether I should just stick
with Class 1 or start all over with Class 2. The problem was that
Class 1 was composed of twenty-six top-ranked freshmen, and
Class 4 of the twenty-four lowest-ranked, and since their levels
differed so vastly, it would mean a lot more work for me, Beth

said, adding that she would ask the counterparts for permission to let me teach whomever I decided on.

I hesitated; part of me feared that more teaching duties would take time away from writing, the real reason I was there, but I knew this might be a great opportunity to experience the extremes of the student body. As I walked into the cafeteria after class, still uncertain, and joined the line for teachers and graduate students, a few of my Class 1 students ran up to me with anxious faces. "Will you be our teacher?" they asked. "Will you stay with us?" It appeared that rumors circulated fast in this tiny community—not surprising, perhaps, since most things were visible from every corner. "Is that what you all want?" I asked. They nodded eagerly as though I were about to present them with the biggest gift of their lives. So it was decided right then, and, though I did not understand it at the time, it was more than the decision to be just their teacher.

When I found Beth in the cafeteria and told her that I would stick with Class 1, she reminded me that it would be a lot more work, but it did not seem like work, in that moment, to be their teacher. It felt more like choosing one child over another, and I have often wondered how my experience would have differed had I not walked into the wrong room. Because Class 1 was in fact a special group, the smartest, which in that world meant, among other things, that they followed orders very well. And it was that very quality, which seemed more particular to Class 1 than Class 4, that would bother me the most in the months to come.

After my conversation with Beth, I saw the same boys staring intently at me from the lunch line. So I smiled and nodded, signaling to them that yes, I would indeed be their teacher. And the beaming smiles I received in return made that first day of teaching unforgettable. These young men were in many ways like children, with all their vulnerability and innocence intact, hanging on to my every move as though it would determine their destinies. Later I would wonder if it was decided in that moment that I would fall in love with them. We need to feel needed. We love the ones who want us.

4

I AM FROM SOUTHERN STOCK. FOR GENERATIONS, MY FA-
ther's Gwangsan clan of Kim settled in Chungcheong-do, the
only province among the peninsula's eight that is partly land-
locked. People there are known for being mellow in temper-
ament and kind in spirit, although such a reputation might be
exaggerated by their countrymen, who feel sorry for them for
missing out on the sea. I spent most of my childhood there, in
a very big house surrounded by hills. I remember looking up at
the sky for a rush of blue, which might have been a premonition
of my later life on the isle of Manhattan.

According to my grandfather, who often sat me and my
brother and sister down to review the superiority of our lin-
eage, the Gwangsan clan was known for producing the leading
Confucian scholars in Korea. We were the noblest of all Korean
families, he said, and certainly the most dignified of the hundreds of different Kim clans. We were not warriors like the
Kimhae clan, or blinded by earthly ambition and titles like the
Andong clan. We preferred thinking to fighting and had often
served as teachers to kings. The most eminent of my ancestors

were the father and son scholars, Kim Jang-saeng (Sagye) and Kim Jip (Shindokjae), from the sixteenth century—both enshrined among Korea's eighteen sages. Today, whenever I visit Seoul and pass the ancient imperial palace that housed our kings for centuries, I remember my grandfather's smug grin and the inevitable mantra of how without our great-great-great-grandfathers, Korea would be without its guiding philosophy.

Years later, I traveled to the beautiful, temple-strewn Gyeong-sang province, in the southeastern corner of the country, where I was stopped on the street by a very old man costumed in a traditional linen robe and hat, made with horsetail hair and bamboo. The area was famous for its orthodox traditions. Unlike the rest of the country, where the eldest sons of family clans performed ancestor worship rites for their dead parents on lunar New Year's Day, *Chuseok* (Harvest Day), and the death anniversaries, families there conducted the rites on all sorts of special memorial days even for ancestors many generations removed. It was said that no mothers wanted their daughters to be married off to the men from that region since daughters-in-law worked year round, cooking, cleaning, and washing, never mind being perpetually pressured to produce a male heir. Hearing me speak English with my companion, the old man asked where I was from. I told him, in Korean, that I was born in Seoul but lived in New York, and that my people were originally from Chungcheong province. At this, he nodded approval and asked, "So where is your *bonjuk?*" meaning where did my clan originate. When I told him Gwangsan Kim, his face brightened. He nodded again, looking very thoughtful, and said, "Why, you are from a very noble family! Most noble, I might add. Yours is the *second* noblest family in all of Korea!" When I asked him who was the first, he exclaimed, as if he could not believe I did not already know, "Of course, my family of Poongsan Yoo!"

Then he began telling me about an ancestor of his, who in the sixteenth century had saved Korea from a Japanese attack. "Without my great-great-great-grandfather, our country would not exist!" he said proudly.

My father still attends biannual, regional Gwangsan Kim meetings, which take place in a Korean restaurant near where he now lives, in Fort Lee, New Jersey. About twenty members sit around the Korean meals of *kimchi chigae* and *gamjatang* and discuss the greatest achievements of our ancestors, who are buried in Yunsan borough in Nonsan City of Chungcheong province, including my grandparents. Unable to tend to their graves the way a good Confucian son should, my father is plagued with guilt. One year I traveled to South Korea in his place, although the gravesite was hard to get to without a car. The train took about two hours, and after that I had to take a bus to Yunsan. Everyone within a ten-mile radius was Gwangsan Kim, according to the bus driver, who asked me, "Who's the caretaker of your plot?" I told him, and he nodded in recognition. It was a rural area, and everyone either knew one another or was related. He helped me find a taxi, which took me to a particular turn in the road shown on a map hand drawn by a relative. There was no sign, but I got out of the taxi and trekked along the path, endless burial mounds unfolding before me, tiny hills that had held the bones of my ancestors for hundreds of years, each one with a stone tablet as a marker. There they were, the people who made me, whose unions had led me to stand there in that time—the history of me.

Except that the letters on each tablet were in Chinese, as Koreans still relied on written Chinese for matters relating to death. Throughout history, China was always the big brother to neighboring Korea, this tiny kingdom unfortunately located adjacent to the massive empire, and in some ways, that tradition seemed to have held up. Anyone following North Korea would tell you that it is China that really holds the power.

Since mandatory instruction in Chinese did not begin until the seventh grade, which was when I emigrated, all I knew of Chinese was my name. Every gravestone featured the character "Kim," followed by individual names, which I could not read. The Gwangsan clan of Kims were all gathered there, and had I not been a woman—according to Korean custom, a woman is buried with her husband's family—and had we stayed in Korea, I too would have ended up there, along with my father. (As for unmarried women, I have no idea where they are buried. For a very long time, in Korea, no one talked about them.)

For thousands of years, scarcely anyone left. Korea was the hermit kingdom, with its spiritual basis in Confucianism, Buddhism, and Shamanism, until 1910, when it was annexed by Japan and colonized for thirty-five years thereafter, followed by the Korean War in 1950. Having been born and raised under these brutal colonizers, my paternal grandfather spoke fluent Japanese. Shortly before his death, in the mid-1980s, he came to stay with my family in Queens, where he befriended a young Japanese woman, a missionary from the Unification Church. When my father confronted him about his sudden interest in the cult, my grandfather answered that he didn't care about the Moonies, he only enjoyed the chance to speak Japanese with his new friend. Like others from his generation, he suffered from a sort of Stockholm syndrome and missed the language of his oppressors. Koreans' love–hate relationship with Japan carries on to this day, compounded by their relationship with the superpowers who took over where Japan left off: the United States and the Soviet Union, who together liberated Korea only to carve it up as a proxy for the Cold War.

Today, South Koreans are largely mixed in their attitude

toward the United States, which keeps almost thirty thousand troops stationed smack in the middle of the capital, occupying prime real estate.* Many of them resent the presence of these foreign protectors, more than sixty years after the armistice, and yet they readily acknowledge that it is their alliance with the United States that has helped South Korea become a democracy as well as a first-world nation. If South Korea is indebted to the United States for its prosperity, North Korea has been largely indebted to China for its survival since the fall of the Soviet Union. Although both China and the Soviet Union had a hand in the division of Korea, North Koreans do not speak of that; they blame only the United States and Japan. Alliances can be hard to break. History is a record of many such irrationalities.

On that visit to my ancestors' graves, it occurred to me that tradition is not well suited for globalization. Traditions are about holding on to the past, whereas I belong in a new world, and in my new world of America, one reinvents oneself constantly, which is a certain kind of privilege. It was in 1983, following decades of military dictatorship in the South, that my parents finally left the old country. They were the first generation of Gwangsan Kim to turn their back on all that was in front of me in those burial mounds, and here I was, years later, the descendant who had crossed the ocean to return, unable to identify my grandparents' gravestones until the caretaker came and led me to them.

MY MOTHER'S SIDE is more humble, at least according to her. I don't know how true that is, as my mother deferred to my father on almost everything, including the degree of nobility

---

* The United States plans to relocate its military base outside Seoul by 2016.

in their backgrounds. Although her Yoon clan had originated from the ancient region of Papyeong in Gyeonggi province, she was born and raised in Seoul, as were her parents. The Papyeong Yoons were known for their queens. Often the bride of the future king was selected from faded noble families who lacked ambition, since those holding power in the court tried to guard against anyone who might usurp their power. Her preoccupation, however, was with more recent family history.

As my mother tells it, June 25, 1950, was a quiet Sunday. She was just four years old, although she remembers it all as if it happened yesterday. That was the day when North Korean bombs first fell over the southern capital of Seoul. That day marked the end of a childhood that never really had the chance to begin.

So it goes like this, our conversation.

The bombs were coming, and we ran, my mother says. She is not sure if she heard them, but she knew they were coming because everyone in the neighborhood was fleeing.

Where were you going? I ask.

Her reaction then is always the same—incredulous at being asked something so obvious.

To the south, of course! Anywhere, so long as it was toward the south. We knew that if we stayed there, we would die. At least that was what my mother said when she was packing.

Her father is away on a business trip to Busan at the southernmost tip of the country. This is unusual. He is an administrator at the local community center—not a job that requires business travel. But the family is lucky that he was sent south, not north, for work. An overnight trip north, a couple of hours away, and some families are separated forever. The war announcements must be airing on the radio because almost no one has a telephone or TV. The mood is urgent, panicked even, and my mother remembers a sudden cold breeze sweeping across the living room, even though it was summer and humid. The neighbors have begun fleeing, carrying their possessions on their backs, checking in to see what Mrs. Yoon is up to, why she has not left yet.

"*Palgengis* [the Red] are coming!" they scream. "There's war!" These people have lived through the Japanese rule. They are accustomed to catastrophe.

My grandmother must make the decision alone. The children must be fed and dressed, and the youngest one will have to be carried. My mother is a quiet child, but she is even quieter than usual; she can tell something big is about to happen. My grandmother tells the children to start packing. They all gather their things frantically.

Five children in total, but not really.

What do you mean, five children, but not really?

My mother would pause here. She might be in the midst of cutting up daikon or roasting seaweed for my lunch box. She might be getting ready for a night out with my father, standing before a dressing mirror in her green silk wrap dress and matching leather gloves. I can still see her reflection in the mirror, her hair blow-dried into a windswept Farrah Fawcett do, not a trace of the war-fleeing child visible. She modeled once, in the sixties, for a Japanese photographer who spotted her in a restaurant in Seoul because of her striking resemblance to a Japanese movie star. This resemblance inspired a Korean TV producer to pursue her for months and cast her in a weekly soap opera, but the week before filming she took off on a seaside outing with my father and never showed up. She was not irresponsible by nature, but she wasn't sure what a model or an actress did because in postwar Korea, TV and magazines were still new and mysterious. At the moment, her beauty seems even more exaggerated as she pauses and gazes into a distance. My mother is still young. Just barely in her thirties, the wound still raw.

What do you mean, not really five?

You see . . . there were nine originally. Four died in infancy. Babies didn't always live back then.

This part always mystifies me. I am a child, and death is something someone invented somewhere. I am lost as to where those other babies went.

My mother sighs over the deaths she did not witness. She is the lucky one. She came last—the youngest of the nine. She survived and grew into a beautiful woman, a wife, a mother. Four others never made it. As a mother, saying these things aloud scares her, and she pulls me toward her and squeezes me very hard as though she is afraid of losing me too. I don't like this moment. I don't like the fear in her eyes, but I keep on asking so that it will distract her and she will finish telling the story, although this story has no ending. A loop that does not complete a circle. A gap that will never be filled.

All she recalls is the sudden chaos, her mother and her siblings in a great hurry. Her eldest brother takes charge. He is only seventeen, but with his father missing, he is the man of the house, telling his mother to get some rice balls ready for their train journey. It is decided that they will first go to Suwon, nineteen miles outside of Seoul, where they have a relative, and from there, they will make their way to Busan, where her father is. She is soon picked up, in the arms of her eldest brother. The other three children follow, each with a parcel of things on his or her back. My grandmother gazes at the house one last time, afraid she might never set eyes on it again. It will be three years before she does, but she does not know that as she reluctantly turns away to begin the long walk to the train that will take them to safety.

You see, it was all farmland up there in the hills, a good hour walk to Seoul Station.

Tucked beneath the rocky Bukak-san (Mount Bukak) towering above and adjacent to the Gyeongbokgung imperial palace and the Blue House, where the president resides, my mother's childhood neighborhood of Samcheong-dong was long ignored as a sleepy corner where public transportation was inconvenient and the daily patrol by armed guards made even a casual walk difficult. Although the view from there has always been spectacular, Samcheong-dong, for a long time, remained a poor cousin to wealthier nearby districts.

Samcheong-dong today bears no resemblance to the forgotten hills of my mother's recollection. In 2009, when I was living in Seoul on a fellowship, I took tennis lessons in Samcheong Park, about a hundred yards from where my mother's childhood home had been. Nobody lived there anymore. My uncle had long since sold the family house and moved to the suburbs as the neighborhood began to attract real estate developers. Many of its run-down *hanok*s (traditional Korean shingle-tile roofed houses) had been converted into cafés and boutiques, and the area had become one of the city's most popular destinations for couples. I would walk past the imperial palace every morning, up the winding road that was oddly reminiscent of the picturesque Montmartre one sees in romantic movies. The fashionable trend that year was young male baristas. Everywhere it seemed that handsome young men in their early twenties were taking orders with their iPads and pouring coffee with exaggerated precision and explanations—slow drip, siphon, Chemex. Seoul in 2009, Samcheong-dong in particular, seemed hipper than anywhere else I had recently visited, but when I told my mother about it later, back in New Jersey, she looked at me blankly. Then, after a long pause, she said, "What about the creek? I used to take our dirty laundry and wash it there." I told her that no one did laundry in creeks anymore and that I hadn't seen anything resembling a creek in my walks. In her mind, though, she was back there, the youngest of the family, taking the washing to the creek on afternoons when she was let out of school early.

Again the mind does a loop, and all roads converge on a single moment on June 25, 1950. For those of her generation who lost somebody, life is forever divided between before that day and after.

It takes the six of them several hours to reach Seoul Station because the streets are packed with people fleeing. The older children take hold, protectively, of the hands of the younger ones. The walk is about two and a half miles, but my grandmother is alone with five children, carrying as much as she can on her back. My seventeen-year-old uncle must have led the group.

No family photograph remains from that day or those immediately thereafter. Photographs are an indulgence when you are running for your life. I have looked up black-and-white pictures of Seoul from that day, faded evidence of refugees who could be from any Asian country fleeing any war. They put their heads down and made their way to the south, where the bombs from the North would not reach. No one complained. No one questioned. This was the generation that had seen it all, the heartache of having their country taken by Japan, their mortal enemy, and now the heartache of this division that seemed to have happened overnight. Those years, from 1945 to 1950, had been confusing, with Kim Il-sung, the Red Army major, in the North, and Syngman Rhee, the American protégé, in the South. Cold War politics knows no bounds, and the people had no say in its dreadful consequences. Resignation is a habit, and it is contagious.

It was a miracle that we made it to the station before nightfall. We were lucky . . . at first.

It is this "at first" that makes my heart sink. I don't like the part that comes next, but I let my mother continue because I know that we must.

After fighting her way through the jam-packed station, my grandmother learns that all tickets on all southbound trains are sold out. She sees people climbing onto the roofs of departing trains in desperation. After waiting there for hours, she hears about some trucks giving rides to families with young children. So she and the children run, small fists tightly folded over the smaller ones. And, miraculously, there is a dusty truck with people in back but with room for more, and they hop on, and my grandmother, soaked in sweat, makes sure that all five children are there, including the baby girl in her arms, my mother, placed there by her eldest son. These are good children, good eggs, the ones who survived against all odds.

She plops down, leaning against the tailgate, and takes a deep breath, her tremendous breasts heaving, these breasts that fed nine infants, although she has only five to show for it. She is forty-five years old, but she looks and feels older, and she realizes she is tired, exhausted in fact, not the optimal emotion to feel at the dawn of a war, although she is not yet sure if it really is war. All she knows is that they are on a vehicle, away from the bombs, and that somehow, without her husband, she has managed to get all of them here. She feels smug for a moment and wants to congratulate herself for this accomplishment, but instead casts a lingering glance at her oldest, the son, the one who survived. He is her lucky charm. It is with him that the tide turned. He lived, and each successive baby lived, as though with him came this beautiful gift of life; and look at him now, all grown and handsome at seventeen. She can barely contain the overwhelming love in her heart and tries to pull away her gaze although she is incapable of doing so, and it is then that a shout is heard from somewhere.

As my mother tells it, no one could clearly remember that moment afterward. There is so much confusion and commotion. Suddenly dirty faces are peering in, and people are clutching the side of the truck in a desperate attempt to board this ark that will take them away from the coming flood of violence; the only way to flee the bombs, away from Seoul, the mountainous, sprawling capital that has housed Korean royals for centuries, the epitome of every Korean's desires, but in this moment, all at once, everyone wants to chuck it into the nearest trash can and run. The goal is to get the hell out of Xanadu, if only the truck would move.

If only it had pulled out right then and there . . .

There it is again, the mantra "if only." I am always made aware of the alternative universe where things turned out differently, in which lives were saved. I am used to the mantra. For immigrants, regret can become a way of life.

Shouts are coming from somewhere. Somebody, some panicked mother or father, a desperate voice pleading with young men to give up their spaces to women and children. Before the shouts register, before my grandmother has a moment to ponder the words or protest, the seventeen-year-old rises. "I'll go," he says, then reassures her: "I'll find another ride, Mother. Don't worry." Then, just as quickly, he is out of sight, followed by the sound of the engine. It all happens in a blink, and my grandmother, bewildered by this unexpected twist, turns frantically in the direction where her son has gone, and the truck is moving suddenly, too fast for her to think clearly, and only later does it occur to her that she should have jumped off right then and dragged him back. She should have sought out the one who had shouted and gouged out his eyes. This is war, and a split-second decision is costly. There she is, my grandmother, dumbstruck on a speeding truck, without her oldest child. The baby that lived.

Seoul was captured three days later.

The finality in my mother's voice comes without emotion. "The end," her voice seems to say, although this story has no end. The war ensues, and the family moves from town to town, staying in makeshift tents and in the homes of relatives and strangers. For three years, most of the country is on the move.

My mother's family stops in the city of Suwon to wait for my uncle, but he never arrives. Some days later, they run into neighbors who report seeing him dragged away by North Korean soldiers. His hands were tied behind him with a rope, they say. The road back to Seoul is blocked now, and my grandmother waits in vain.

How long did you wait? I ask.

How long is long enough?

My mother is not sure. She was only four years old, after all, but the others, including my younger uncle, who lives in Seoul, are not clear on this either. What my mother recalls is the image of her mother, half-crazed and wailing, wearing her skirt over her head as though it were a scarf and roaming the neighborhood in the evenings. Every evening the older children would go out in search of her, and she would inevitably say that she had been looking for her son. This behavior never stops. Some days she wanders and searches, and other days she remains quiet and stares into space.

Growing up, this story was repeated to me often, and each

time, I wished for a different ending. A different plot. It was a story then, sad and yet morbidly exciting because my mother was a part of it. But later I came to see it was also a sort of therapy, the way my mother kept on telling it over and over, as her mother had done for years. And the storytelling continues as I type these words here in New York, in a language alien to those who lived through the division, a language that shields me from the worst of my grief. For even now, decades after I first adopted it, English does not pierce my heart the same way that my mother tongue does. The word *division* weighs less than *bundan*, and *war* is easier to say than *junjeng*.

Years after the war was over, the only thing my grandmother liked to do was visit shamans. The eerily accurate shaman of Inwang-san (Mount Inwang), the baby girl shaman famed for locating the bones of the neighbor's missing child, the virgin shaman, the old maid shaman, the fat matron shaman—she went to see them all. They all said the same thing: *Yes, he's alive. He's up north. He's in Pyongyang.* I would like to believe this is true, as she must have. Their assurances kept her going, though by the time I was born, she had suffered a stroke and spent her days in bed. She was sixty-five. I would say that the stroke took her soul away, but by everyone's testimony, her soul was already long gone.

5

On my third day, the students collectively showed up at dinner around 7 p.m., far later than the scheduled 6:30 p.m. arrival. This was unusual since their timing had been exact until then. When I sat down with a few and asked why they were late, they looked nervous. Finally, one said they had had a social studies class for two hours in Korean. Although that still did not explain why the class had run over by thirty minutes, I did not probe further. From their letters, I knew that they spent afternoons studying Juche, though I had no idea where. Maybe the powers that be had decided they needed to counteract any brainwashing of their elite youth that we, the foreigners, might attempt.

Then I saw six of my students wearing khaki army uniforms rather than shirts and ties, and asked the others why. "They're on duty," one said. The rest lowered their heads and stared at their food. I asked them what kind of duty, but they would not answer. So I made a joke of it and said, "They look older in uniform, like fine young gentlemen!" At this, their faces softened, and they seemed to forget whatever they might have done that afternoon to make them so tense. The word *gentleman* always made them blush and giggle.

Katie came up to me after dinner and whispered brightly, "Don't you think Choi Min-jun is the cutest boy you've ever seen?" It had not occurred to me until then that at twenty-three, she was not much older than the students. It was entirely possible that they might have crushes on one another. For the first time since we arrived, her face was filled with girlish giddiness, and for a moment, life seemed almost normal. Boys and girls. The stuff that makes the world go around, or at least a tad brighter. It was happening here in Pyongyang too, even across taboo lines.

"He looks so nice in his military uniform, so I asked him why he was wearing it," Katie continued. I was hoping she might have found out more than I had. "He wouldn't say and just blushed."

Teachers in this tiny, locked compound were like superstars. The students competed to sit with us at all three meals. For them, we seemed to be everything—walking English dictionaries, a window to the outside world. Although we were forbidden to tell them anything, they knew we had the answers. Some were bold enough to approach me directly and ask, "Professor, would you care to join me?" Their English was often quite formal because, since middle school, they had been taught British English. Others were so shy that we had to assign them to eat with us.

The question of seating could be complicated. Each table seated four people, but we had been warned that the counterparts discouraged sitting with the same students more than once. We were told it was so that the students would have an equal chance to practice their English, but it also appeared that they did not want us to get close to any particular one.

However, we inevitably ended up sitting with the same students more than once.

Breakfast was porridge and boiled eggs. Lunch and dinner were almost always the same too: rice and some sort of watery soup, often with just a couple of marinated vegetables such as kimchi, bean sprouts, or potatoes. Even kimchi, the Korean staple on both sides, was tasteless because it was made with hard green cabbage instead of traditional Napa cabbage, which was scarce that year, supposedly due to a bad harvest. There was hardly ever any meat.

The students usually led the conversation. "How can I learn English better, Professor?" was the question I heard at almost every meal. Improving their English was our mutual concern, but also our cover, which is ironic, given how much they are taught to hate imperialist America. We both hid behind that question.

They admitted to being a bit daunted by the different accents they heard at the school. For example, Joan, who was in her seventies and originally from Alabama, spoke with an accent that was very unfamiliar to them, and they found it quite difficult to understand her. Other teachers had New Zealand, Australian, or British accents. One student asked whether an American or British accent would be more advantageous for his future. It was a valid question, although I did not know in what capacity they were expected to use English when so few North Koreans were allowed to travel. I wanted to tell him that he should watch foreign news on the BBC and CNN and decide which accent he liked better. But I knew the only TV channels he had access to were the North Korean ones. I also wished he could watch Hollywood films so that he would be exposed to everyday English. Of course this was not an option, either.

On rare occasions when questions strayed from the topic

of how best to learn English, they usually went something like this:

> *How long does it take to fly here from New York?*
> *Do you miss your mother?*
> *Who would you marry, an American or a Korean man?*

But they never deviated further than that.

THE NEXT DAY was Park Jun-ho's twentieth birthday, and he was in high spirits. He was popular and sharp, and could be playful, though his laughing eyes sometimes turned cold at a moment's notice. He said very proudly that his family of four lived in the center of Pyongyang, and he was cocky enough to declare that his own speaking skill was excellent, since his father had spoken to him in Chinese and English from the time he was little. That day being his birthday, his mother would have made him noodles—a Chinese birthday tradition, but not a South Korean one—but since he was not at home, the students in his class had planned a celebration.

"Hong Mun-sup will play guitar, and Park Se-hoon is the class dancer! Then Kim Tae-hyun plays the girl in this skit, and Ri Jin-chul the boy," Jun-ho explained. The plan was to gather in one of their rooms that evening and amuse the birthday boy with performances. One by one, they would sing him a song, and this would last a couple of hours. When I asked what kinds of songs, the students just shrugged and said, "Songs about friendship." Here there were no bars, no girls, and no computer games. Other than soccer and basketball and weekly gatherings to watch the TV drama called *The Nation of the Sun*, about the heroic actions of their Great Leader, their only form of entertainment was one another. It was saddening that they had so few ways to amuse themselves, but also lovely. The last time I had made up stories and acted them out with friends was as a child in South Korea, during the seventies, and we did it because we too had little else to play with and no choice but to be creative. Memories of throwing on my mother's clothes to playact a princess, a prince, a pirate rushed back to me, and I felt a yearning for a time long gone.

Park Jun-ho began teasing Choi Min-jun, his roommate, at the dinner table. He told me that Min-jun was known among the boys as the serious one, and they often called him a "romantic." Min-jun became embarrassed and waved his hands in denial. He said Jun-ho was always jesting, and that he regretted telling Jun-ho about his pretty younger sister, who was sixteen, because Jun-ho had said that if they ever met, he would say to her, "You just wait for me."

They all cracked up at this. After all, their only interaction with the opposite sex was with their foreign teachers or the guards who occupied the lower floors of their dormitory. Dr. Joseph told me that initially the school had wanted to bring in male guards, but they felt that they might appear too threatening to the foreigners. With female guards, there were instead concerns that the boys might be distracted, but it turned out that they were from such different social strata that the boys pretty much ignored them. Thus, for the moment, girls and casual dating were just a fantasy. Jun-ho said, "Maybe Min-jun's sister is pretty, but I bet she's too shy for me." It was then that quiet Ryu Jung-min at the table leaned in and said, "But the really funny thing is that this boy talks like this, but he has never had a girlfriend in his life! He is a disaster with girls!"

At the mention of Jun-ho's disastrous ways with girls, all four of us burst out laughing. *Disaster* would become a favorite word for the boys that summer, almost a private joke. They loved saying it under any circumstances—sometimes they would say "disaster food," or that an exam had been a disaster.

At such moments, it was as though we were sitting in any school cafeteria anywhere. They were simply college students who were interested in the one thing most boys their age were interested in: girls. At moments like those, I forgot where I was. Or if I did remember, I quickly made myself forget. And my guard came down, and I felt a sudden freedom from the constraints that wound all of us so tight, and I looked across at their mischievous faces and felt such tenderness for them, and I became a momentary confidante for their gossip about girls and a well-wisher on the twentieth birthday of my charming student, and I felt pleased and relaxed until my eyes would catch the shining metal pins on their chests, the eternally present face of their Eternal President, there on each of their hearts, marking his territory, although they were just badges, and these young men could easily pull them off and throw them into the trash along with the uneaten grub on their trays, but then it would dawn on me that such a thing would never happen, and that this glimmer of hope was only a mirage.

DURING THAT FIRST week, I kept noticing things that bothered me. Once we asked the students to put together a skit, and they chose to write about two Canadian teachers going to a local hospital. One of them was injured so the other offered to sell his blood to help him, but they discovered that medical care was free due to the solicitude of the Great General Kim Jong-il.

Katie pointed out to them that this made no sense, since 1) a foreign teacher would be allowed only in a foreign hospital, which was not free, 2) people generally are not paid for donating blood, and 3) emergency rooms do not require patients to pay up front. The students became puzzled and said, "Well, okay, the friend who is not injured needs to tell the wife of the injured one, so he goes to the airport to fly to Canada to let her know." Katie asked why he wouldn't just call the wife instead of flying all the way to Canada. The students stumbled and said, "Okay, in that case, the friend could use the phone at the hospital, and maybe the doctor will call for them, but how would the doctor speak to the wife in Canada when he speaks no English?" Katie asked why the friend would not just talk to the wife directly. And on it went. Each answer depressed us further, because it was plain that a simple thing like calling a family member in a foreign country was inconceivable to them, at least not without special permission.

Another time, we played a game of Truth or Lie. We asked students to come up with two true statements about themselves and one false one, and the rest of the class had to guess which was which. When one student got up and said, "I visited China last year on vacation," the whole class burst out laughing and shouted, "False!" They all knew that this was impossible.

Then another student said, "When I was a child, I ate tough beef," and many students nodded and shouted out, "True!" I recalled a defector telling me that the first time he ate beef, it was strangely leathery. According to him, during the 2001 outbreak of foot-and-mouth disease, hardly anyone was buying beef, and the rumor was that instead of throwing the aged meat out, Australia had given it to the people of North Korea. It was entirely possible that my elite students had eaten this very beef, especially since that was soon after their great famine. I looked around the classroom and wondered what else they might have experienced as children, and how it had shaped them. So many of them already had at least a few gray hairs. Perhaps it was the lack of nutrition, even for these privileged young men.

At times my students revealed a cluelessness that surprised me. Once a student asked me if it was true that everyone in the world spoke Korean. He had heard the Korean language was so superior that they spoke it in England, China, and America. I did not know what to say. Perhaps he was testing me to see if I would contradict all he had learned thus far and would later report me. Or maybe he was just curious. So I took the safe road: "Well, let me see, in China, they speak Chinese, and in England and the United States, they speak English, the way we speak Korean in Korea. However, I live in America and I speak Korean when I speak to my parents, so one might say that the Korean language does get spoken in America." That took some very quick thinking. Even the simplest question could be a minefield.

They emphatically insisted that Juche Tower was the tallest in the world; that *their* Arch of Triumph was the highest, certainly higher than the one in Paris (true); that their amusement park was the best in the world. They were always comparing themselves to the outside world, which none of them had ever seen, declaring themselves the best. This insistence on "best" seemed strangely childlike, and the words *best* and *greatest* were used so frequently that they gradually lost their meaning.

Another time, a student asked me what my favorite food was. They often asked about my favorite flower, favorite sport, or favorite musical instrument. I wondered sometimes whether they had been given a list of safe questions. I soon learned to answer in the way I thought they expected. I liked tennis. I played piano. I enjoyed *naengmyun,* a cold noodle dish that was popular in both Koreas but happened to be the regional specialty of Pyongyang.

(North Koreans call it *raengmyun*.) I did like *naengmyun,* but I could not tell them that I preferred pasta or soba noodles. Although I had seen one hamburger restaurant in Pyongyang, I did not know if any of my students had been there, and they certainly did not talk about international cuisine. So when asked about my favorite food, I stuck to *naengmyun*, which always brought smiles of approval as they inevitably said, "Yes, I hear *raengmyun* is enjoyed all over the world and is hailed as the best food." I felt unable to break it to them that that particular noodle dish had never taken off abroad the way spaghetti had.

Sometimes a meal felt like an interrogation, either vocal or silent. Once, a student, who turned out to be a class secretary, motioned to another student to ask me a question. "Why must we write those letters?" the student asked. "We never learned them at our former university." His tone was suspicious. I had been expecting such a question for some time, since I had turned the letter writing into a weekly exercise. I told them that a paragraph was the basis of any writing in English and that they must learn how to write it, and letters were a good place to practice them. I knew that the questions came from the counterparts.

There were only a handful of times any student veered from the script. During our conversation about Park Jun-ho's birthday party, one of the boys blurted out that he liked singing rock 'n' roll, and then he turned red, quickly checking to see who might be listening. I had never seen anyone scan the room so fast, and the other students went quiet and looked down at their food. There was no explanation for such an instinctive reaction except for a sort of ingrained fear that I could never fathom. In that fleeting moment, I realized that I had been waiting for that slip. It was even possible that I had engineered it. And when the slip came, the truth was so pathetic, just the revelation of a nineteen-year-old boy singing songs in his dorm room, yet for admitting that in public, he might now be in serious trouble. I did my own nervous check to see who might have witnessed the slip and, just as quickly, I changed the topic of the conversation.

We were always wary of one another. And this incessant circling around the boundary and our efforts not to breach it were exhausting. We wanted to discover things about one another, yet if we stumbled across such information, we both froze.

It was a fine dance. I wanted to push them but not too much; to expose them to the outside world, but so subtly that no one would notice. The missionaries wanted to convert them, but not in any obvious way. (During a previous semester, one of the teachers had been expelled from the DPRK for leaving Christian texts in the men's bathroom, and we had all been warned never to say anything about Jesus. As far as I could tell, the missionaries contented themselves with showing North Koreans the love of Christ simply by being kind to them. Theirs was a long-term project, so that when North Korea did one day open up, they would already have a foothold here.)

Was this really conscionable? Awakening my students to what was not in the regime's program could mean death for them and those they loved. If they were to wake up and realize that the outside world was in fact not crumbling, that it was their country that was in danger of collapse, and that everything they had been taught about the Great Leader was bogus, would that make them happier? How would they live from that point on? Awakening was a luxury available only to those in the free world.

NOT ALL OF us knew it then, but it was a time of upheaval in North Korea. During my first week, at a staff meeting, President

Kim told us that every university in the entire country had shut down, except PUST. The reason PUST had been spared, he said, was that the Great Leader "believed" in him personally. This bit of news was related to us with no further explanation, but it was consistent with outside reports that Kim Jong-un, the "Precious Leader," was being positioned to take over for the sixty-nine-year-old Kim Jong-il, who had suffered a stroke in 2008, and that every university student had been taken out of school and sent to do construction work until April 2012, when the entire nation would celebrate Kim Il-sung's one hundredth birthday.

I was not sure what to think. Western news reports about the DPRK were often unreliable, and the closing of all universities other than PUST seemed an extreme measure, even for North Korea.

It seemed strange that in a country where organized religion was not permitted, and where anyone who did not believe in the Great Leader was considered a heretic, only this school— the "embassy from the kingdom of heaven," according to President Kim—would be permitted to operate. Perhaps the Great Leader believed not in Kim, but in the cash the Christians raised to fund this free, relatively posh school for the North Korean elite. Moreover, I knew of no science teachers at the school, despite the fact that it was called the Pyongyang University of Science and Technology. I wanted to know why my students had not been sent to do construction like the others, but there was no one I could ask.

WITH EACH PASSING day, we, the teachers, wondered why we were so tired. Sarah, a teacher from New Zealand, said that she slept for hours in the middle of the day. Ruth, another New

Zealander, but of Korean origin, said that she felt as though she were still jet-lagged although she had flown in from Yanji, China, which was only one hour behind. I would fall into such a heavy sleep that my body felt almost numb. Katie said that it was because we were all so cautious all the time. Every evening, I thought back to the conversations that had taken place earlier that day during each meal, trying to determine whether I had said something I should not have. It takes tremendous energy to censor yourself all the time, to have to, in a sense, continually lie.

There were mornings when I looked out my window and stared at the wall that separated PUST from the outside. Some teachers whispered that this was a five-star prison. We knew that we could never pass through the gate except on trips to go grocery shopping at the diplomatic compound or on organized sightseeing tours at designated times, when minders planned our outings down to the minute and accompanied us.

On weekends, there were trips outside when teachers could stock up on groceries. The school van took teachers to Pyongyang Shop, a Japanese-owned grocery, and an Argentinian grocery. All of them carried canned products, cheese, fruit, cereal, and long-lasting milk. The Japanese shop sold Japanese-made pancake mix for about five dollars, as well as wheat germ, which cost twice what it did in the United States. The Argentinian shop sold a variety of 100 percent fruit juice concentrates and some canned pasta from France. These stores took euros, Chinese renminbi, and U.S. dollars, but not North Korean won. As per the rules, we were only allowed to use the local currency in places where the locals shopped alongside us. The newly constructed Potonggang Department Store carried every kind of import, from refrigerators and cosmetics to groceries, laid out on two floors connected by an escalator, a rare sight in North

Korea. The people who shopped there looked wealthier than those on the streets.

On those outings, we were escorted out and brought back in as a unit. We never crossed the boundary on our own. Would I be shot if I were to run out the gate while jogging? Was there a watch post from which someone surveyed us at all times? Even in my room, I never felt free. This vigilance was so exhausting that I welcomed it when Sarah came over one night and said, "Let's see if the students would invite us to play soccer with them!"

Basketball and soccer, and sometimes volleyball, were the sports of choice among the students, for the obvious reason that the only equipment required was a ball. After dinner, they gathered and played either in the cement basketball court by their dormitory or in the grass field in the center of the campus. They did not have jerseys, so the teams were divided between those students with shirts and those without. On hot July evenings, they played with a zeal I had not seen them show anywhere else. They shouted at each other in jest, burst into laughter, sweated profusely, and moved with the unique grace and beauty of youth. I often sat on a rock nearby and watched them. The sun would be setting in the distance, so slowly that sometimes it appeared as though even the sun moved at a different speed there, like the slow smoke billowing from the distant tower. That smoke, on such evenings, looked as ethereal as those moving bodies, and in that moment, I forgot all of it, the taboo subjects we never spoke of and the secrets hidden all over campus. Instead all I saw was their heartbreaking youth and energy, and I wished then that they could have the whole world, all of it, that which had been denied to them for twenty years of their lives, because none of them had any idea that as their bodies bounced, their minds stood so very still within that field in that campus locked away from time.

On that particular evening, Sarah and I walked past them and lingered, hoping for an invitation, until one of them asked, "Professor, would you like to play with us?" Sarah broke into a huge smile and said, "Yes!" and it was as easy as that. Surprisingly, the counterparts, who must have been informed, never intercepted her. Before we knew it, it became a ritual for Sarah to play with the students in the evenings. Sarah had played back in college, just a few years ago. At about five foot two, with bright blue eyes, sandy hair always in a ponytail, and freckles covering her childlike features, she looked like a quiet, church-going country girl, but on the field she was ferocious, with quick foot movements and remarkable stamina. The boys were impressed. They weren't used to playing with girls. But this wasn't just any girl. This was one of the first foreigners they had ever met. Their professor, no less. They loved the novelty of it, and Sarah became a mini-star on campus. A few other professors, including me, joined in at times, but never with her expertise.

During a break in the game, Sarah came up to me and said, "Oh, I feel good being here now, really good, I could really imagine living here." The boys must have felt just as relaxed because some who had been standing in front of the big gray building across the road walked over to watch as well. They were wearing the same uniform Choi Min-jun had been wearing a few nights ago at dinner. "So why are you wearing that?" I asked casually. "Oh, we guard our Kimilsungism Study Hall," one said. I learned that six boys took turns guarding the large, austere building all night long, from dinnertime until breakfast. I could not imagine what could be inside that needed guarding; it seemed that their demonstration of devotion was itself the point. The mystery of the uniform was not that mysterious after all, so why had some of them been so afraid to tell us?

6

THE WORLD WIDE WEB WAS NOT REALLY WORLDWIDE, IT turned out. None of us ever breathed a word about it. A few students who had transferred from Kim Chaek University said that what they most missed from their old school was how they had all been connected by an electronic network. I understood that they were talking about their intranet, a heavily censored network that allowed them access only to already downloaded information and state-sponsored websites.

I was not allowed to tell them that their intranet was not the same as the Internet—that the rest of the world was connected while only they were left out. I would look for signs that one of them guessed the truth, but I saw none. Without having experienced the World Wide Web, could I have imagined it? Even if someone had described it to me, I would never have been able to fathom it.

I asked innocently whether they could communicate with their parents over this electronic connection, and they answered, "No, just by phone, sometimes." I asked whether their parents knew how to use a computer. Most said their fathers knew how, but not their mothers. One said that his father was a government official so he was good with computers, and another said that his father was a doctor so he also knew how to use them.

They had all heard of Bill Gates from their former universities, but I wanted to tell them about Mark Zuckerberg, who at their age had revolutionized the way we communicate with one another. How very much they would have enjoyed learning about the boy wonder and his invention of Facebook, the magic of connecting with people all over the world! Sometimes I would fantasize about smuggling in _The Social Network,_ writing subtitles, and secretly distributing it throughout the student dorms, but I was not a superhero, and all I could do was smile at their claims about their amazing intranet across our trays of dull-tasting kimchi and rice.

By the second week, with the counterparts' approval, the teachers had begun to introduce the students to various parlor games—trivia contests, spelling bees, Pictionary. Right away I was struck by their astounding lack of general knowledge about the world. These were North Korea's brightest students, yet photos of the United Nations, the Taj Mahal, and the Great Pyramids of Giza elicited only blank expressions. A few guessed the names and locations of the Eiffel Tower and Stonehenge, but only after much hemming and hawing. Hardly anyone knew what country had first landed men on the moon, despite the fact that they were science and technology majors. Asked what year computers had been invented, most had no idea.

At the same time, they all knew that Alaska had been sold to the United States for the absurdly low price of $7.2 million—a clear lesson in American imperialism. And though their English vocabulary levels were uneven, there was one phrase everyone knew: *brain drain*. Was the regime so afraid that members of the elite would defect that they had drilled them on that word? When we decided to make origami together, we learned that they knew how to make nothing except war planes.

Of course, in response to any question about their own country—such as when their first satellite, *Kwangmyongsong-1*, was launched into space (an event much boasted about by the DPRK, although the rest of the world deemed it a failure)—they all shouted out the exact date and year.

They enjoyed games that pitted one group against another, perhaps because they did everything in groups. They came to the cafeteria in groups and lived on assigned floors in groups. They played only group sports, and when I mentioned that I liked tennis, they barely responded. They knew what it was, but it was unfamiliar to them. Being divided into groups and ranked in hierarchies—that was what they knew. An individual action was unthinkable.

Group spirit dominated everything. Even when they were competing, they looked out for one another. During the all-freshmen trivia game, which took place in one of the bigger classrooms, some of them whispered answers to others. And spelling bees were nearly impossible, since if one got stuck on a word, the whole class would help him along by mouthing the correct spelling.

When Class 4 finally won the trivia game, their excitement was boundless because they had always been the underdogs. As Katie and I entered their classroom afterward to congratulate them, they all got up and applauded to express their gratitude, which brought us to tears. The class did not settle down from their high for some time. Those were fine moments. Sometimes I wonder whether they, too, will one day reflect on that summer afternoon when they were young and played a game and won and cheered with two teachers from America who cried with happiness.

As I spent more time with them, I began to notice many peculiar habits. For example, they did not like to volunteer answers during class. These were excellent students. They prepared so thoroughly that it often seemed pointless to go over their homework. The margins of their textbooks were filled with scribbled notes. Yet they hesitated before raising their hands. When I would call on them, they would immediately get up to answer, but volunteering seemed foreign to them.

Another thing that baffled the students was the pronoun "my." When referring to Pyongyang, they never said "my" city, but rather "our" city. The DPRK was never "my" country but "our" country. In fact, the words *Pyongyang* and *DPRK* were always modified with "our," as in "our Pyongyang" or "our DPRK." Even when we gave them a special lesson on "my" versus "our," and made clear that they could drop "our" altogether with proper nouns, they seemed confused.

They also seemed to fear office hours. This came up because, even though it was only our second week, Class 4 was already falling behind, and we were told that the counterparts had instructed us to give them extra help. However, when Katie and I set up office hours for those who needed tutoring, we could not persuade anyone to show up, no matter how much we pleaded. The students did not understand what office hours were and viewed them as punishment. We also realized that they were frightened at the idea of being with us one on one, and so we told them they could come in pairs. Still, one student insisted, "Please, can you tell me *in* the classroom?" Finally we told them that it was mandatory for them to come, and they seemed pleased to obey.

During that second week, some of the teachers were called to the office of Dr. Joseph, our liaison to the counterparts. On his desk were slips of paper that the counterparts had demanded to know the nature of. On the slips were messages such as "The place where dough rises." These were clues from an afternoon activity all the teachers had planned—a treasure hunt in which clues and pictures were to be hidden in various locations across campus. The pictures were innocuous images of the sun, moon, and other objects that teachers had randomly printed out from the Internet. Each student would be given a sort of scorecard with a set of boxes, and at each location they would draw the image they found on the card, eventually filling all the boxes. Although the activity itself had been preapproved, the counterparts were furious that the clues and images had not been submitted for approval beforehand and demanded to know what each one meant.

Dr. Joseph looked upset. He had been reprimanded by the counterparts. We, in turn, panicked since we had no other activity for the afternoon. Still worse, we were worried that the counterparts would not let us plan any further activities. We promised to submit a detailed explanation of the clues and quickly replaced the treasure hunt with the viewing of a documentary.

This was how the treasure hunt came to be replaced by a showing of *March of the Penguins*. It was easy to narrow down our choices: only nature documentaries or animated films were allowed, and *March of the Penguins* was already approved. Unfortunately, the classroom was designed in such a way that projecting a movie against the wall was not simple. The side walls had windows, and the front and back walls featured blackboards, as well as portraits of and messages from the two Great Leaders, which could not be moved. Throughout the school, it was impossible to find a blank wall not adorned by both men. So the one hundred freshmen gathered in one of the bigger classrooms to watch a movie that was half the size it could have been.

Wherever we were, the Leaders were too. And I wondered what would happen when Kim Jong-il died and Kim Jong-un took over, not knowing how imminent this was. Would a third portrait be added to every wall in the country? Would they have to take down some of the paintings of the father and son to make room for the grandson? Would they have to move some of the slogans and insert his sayings there as well? What about songs? What about books? What about bronze statues? It was endless, and it would be a major project. Katie remarked how much easier it would be if they could just Photoshop an image in rather than doing it manually.

AT MEALS, THE boys flirted with Katie. Park Jun-ho quizzed her on the qualities she looked for in a man. When she named them, he said: "I have them all!" So she asked, in return, what he liked in a woman. "Obedience," he answered. When we gave them a writing assignment entitled "How to Successfully Get a Girl," some of the boys seemed mystified. They came up to me at lunch and asked, "Teacher, this is very difficult for us. How can we write this? We have never had girlfriends!" They were technically college juniors, having spent two years at other universities that were mostly coed. With such a fine pedigree and having grown up mostly in Pyongyang, these were some of the most eligible bachelors in the country, and yet the methods they came up with to woo their dream girl were almost childlike.

One wrote that if you saw your favorite girl drowning, you should rescue her, even if you did not swim, and then she would see that you are nice, and you would become boyfriend and girlfriend. Another wrote that if it rained, you must share your umbrella with your favorite girl if she did not have one. No one suggested anything so bold as going with a girl to a café or movie, but several wrote about meeting up at the Grand People's Study House, their national library, which made me think that perhaps that was the main place where boys and girls met in Pyongyang. More than one described his ideal girl as one who would obey him, listen to him, and be a good mother to his son. After all, this was a country where the most important thing a woman had ever done was to give birth to the Great Leader— not unlike the Virgin Mary. Kim Jong-suk, Kim Il-sung's wife and Kim Jong-il's mother, has been immortalized as the revolutionary female general, one of the holy trinity of "Three Generals" (the others being her husband and son). However, Kim Jong-il's various wives were never even acknowledged.* Most students wrote postscripts about how they really had no interest in girls and would rather study to help build their powerful and prosperous nation and make their Great Leader proud, as though they were conscious of who might read their words.

Some of the young teachers in my group were just as innocent. Sarah talked about a past romance, and yet after some time, I realized that the relationship had not involved any physical contact. I asked her what made it a romance and not a friendship, but she just smiled shyly. Katie also talked about dating but never allowing kissing. She kept repeating that she was okay being alone because God fulfilled her. I wondered whether my students were equally fulfilled by their devotion to the Great Leader.

One evening, after dinner, Sarah stopped by my room,

---

* In 2012, when Kim Jong-un brought his wife out in public, it was considered a radical break with tradition.

looking like a teenager in her T-shirt and baggy soccer shorts. She told me that she had written a will before leaving home. She had no idea what it would be like in North Korea and asked God whether it would be all right if she died. And he told her that it would be. And she knew that he would show her the way. "I want my life to count," said Sarah with wistful eyes, and for a moment, I felt a kinship with her. She said that she wanted to marry soon, now that she was approaching thirty, but there were no men for her at PUST. If she met someone who shared her dreams, she could imagine marrying him, moving here together, and dedicating her life to bringing Christianity to the people of North Korea.

She asked me if I had a boyfriend. I told her I was not sure, although there was someone I liked. I immediately regretted admitting this; I barely knew her, and she was a missionary. I was lonely, I guess. With each day, I felt more isolated. It was odd that I should have felt so in need of a human connection in this communal space. Every meal was shared, every second of the day spent in the company of others. In New York City, as a writer, a whole week sometimes passed in which I was holed up in my apartment and did not see a person and felt content, and yet here I wanted to pour my heart out to someone, anyone. And for that moment, it felt as though we were just two girlfriends whispering secrets to each other.

"What's he like? Did you meet him at church?" she asked with a smile in her eyes, lowering her voice to say the word *church*.

I said no.

"Is he someone who could join you here?" she asked. She had a habit of opening her eyes unusually wide as though she were permanently surprised.

I knew what she was after, and I felt uneasy about where the conversation was going. So I just said, "Probably not."

Her eyes widened even more. "He's Christian, right?"

I was not sure how to answer this since I did not want to reveal myself, so I answered as truthfully as I could, reflecting on the fact that my lover was a writer. "He's . . . spiritual."

She asked again, "But does he *not* believe in Jesus?"

I could see the beginning of a rift, the disapproval in her eyes. I liked her, and I did not want to lose her. So I just repeated, "He's spiritual."

She seemed confused, but she asked no more questions. There was no doubt in her mind that I was just like her, a missionary, because why would I work without pay in this bleak land if I were not following a higher calling? But no real believer would be interested in a nonbeliever for a mate.

Life was about serving a purpose, and yet there was a gulf between us. Her life's purpose was to serve God. Without him, life would lose its meaning and she might as well not exist.

What I did not tell Sarah was that during the first ten days, I had received just one email from the man in Brooklyn. *When are you coming home?* he asked. That's all he wrote. He was a man of few words to begin with, and perhaps he felt nervous sending emails to this forbidden place on the other side of the world. For newly connected lovers, two months apart was an interminably long time, especially when our lives were moving at such vastly different speeds. Since I had arrived in Pyongyang, England's *News of the World* had shut down after the phone hacking scandal exploded. The final Harry Potter movie had come and gone. Mumbai had suffered another bombing. A new nation had been born in Sudan. Amazon had just announced a new tablet to rival the iPad. I knew all this because I was one of the very few in all of North Korea who had access to global news. In my room, I always had CNN Asia on, often with the sound muted. In the past I had never watched much TV news, but here it felt comforting, a window to the outside world.

One evening, I was grading papers when I happened to look up and see the Brooklyn Bridge and the Empire State Building on the screen. I burst into tears, seized by such a profound longing for home that I could not stand it. I paced back and forth, wanting to pick up the phone and call home, but of course we had no phones that could call outside. Nothing went in or out. It felt so stationary that it was sometimes hard to put dates to things.

I had asked my students when their favorite drama, *The Nation of the Sun*, was made, and they had no idea. Ten years ago? Twenty? They seemed to think it was about twenty, which made me realize that even their favorite TV program was not currently produced. Both Great Leaders always looked to be in late middle age. No one knew the exact age of the Precious Leader; it was not until later, after he came to power, that various media confirmed his age as twenty-nine. Their newspaper was filled with vague events with nonspecific dates, and on the one trip we had taken outside the gate, I had seen store signs with words such as *namse* (a word for vegetables no longer used in South Korea) that harkened back to decades ago. The entire country was like a linguistic and cultural Galápagos.

So time moved on—or didn't—on this strange campus that seemed even stranger than the strange country beyond its walls, and, to find an anchor, I hung on to my lover's email. *When are you coming home?* Those five words carried me as I woke up at 5 a.m. and opened the curtain to face each new day.

"So are you a writer?"

Sarah's question shook me out of my reverie.

For a moment I was caught off guard, but then I said yes, I was a novelist, but I was there as a teacher. To my relief, she seemed satisfied with my answer and never brought the subject up again.

Shortly after my conversation with Sarah, I discovered that one of the teachers, a man from a Christian university in Mississippi, had Googled everyone from the group. Some of the missionaries seemed oblivious to their surroundings, even naive, often forgetting that our Internet connection was constantly monitored. A teacher from Texas told me that he got on the Internet and tried to pay for something with PayPal, but it was denied because the company blocked usage from countries under international economic sanction. Another teacher seemed surprised to learn that this country had gulags.

When Katie heard about the teacher who had Googled everyone, she panicked. She had done some NGO work helping defectors. Though I did not say anything to Katie, I was afraid that my cover had been blown. So far, no one in our group had asked me directly whether or not I was Christian, perhaps because they kept a low profile themselves. All I could hope was that the counterparts did not learn the truth.

Yet it was understandable that we would sometimes forget to be careful, since we had not been raised in an atmosphere of hypervigilance. With each day, I found myself slipping, usually at meals, where our conversations were more informal. Sometimes after teaching all morning, I became clumsy from fatigue. Other times I slipped on purpose.

Once, we were discussing sports—the students were uniformly passionate about sports—and they were curious about the NBA, but the only player they knew was Michael Jordan. Their knowledge was never up to date. Even the North Korean basketball superstar they talked about—Ri Myung-hoon, the tallest player in the world, according to them—had played little since the 1990s. They all claimed that they had never seen an NBA game, but some of them seemed more aware than they let on. One student asked, "Who is the best player now?" So he knew that Jordan had retired. I told him that it was Miami Heat's LeBron James, but then decided I would be on safer ground with tennis and told a story about seeing two top-ranked players, Rafael Nadal and Roger Federer, play at the U.S. Open a few years before.

"You saw them in person?" one of the students asked, incredulous.

We were not supposed to say things that could be seen as boasting about America, but I wanted them to know that seeing professional sports in person was very much a reality in the rest of the world, and that it was perfectly normal for players from Spain and Switzerland to travel to New York, and vice versa. I wanted them to know that no one told us where we could go and where we could not. So I just shrugged and said, "Of course, the stadium is only about forty-five minutes from my apartment by subway, so I go to the U.S. Open every year." They said nothing, and I was not sure if they believed me.

Other times I would say things like "Yes, I learned to play pool when I did an exchange program in London during college." Or "I backpacked across Europe when I was your age," or "I was born in Seoul and still have family there, so I visit Seoul often." They never asked, "How was it?" or "What is London like?" but I knew they noticed the fact that, unlike them, we teachers were able to travel freely. Their only response would be to suddenly go quiet, and I would pick up the conversation, saying something about Pyongyang instead, at which their faces would brighten.

They would ask me what I had seen in Pyongyang, and they

would describe other worthy sites. There was a place called Golden Lane, they said, which was a bowling alley as well as a billiard hall. There was Changgangwon, a "service" place with a swimming pool and barbershop. Pyongyang Indoor Stadium was another place they were quite proud of. But none of them offered the phrases that usually accompany locals' advice to visitors: *You must go there next week*, or *Let me show you*. No one here was allowed to go anywhere of his own accord, without permission.

The teachers had been talking about a possible trip to Kaesung next semester, so I asked the students how many had been there. Kaesung had been an ancient Korean capital as well as a bargaining chip during the Korean War, when both sides stalled in signing the armistice in hopes of securing it. Because of its proximity to the 38th parallel, the city had served as an inter-Korean trade zone since 2002. It was possibly the second most important city in the nation, only a couple of hours from Pyongyang, yet only one student had been there. During their time at PUST, they weren't even allowed to visit their parents in downtown Pyongyang, only ten or fifteen minutes away by car.

Not only were the teachers' movements similarly restricted, but communication was heavily constrained. Joan said that her daughter was mining her regular emails back home and had promised to tell her about anything urgent. Katie said that she was in contact with no one but her parents, and she generally wrote only one sentence to tell them she was okay. Sarah also kept things very short and to the point. I never emailed my parents from PUST. My mother was so upset and worried about my being there that she could barely look at me before I left. I sent a weekly email saying "I am safe" to my brother-in-law as a way of checking in on my sister, as well as letting the rest of the family know that I was alive.

We were always obedient. If any one of us had been wild

and rebellious, that person could have tried to slip past the guards or climb the walls that surrounded PUST, but nobody ever dared. The constant surveillance by the counterparts and the minders evoked fear in us. We knew that the consequences were unthinkable, so we did what we were told.

We accepted our situation meekly. How quickly we became prisoners, how quickly we gave up our freedom, how quickly we tolerated the loss of that freedom, like a child being abused, in silence. In this world, there were no individual demands, and asking permission for everything was infantilizing. So we began to understand our students, who had never been able to do anything on their own. The notion of following your heart's desire, of going wherever you chose, did not exist here, and I did not see any way to let them know what it felt like, especially since, after so little time in their system, I had lost my own sense of freedom.

BY THE END of the second week, the students seemed to have gotten used to the idea of office hours. Now that they had been commanded to come, they arrived in swarms. One afternoon, as Katie and I were getting ready for the students, Mr. Ri appeared at our door. Until then, no counterpart or minder had randomly turned up at my office. He made small talk and told us not to be nervous, which of course only made us more so. He then sat down in one of the spare chairs and began to page through the textbook on my desk. The book had already won the counterparts' approval, so there was no need for us to be worried, and yet his behavior was vaguely threatening. Katie sat in one corner and began reading through student compositions, which made me panic slightly in case any of them revealed too much. So while exchanging pleasantries with Mr. Ri, I casually took a notebook and flung it over the pile of papers in front of Katie. Luckily, she caught on right away and pretended to be rearranging the desk, efficiently hiding the pile. Mr. Ri seemed not to notice. Continuing to skim the textbook, he remarked how hard English was. I told him in simple Korean, so that Katie could understand, that he should join our class if he wanted to learn more, but I joked that he would have to do his homework, and my invitation seemed to please him. It was hard to believe that only three years before we had shared tears at the airport. If he remembered it, he did not show it, and I certainly never mentioned it. In this world, sentimental reflection on a shared history was not a thing we could afford.

I then noticed several students at the door, who swiftly recoiled when they saw Mr. Ri. These were the most garrulous ones from the group, so it was eerie to see how they stiffened at the sight of him. Even Park Jun-ho, the student with perpetually smiling eyes and devilish charm, looked nervous. Mr. Ri seemed to want to stick around, but I put my foot down. "My students can't really focus with you around," I said with a smile, and he laughed awkwardly and left. Immediately, the boys visibly relaxed. Soon more boys arrived, and before we knew it, we had an office full of students. Some had questions about the textbook, but mostly they wanted just to talk. "Free talking in English!" they insisted.

While Katie told them a story about setting her kitchen on fire in China while trying to roast a chicken, I thought about what I could possibly tell them, but almost everything about my life was taboo. So instead of opening up about myself, I brought up their recent homework topic, "How to Successfully Get a Girl," and asked whether people still subscribed to arranged marriages in their society. They said yes, some, but they themselves preferred the idea of marrying for love. However, they really did not think about it, since women typically married at twenty-seven and men around thirty. This was probably due to the fact that most men were required to serve in the military for ten years, starting at seventeen, although my students were exempt from such duty, as most children of the elite were. Then they asked how it was done in America, so I told them there were no arranged marriages, but some people now met via computer. I caught myself in mid-sentence, before I spoke the word *Internet*. Unable to explain about dating sites or speak freely as they had requested, I could do nothing but return to the topic of English grammar.

THE FOLLOWING SATURDAY, I found myself at a table with three students wearing their khaki guard uniforms, by now a familiar sight. The students seemed more relaxed, and when I asked them why they had to guard the Kimilsungism Study Hall every night, they told me that they were guarding the spirit of their Great Leader. Then I asked them what was inside the building. Just classrooms, they said. This same building was where they disappeared in the late afternoons to study Juche, so it occurred to me that it was a bit like a church for them.

As I imagined all the more productive ways those young men could spend their Saturday nights, Kang Sun-pil added, "Oh, but it is not tiring at all. There are six of us. We take turns. It is really not difficult. We read and study English to pass the time, and if we learn English, we will be able to better serve our country and our Great General Kim Jong-il." This was so clearly articulated that I did a double take. Until then Sun-pil had been so quiet in class that I had hardly noticed him, but in that moment I could not help thinking that if I ever slipped, he would report me. Then I looked at the other two at the table. Suddenly I did not trust any of them. These moments of doubt were like poison. I was not sure who they were, and I felt like a mother terrified of her own children, an extremely ugly feeling. But then one of them would say something adorable, and I would shake it off.

To change the subject, I told them that the teachers had been taken sightseeing that day. When I said that I had seen their subway system, they immediately guessed that I had been to the Buheung (Revival) and Yunggwang (Glory) stations, the designated stops for tourists, which I had been shown each time I visited Pyongyang. I also told them that I was taken to the Grand People's Study House. At this, Ryu Jung-min suddenly perked up and asked if I had seen any students there. He looked at me intently, and from his expression, I gathered that this was an important question. To ponder its implications, I asked him to repeat it.

"Were there students like us? University students?" he asked.

Now that I thought about it, I did not recall seeing a single student their age there.

"No, everyone looked a bit older," I said slowly. "Maybe the young people were in their mid-twenties? So I guess no university students." He looked down with something akin to resignation.

"When were you there?" another student piped up. "Perhaps it was morning, and university students were all in classes there instead. They give classes at the Grand People's Study House, and those classes are free, all because of the solicitude of our Great General Kim Jong-il."

Although we had been shown two lively classes in session, I

could not remember seeing any college students there, except perhaps a few young women. When I said this, it seemed to make everyone at the table anxious.

Later that night, I thought I understood why the students had been so inquisitive, and so tense. Jung-min and the others probably had so little communication with anyone outside the university that they had no idea where their friends were. Whenever I asked them if they corresponded with their family and friends, they never answered directly. One student said that he called his parents when he missed them, but when I asked whether there was a phone in the dormitory, he did not answer. Another student said that he was waiting for a package from his sister, and when I asked him if he wrote letters to his parents too, he also did not answer. My suspicion was that contact was rare. Or if they had a way of contacting home—some of them might have owned cell phones—perhaps they could not converse freely without fear of being listened in on.

But something else struck me about Jung-min's question. He wanted to know if we had seen any university students in the one place in Pyongyang where they usually congregated. We had seen none. Could it be that PUST really was the only university open in all of North Korea, as President Kim had told us? And did the closing of the universities have anything to do with the fact that Kim Jong-il's health was failing and that a change of regime might be imminent? Our students were the crème de la crème of this society. Of course they would not be sent to construction fields like the rest, but instead sent here, to a boarding school within their own city, where they could practice their English and wait for the political storm to pass. Was it our job, then, to provide the sons of the North Korean elite with a temporary sanctuary?

7

ONE AFTERNOON I WAS HAVING LUNCH WITH THREE STU-
dents as usual, and just as I was finishing, Katie rushed over to
my table and asked to talk in private. There was nowhere we
could go where we would not be overheard, so we decided to
take a walk around the campus, hoping it would look as though
we were strolling and discussing the day's lesson. Taking a walk
was the only way we could speak freely. So as not to appear suspicious, we stopped occasionally to take pictures of each other.

Katie was panicked about a conversation with one of the
students at her table. The student had asked to sit with her,
even though he did not belong to either of our classes. Sometimes students were so eager to practice their English that when
they could not sit with their own teachers, they approached any
teacher they saw nearby. There was no clear rule about eating
only with those you taught, so occasionally we ended up sitting
with students we did not know.

It had started innocently enough when the student asked
her why higher education in the United States was not free as

it was in North Korea, as made possible by their Great Leader. This was not a surprising question. During previous visits, I had been asked the same thing, which made me think the regime must use the costly higher education system in America as an example of the failure of capitalism.

Katie said that she did her best to explain scholarships and loans, as well as the meaning of private and public education, but she knew that she was not supposed to discuss any of it and became nervous. This particular student, however, probed further. He had never even heard the word *tax* until he came to PUST, where it was mentioned in one of his textbooks, and he found it impossible to understand.

"What are these things called 'tax'?" he wanted to know. "Why do people pay this money to the government?"

Katie tried to explain, but she felt stuck on what she should and should not say. She was worried that perhaps the student had been testing her and would write up a report on her. We circled the campus a couple of times, discussing how to best deal with the situation.

Finally, we decided that I should eat with him to see if she should worry about any of it. So, at the next meal, Katie pointed him out to me, and I approached him and asked if I might join him. He seemed surprised and pleased and introduced himself. His name was Ryu Ji-hoon. His English was good, so maybe he was a sophomore.

He was not interested in small talk. As soon as we sat down, he told me that one of his teachers had insisted that both humans and animals were capable of creativity. However, he thought that only humans could be creative. What were my thoughts? I had never thought about the topic until that moment and told him as much. I said I could not be sure, but dolphins, for example, were known for being very intelligent.

But I felt that he was not really interested in my answer, as he moved on quickly.

"Have you heard of 'The Song of General Kim Jong-il'?" he asked.

"Yes," I said cautiously.

"What do you think of it?" he asked me, point blank.

I froze. Complete honesty was out of the question, but I wanted to answer as truthfully as I could. So I said, "You and I come from different systems. Americans have their national anthem. Britain has theirs. South Korea has theirs, too. I understand that that particular song is basically your national anthem, and I respect that."

He seemed to reflect on my answer for a while. Meanwhile, the other two at the table looked nervous and remained quiet until one of them blurted out a question about soccer. But this particular student was not deterred, and he shot out another question.

"National assembly . . . tell me about it."

"National assembly? Which national assembly? Whose national assembly?" I said, slightly panicked. "You mean in South Korea? Or the U.S. Congress? They're all different, so it's impossible to say."

He was not so easily dissuaded. "Any country, doesn't matter. Tell me the general idea. You are American, so tell me about how it works in America," he said, meeting my eyes.

Uncertain how much I was allowed to reveal, I took a deep breath and answered in the simplest way I knew. I told him that the United States is made up of fifty states and that the people in those states elect representatives to Congress. We have an elected president, too, I said, and that the president and representatives have to work with one another to pass laws. So in fact it is the people who make decisions.

"But I think the president is the one who should make decisions," he fired back. "He has the power, no?"

I believe I closed my eyes in that moment. I felt weak in the knees. Perhaps living among such devout missionaries had made me religious because I broke into a mental prayer then to anyone anywhere to give me the strength to tell the truth. This was the exact kind of discussion we had been warned against. I knew that this student might be trying to trap me, or worse, that I might get him in serious trouble.

"It's like this," I said cautiously. "For example, at this school, President James Kim is the face of PUST, but the real power is not his, nor should it be his. This entire school is about the students, not President Kim. It's the same in our system. Our country is not for the president but the people. The president is just the face, the symbol, but the real power belongs to the people. The people make the decisions."

What I had just described was, more or less, democracy. I could not read the expression on his face, but almost immediately afterward he said, "Thank you, Professor. I do not want to take up too much of your time. It was my pleasure to have dinner with you."

That evening, Katie and I circled the campus a few times again, discussing our growing fears about his motives. Perhaps he was on a mission to earn some sort of reward by trading information about us.

"So what?" Katie said. "The most they could do is deport us. So we get deported and get sent home, which would be just *fine*. But what if that's not the case? What if he's genuinely curious?"

The second scenario made us both grim. What if we were the instigators of his doubt, what if he was beginning to realize that everything he had known thus far was a lie, and that we were the ones who held the key to truth? We agreed that we would never sit with him again, not even if he asked. "A dinner with us might get him killed," Katie said. I wanted to dismiss the comment as the melodrama of a twenty-three-year-old, but I knew it wasn't that. In North Korea, such a consequence was entirely possible.

THE NEXT DAY, I was almost done with dinner when a student approached and pulled up a chair. He had heard from a group of students that I had said animals demonstrated creativity, and he wanted to refute the idea. I burst out laughing and told him that I had never studied animal intelligence or behavior and had only been guessing. I told him I had simply pointed out that among the millions of species of animals, some, like dolphins, were known to be smarter than others. He seemed greatly disturbed by this and pointed out that clever and creative were two different things, and then proceeded to tell a long story involving a monkey, to illustrate the point that animals could not think creatively. Other students gathered around us and chimed in. They had all majored in some discipline within science and technology and had a lot to say about the creativity of animals versus the creativity of humans.

"Well, you are all philosophers, and so to each his own," I finally said. "We as humans are imperfect. We are changing so rapidly, every second, every month, every year. Look at the way technology is altering the way we think about everything. Perhaps the study of animals is changing too, and we can't really rely on discoveries that are many years old. I think being human, with an infinitely expanding mind, means being open-minded. I'd like to be open-minded about this question."

They seemed amused by my answer, and mildly satisfied.

Then one of them leaned in and said, "I am Ji-hoon's room-mate, and he is with you." This was so unexpected that at first I was not sure if I had heard him right.

"Ji-hoon's with me?" I said, haltingly.

"Yes, he thinks like you," he said shyly.

That night I lay awake, unable to fall asleep. I was anxious and scared. Our fears and hopes were justified: Ji-hoon was thirsty for information, not trapping us to make a report. Perhaps this was why the regime had shut down universities across the coun-try. Perhaps some small efforts to overthrow the dictatorship of the Great Leader had begun percolating in some corners of this oblique country—the beginnings of a North Korean Spring.

Katie had said that we could get him killed, and that we shouldn't talk to him anymore. But if we did not talk to him and avoided giving him any more information, then what was I doing here?

It was the parents of our students who were at the helm of this country, responsible for making it the way it was, and these very young men would inherit that task. Most of them were being groomed to hold top positions and to help their Precious Leader suppress and isolate the people, which would ensure that he remained in power. Such was the prescribed course of their futures as the offspring of the privileged class. Such was the *best*-case scenario. And, as their teachers, we were the ones who would arm these young men with enough English to com-bat the world they were conditioned to view as the enemy.

Until then I had hoped that perhaps I could change one student, open up one path of understanding. But what kind of a future did I envision for the one student I reached? Opening up this country would mean sacrificing these lives. Opening up this country would mean the blood of my beautiful students. I recalled Ji-hoon's face and tried not to think of the terrible consequences, and that night, and many nights afterward, passed like this in Pyongyang. This particular night there was an endless, mournful rain. Fear can creep up on you anywhere, but when it does in North Korea it is a lonely feeling.

I gave up trying to sleep and turned on the TV. CNN Asia reported heavy rain in all of East Asia, eastern China, and most of South Korea. "How about North Korea?" the anchor asked. The question sounded almost cheeky, and the weather woman replied, "Probably. It was raining last week, but that information alone took four days for us to obtain, so we just don't know!"

From that night on, when I looked at the faces of my boys, I would think—and then try not to think—of what lay ahead for them. One of the vocabulary words I had to teach them was *fleeting*. I would use the phrase "Youth is fleeting," and while gazing at them, repeating the phrase aloud, I would think how much briefer their youth was than that of young men their age back home. But I did not like to reflect on this. Anytime I imagined the gloom of their future I shook it off as quickly as I could so that I could stand being there, in that time, teaching them the English language to the best of my ability.

Now, a few years later, their faces still come to me, one by one, and this motherly feeling overwhelms me. I taught them how to speak, this strange breed of children, unaware of the world outside. Yet I hope they have forgotten everything I inspired in them and have simply grown to become soldiers of the regime. I do not want to imagine what might happen if they retained my lessons, remembered me, began questioning the system. I cannot bear the idea that any of my students—my boys who so eagerly shouted, "Good morning, Professor Kim! How are you?" every time I walked into the classroom—might end up somewhere dark and cold, in one of the gulags that exist all over North Korea. The thought keeps me awake at night still.

8

After two weeks, the teachers were elated to be taken on our first excursion outside the city, to an apple farm thirty minutes away. It was a weekend, yet on either side of us we saw people working in fields so lusciously green that they looked as though they had been painted. For a moment, the stories of bare land and bare mountains and the SOS from the World Food Program and the sanctions from the United Nations condemning the DPRK for human rights violations seemed like stuff that people had made up out of boredom or malice. For a moment, I wanted to believe what was before my eyes—an immaculate landscape and clean air. I could almost imagine families with picnic baskets in tow on their way to pick apples, but the road remained empty the whole way there.

At one point, in the distance, we saw what looked like dark straw houses. The minders told us they were part of a model folk village for tourists that was under construction, and that this land had once belonged to the capital of Koguryo Kingdom from Korea's Three Kingdom Era. For a moment I felt excited, remembering how, as a schoolchild in South Korea, I'd learned about this fantastic kingdom famed for its horse-riding warriors and exotic costumes for much of the first millennium. And here it was, this land still here with the low mountains shadowing the horizon, and green patches of land stretching in front of us.

Then the bus swerved closer to the edge of the road, and I saw a few people walking alongside it. Their faces were ghastly, as though they had not been fed in years. A skeletal woman held out a pack of cigarettes as though offering it for sale to any passing bus, although there was none but ours. When we passed closer to one of the construction sites, the workers became visible, with hollowed eyes and sunken cheeks, clothing tattered, heads shaved, looking like Nazi concentration camp victims. The sight was so shocking that both Katie and I drew in sharp breaths. We could not say anything or show our feelings, since the minder sat nearby, but we exchanged glances and Katie mouthed the exact word that struck me at that moment: "Slaves."

It was clear to me that there was one set of people in Pyongyang—among them my students, the party leaders, the minders—who were well fed and had healthy complexions and were of regular height, and then there were all the other people, the ones I glimpsed through the windows of the bus. On weekend shopping trips, I had seen them on the streets, cutting trees or sweeping the sidewalk or riding trams. They were often bony, their faces almost dark green from overexposure to the sun or malnutrition or something worse. They were generally shorter and markedly smaller in every way, with haunted eyes. The old ones almost always walked stooped, and I always wondered whether any of them could be my mother's brother. He would have been seventy-five years old if he were still alive, but the more I saw of North Korea, the more certain I was that he could not have survived. They seemed to belong to almost an entirely different race than my students. Yet these people we had just passed appeared even more emaciated.

We were barely twenty minutes out of Pyongyang. One of the slogans posted everywhere at the school and on the buildings in the city was Kim Jong-il's dictum "Let's Live Our Way." Juche meant exactly that: to live on your own without relying on anyone else. But "our way" did not seem to me much like living on your own; it seemed more like living off the blood of the rest of the country without having to see them. And not relying on anyone else seemed more like total isolation. I thought of Edgar Allan Poe's "The Masque of the Red Death," in which the princes and nobles lock themselves in a castle to avoid the plague, but of course the plague knows no boundaries and all of them succumb to its "darkness and decay."

Just thirty minutes outside the city, we pulled up at the apple farm, endless fields of fledgling trees in perfect rows spread out before us. Our minder told us that these hundreds of thousands of apple trees were so special that they bore fruit within a year, while trees everywhere else took several years to produce apples. The farm was about fifteen hundred acres, he continued, and produced thirty thousand tons of 106 varieties of apples. We were becoming used to North Korean hyperbole. A student had once told me that his former college, Pyongyang University of Printing Engineering, was the only such college in all of Asia, and one of only two such universities in the world, the other one being in Germany. Several other students insisted that their former universities were the best in the world for this or that. The idea that North Korea alone excelled while all other nations were falling behind seemed a near obsession.

Waiting for us at the top of the hill were three men in khaki uniforms and a female guide in her twenties—quite pretty, as female guides always were. In the distance was a set of long, low buildings with bright blue roofs, which the guide explained was a factory for slicing and drying apples, and I recalled the packaged snack, labeled simply "Dried Apples," sold at the city's Potonggang supermarket. Other than alcohol, cigarettes, and water, this seemed to be one of the few locally produced products. In the future, the guide told us, they would also grow other kinds of fruit at the farm, and there were plans to raise turtles.

Then she launched into a very long description of the two-year history of the farm, highlighted by the times that Kim Jong-il had visited. Among his comments: The apples were very big and round, and he was happy that now his people would be fed apples. Then he worried about the working conditions of the farmers and sent tractors to transport them from tree to tree and from their homes to the farm. He even sent every worker a color TV and ordered that they be given access to a signal, like the citizens of Pyongyang. When he returned the next year he commented that the apples were so good it was a shame for him alone to see them, and that he wished he could share the sight with everyone. So it went, with detailed accounts of everything Kim Jong-il had said, and even where he stood as he spoke the words. "Our Great General Comrade Kim Jong-il is not only the greatest in leading our powerful and prosperous nation but even well versed in apple growing," the guide declared. As she launched into an anecdote about an Italian diplomat who had visited the farm and applauded the Great Leader and donated even more apple seeds, I began to feel restless.

Luckily, at that moment, two women from our group asked to use a toilet and got one of the men in charge to drive them in a car to the village at the bottom of the hill. I did not need to go to the bathroom but seized the opportunity to escape more tales of the Great Leader and the wondrous apples, and see the neighborhood below. Two minders, of course, came along. The village consisted of a cluster of fifty or sixty houses and a huge Kim Il-sung mural at the top of concrete steps like a shrine. The one-story houses looked identical, each with a blue shingled roof and a small garden. The minders took us to the first of the houses and pointed to an outhouse in the yard. The stench was so unbearable that I felt nauseated just standing in line. Since we were all women, the minders remained about fifty yards away on the other side of the stone fence.

Just then, a wooden door slid open from the house and an old woman's face appeared. She was so wrinkled and small and missing so many teeth she could have been a hundred years old. "Who's here? Where do you girls come from?" she asked. This surprised us since the few locals who ever got this close to us always avoided our eyes. This old woman looked genuinely curious. I said hello in Korean. Almost immediately, one of the minders shouted: "Old woman, these are visitors to the farm! Get inside!" His tone was ice cold, menacing. The old woman did not even reply but immediately shut the door. We were in her yard, using her facilities without permission, and yet she was ordered inside.

Slaves. The word came back to me again. In that brief moment, I felt a paralyzing fear, and I wanted to get out of this country. I was afraid of getting stuck here. I was afraid of the minders who could order the old woman to go away, and the speed with which she listened. I recalled the way my students stiffened at the sight of Mr. Ri. The terror here was palpable.

When we returned to the rest of the group, all of us were suddenly told that, because it was Saturday, the workers were resting so we could not tour the factory. On the way back, the bus took a different route, and we passed no skeletal workers.

AT DINNER, WHEN I told the students at my table that we had visited an apple farm, all three brightened and exclaimed, "Daedonggang Fruit Farm?" I nodded. I told them it was my first visit to such a fruit farm, a fact they found incredible. "I'm a city girl," I explained, "and in America, teachers teach and farmers farm," to which one student responded, "Strange, I am a city boy too, but in our country we, even the university students, all know how to farm."

The students proudly said that the apple farm was the eleventh *songun* (military first) wonder of their country, and that they had helped to build it. They told me that in April and May 2009, college students from throughout Pyongyang had spent every Sunday digging holes for the trees, working in teams. They seemed genuinely fond of their memories of working there, though one student admitted that it had been hard because it was extremely cold that spring. I asked if they had since visited to see—and taste—the fruits of their labor. There was a pause before they told me that they had not seen the farm since the trees had been planted. Yet the farm was less than half an hour's drive from the school.

To ease the sudden awkwardness, I asked about the other wonders. They seemed relieved and volunteered information eagerly. When General Kim Jong-il took over after Eternal Great Leader Kim Il-sung's death in 1994, they told me, there had been only eight wonders, but now they had twelve. The first one was the Sunrise at Baekdu-san (Mount Baekdu), where Kim Jong-il was born. The second was the winter pines at Dabak

Military Base, where Kim Jong-il had first thought of the *son-gun* policy. The third was the azaleas at Chulryong hill near a frontline base, where Kim Jong-il often visited. The fourth was the night view of Jangja mountain, where Kim Jong-il had taken refuge during the Korean War as a child. The fifth was the echo of the Oolim Falls, which Kim Jong-il said was the sound of a powerful and prosperous nation. The sixth was the horizon of Handrebul field, the site of Kim Jong-il's 1998 land reform. The seventh was the potato flowers from the field of Daehongdan, where Kim Il-sung had fought the Japanese imperialists and Kim Jong-il upheld his revolutionary spirit by starting the country's biggest potato farm. The eighth was the view of the village of Bumanli, which Kim Jong-il had praised as a socialist ideal that shone bright during the Arduous March. The ninth was the beans at the army depot, which Kim Jong-il once said made him happy that his soldiers were well fed. The tenth was the rice harvest in the town of Migok, so plentiful that Kim Jong-il had declared it to be a shining example of socialist farming. The eleventh was the apple farm, and the twelfth was the Ryongjung fish farm of southern Hwanghae province whose sturgeons swarmed toward the sea, just as the satellites of the DPRK, under Kim Jong-il, flew toward the sky. The students uniformly remarked that the increase from eight to twelve wonders under the Great General's guidance meant that their country was powerful and prosperous and would continue to be so.

It was at moments like these that I could not help but think that they—my beloved students—were insane. Either they were so terrified that they felt compelled to lie and boast of the greatness of their Leader, or they sincerely believed everything they were telling me. I could not decide which was worse.

Three times a day, the boys lined up in neat rows, divided into groups, and marched from the dormitory to the cafeteria, chanting songs in military fashion. With each day the songs became more familiar to me. There was the ubiquitous "The Song of General Kim Jong-il." And there was another I heard so often that I found myself inadvertently humming the refrain, which went "Without you, there is no us, without you, there is no motherland." By *you*, they meant Kim Jong-il.

Once I asked them the title of the song they had been singing that afternoon, and they said "Victory 727" and explained that it commemorated the DPRK's victory over the U.S. on July 27, 1953. That was the date the armistice was signed, and, of course, the very existence of an armistice means there was neither a victor nor a victory, but I could not tell my students that. Another song was called "Dansumae." When I translated the title as "In a single breath" (Chosun Central TV translates it as "Without a break"), they waved their hands, dismissing that as the literal meaning. The phrase seemed to have some other connotation, since I remembered seeing it as a slogan mounted on top of several buildings around Pyongyang. The real meaning, they told me, was to conquer and destroy instantly. One student said, "For example, it means that we could take over South Korea and conquer and kill everyone there instantly!" I must have looked taken aback because the second boy at the table dropped his face and the third laughed nervously.

Then I would remember that they had been raised with the belief that a war with either South Korea or imperialist America was imminent. For them, this threat was very real, or at least their government told them it was. And, although they were students, their lives were as regimented as those of soldiers in barracks. Beyond guarding the Kimilsungism Study Hall and the Forever Tower, as well as scrubbing the outside of the latter, they tended the grounds for several hours a week and cleaned the classrooms, bathrooms, and hallways. They had to count the spoons and the chopsticks to be sure none were missing. Each group had access to the bathhouse for a shower or haircut only during assigned hours, and every morning and afternoon they did group exercises. In their dorm, four students shared a room, and one was designated as the room manager, responsible for maintaining cleanliness and morale. The room manager reported to the class monitor. The chain of authority was clear.

I began to notice that some of the less savvy boys were paired with sharper ones, who not only roomed with them but sat next to them in class. Naive Choi Min-jun, for example, was never without Park Jun-ho. Ryu Jung-min, who seemed to be without guile, sat with Ri Jin-chul, who never deviated from scripted answers. These duos, which at first struck me as close friendships, seemed, as time went by, more like assigned pairings in which one watched over the other with something more loaded than simple affection.

Yet they were still young, and their discipline was not absolute. Things did slip out. One student admitted that none of them had cell phones, though his roommate quickly added that they all owned cell phones but had willingly given them up upon entering PUST so that they could concentrate on their studies. Yet another student said that he had not seen or talked to his mother since he came to PUST in April, three months ago. He paused, as though he regretted admitting this, but then another and another said that they too had had no contact with family and friends since then. From their dormitory windows, downtown Pyongyang was visible, so close that they could almost hear the sounds of the city, but there was no such thing as a visiting hour. One student's father stopped by the campus to see him but was turned away. All he could do was leave a note.

Just as I began to feel that they were relaxing their guard,

I read their next set of letters, which suddenly focused almost entirely on Kim Jong-il. As a group, they became preachy about his greatness, which they called his "solicitude." If they got a good grade, it was thanks to his solicitude. If their English improved, that also had to do with his solicitude. One of them told a story from his childhood, in the late nineties, when he saw people shouting "Please receive my blood" in front of a hospital. He ended the letter with his own translation of the song "We Envy Nothing in the World."

Another student wrote about the country's CNC (computer numerical control) technology, and how the news of this invention had echoed throughout the world. The reason for this breakthrough, he wrote, was the leadership of the Great General Kim Jong-il. After the collapse of socialism in Eastern Europe, my student wrote, Kim Jong-il led the world's progressive nations to victory. The real meaning of "utility in economy" was different from what I, Dear Professor Kim Suki, must assume to be "profit in economy." Comrade Captain Kim Jong-un had taught them that, as scientists, each of them was a "utility," and that by coming up with great inventions they helped build a powerful and prosperous nation, which pleased the Great General Kim Jong-il.

There seemed to be some confusion about how to refer to Kim Jong-il in English. Even the guides were uncertain. In Korean, they usually called him the Great General, but in English, he was referred to in all sorts of ways: Great Generalissimo, Great General Comrade Leader, Great Leader Marshal, Great General, Great Leader, Dear Leader. Great Generalissimo seemed to be a new one; I did not recall hearing it on previous trips. Had it been adopted in anticipation of Kim Jong-un rising from Captain to Great General?

The student's letter was the first time that I'd heard any mention of Kim Jong-un, other than the red sign that read "Captain Luck" in the hallway on the way to classrooms. But what seemed most peculiar was the way nearly all the students suddenly chose Kim Jong-il as their main topic, and the use of identical words and phrases such as *solicitude, single-unified people*, and *powerful and prosperous nation*. I wondered whether they had gotten a firm lecture from the counterparts during their most recent Saturday meeting, known as *Saenghwal chonghwa* (Daily Life Unity), where, according to Dr. Joseph, they confessed their mistakes and critiqued themselves and others.

THE TEACHERS ALSO had a weekly gathering where confessions were made. Every Sunday morning, in a room on the third floor of our dormitory, we held a makeshift service. Although the students sang all the time at the top of their voices, we were told to sing quietly so that no one would hear. Usually, one teacher brought a keyboard and played hymns while another played the flute. I sang along, but I could not help noticing that if you replaced the word *Jesus* with *Great Leader*, the content was not so different from some of the North Korean songs my students chanted several times each day. In both groups, singing was a joyful, collective ritual from which they took strength. Often I thought how absurd it was that the missionaries and the students could not sing together.

Our service inevitably included testimonies—tearful stories in which personal things were revealed, as if it were group therapy. Stories—this world seemed full of stories. It was rare for anyone to actually see Kim Jong-il, so everything we heard about him was a story. And my Christian colleagues had their stories too, in their Bible.

One evening, I saw Rachel, a thirtysomething Korean Canadian teacher, walking through the small muddy area beside the teacher dormitory. I followed her and asked what she was doing, and she told me that she was looking for the site where "the bell" used to be. According to her, this bell had belonged to the first church in Pyongyang. In the late 1800s, a Welsh Protestant missionary had sailed here from China, but when he arrived, his ship was set on fire by Koreans, and he was stranded here, along with a stack of Bibles. He was soon killed, but a local man found the books and used the pages as wallpaper, and people soon gathered at his house and were converted to Christianity by reading the pages. This was how the first church was born and flourished, only to be shut down once Kim Il-sung came to power. Decades later, while excavating the foundation for PUST, workers found the bell that had belonged to the original church. Until then, no one had a clue that the school's foundation belonged to God.

"That's what's called divine," she whispered.

The cynic in me thought what a good story it was from a PR standpoint. This school needed a lot of money just for its daily operation. Most of it came from churches, and nothing sells better than the story of a miracle. Still, at that moment, I must admit that I wanted to believe the story. I wanted a divine force, any outside force, to intervene here. I very much wanted to believe in this God who had devised a private treasure hunt for believers by hiding a bell under the PUST foundation.

9

TWO WEEKS HAD PASSED, THOUGH I WAS LOSING MY SENSE of time. Most of us were not only tired but restless. "Okay, I've had enough. I like the students and all, but I need to breathe," Rachel said. At times, Katie said, she felt desperate to go home. An American teacher from the Midwest said, "I just want to get in my car and drive to a store when I want to. That seems like such a luxury." They had come to PUST because of their deep faith in God and their desire to spread his gospel, but even they were being worn down by this place.

We found a bit of relief in talk of a teachers' field trip to Myohyang-san (Mount Myohyang), a common tourist destination outside Pyongyang. Mount Myohyang was one of only a few mountains open to foreigners. All others were said to be denuded and barren, due to the economic crisis and famine of the mid-1990s, during which people collected everything for food and fuel and left nothing for the soil, and perhaps also to Kim Il-sung's Find New Land Campaign of the late 1970s, which led to widespread deforestation. My colleagues were excited by the prospect of hiking on the mountain, but to me, a mountain suggested an isolated tourist spot from which I was unlikely to learn anything new about North Korea.

The trip to Mount Myohyang began at 7:30 a.m. Not all teachers joined; some were not interested and some did not want to pay for it. Each outing cost money, from gas and entrance fees to meals. Katie and I sat near the back of the bus in order to avoid the hawk eyes of our two minders, who were like a caricature of the good cop and the bad cop. Mr. Ri was the seemingly easygoing one while Mr. Han was testy, with a penchant for Korean history. Katie whispered to me that I must be careful because Mr. Han tailed me at all times. I could not even go to a bathroom without him asking me where I was going, to which I would answer, "You can just follow me in there if you are so curious," which would shut him up.

Dr. Joseph told us that we must not take photographs without permission during the bus ride, since if anyone outside saw us taking pictures and reported our vehicle, our minders could get in trouble. But there was nothing worth photographing along the 98-mile highway that connected Pyongyang and Mount Myohyang. The scene on either side of us was just as peaceful and immaculate as the scene on the way to the apple farm. Occasionally I spotted what seemed to be farmers working the land, people bicycling or walking alongside the highway, or dirty-looking kids sitting in groups in the middle of the highway as though it were a playground. Every now and then, in the distance, I saw what looked like villages—identical rows of houses and one big concrete building that looked like a school, as well as the inevitable slogans and portraits on buildings and billboards. Most of the houses were one story high, the color of pale cement, with darker, shingled roofs, but some were three to four stories, big enough for several families. They could have been shabby model houses that no one had moved into, or ghost towns from which people had fled. We did not pass a single car during the ninety minutes it took us to get to our destination.

We did, however, pass two checkpoints, where guards with metal batons waved us down. At each one, the bus stopped and Mr. Han showed the guard a document he kept in his front pocket. These guards had on the same uniforms—blue with a white collar—worn by Pyongyang traffic controllers, who are always female and often photographed by foreigners making carefully choreographed, almost robotic movements to conduct relatively little traffic. These guards clearly had nothing to do with traffic.

Our schedule was, as usual, mapped out to the smallest degree. First we had to order lunch at Hyangsan Hotel, then head to the International Friendship Exhibition Hall before going back to eat. Hyangsan Hotel was a distinctly eighties-style structure with a marble interior and the generic feel of a dated, second-tier Hilton. In front, I saw five or six women squatting and cutting the grass with scissors. This was a familiar sight by now, but still strange. At PUST, and even in Pyongyang's parks, I had noticed workers doing the same. Lawnmowers were used in the rest of the world, but not here. Was it about control or was there simply a shortage of gas? If people were perpetually squatting in public spaces for the glory of their Great Leader, would they come to believe in him more deeply? I had heard that the Mayans purposely made the steps of their pyramids very steep so that people had no choice but to climb on their knees.

The previous week, as our bus pulled up to the school after a shopping trip, I had seen my class outside, squatting and pulling weeds, not unlike the women outside Hyangsan Hotel. In his next letter to me, one of them wrote: "You might find it strange when you saw us near your dormitory gardening, but we like it, and it is good for us, and it is our duty to our Great Leader." I thought perhaps his ego had been bruised.

Soon we drove five minutes to the International Friendship Exhibition Hall, which consisted of two similar-looking buildings about two hundred yards apart, designed to look like traditional Korean palaces, each with two soldiers guarding a heavy metal gate. The entrance fee was fourteen dollars per person. As always, we were met by a young woman who served as our guide. First we were told to put cloth booties over our shoes so as not to dirty the marble floors. Then we were told to leave all our things at the coat check and walk through a metal detector. Cameras were not allowed. We were then searched manually as at an airport. Finally, we were led inside to view a set of black cars and a railway carriage given to Kim Il-sung by Stalin and Mao Zedong. A digital display of the number of gifts housed there flashed from the wall: 225,954 items from 184 countries, indicated by flashing red dots on a map. Each room opened into another room full of things, and the guide explained that even if we spent only one minute per one present, it would take one and a half years to view all of them, and that gifts kept pouring in for Kim Il-sung even after his death.

Then she began to describe the presents in front of us, one by one. The replica of Mangyongdae, the house in which Kim Il-sung was born, was made from ivory and had taken ninety-six members of the Communist Party of China one entire year to make. There was a rock from Madagascar that was 100 million years old, she said. There were several presents from Robert Mugabe and Fidel Castro. A silver cup had been given to the Great Leader by Madeleine Albright on October 25, 2000. There was also a figure of a crane given by Billy Graham on April 2, 1992, inscribed "To His Excellency."

We were then led along an extended hallway decorated with

photos of giraffes, elephants, and lions. The guide explained that these animals were also gifts to Kim Il-sung and were now at the Korean Central Zoo in Pyongyang. Finally we came to a room with a big board on the wall, featuring a lot of numbers signifying that Kim Il-sung had visited sixteen countries fifty-four times in total, traveling 52,480 kilometers. Katie and I began to take notes and our minder frowned at us. But when we told him that Katie was interested in pursuing a higher degree in Juche, he softened.

Kim Il-sung had supposedly received 5,050 top government officials and met with 65,000 important people from various countries. In 100 countries, there existed 1,000 Juche research centers. In 106 countries, there existed 69,102,830 translations of Kim Il-sung's works. In 100 countries, there existed 450 streets named after Kim Il-sung. He had received eighty honorary degrees from universities around the world, as well as 180 medals from twenty countries.

One particular set of numbers puzzled me: the board said that 172 countries had given 166,065 items. When I asked why this number differed from the number of presents cited in the first room, the guide explained that the larger number included gifts to Kim Il-sung, Kim Jong-suk, and Kim Jong-il, and this number represented only gifts to Kim Il-sung.

We were then brought to a big room featuring a larger-than-life wax figure of Kim Il-sung himself, standing against a backdrop of pink Kimilsungias (hybrid flowers bred to honor the Great Leader; the ones named after his son are called Kimjong-ilias) and what looked like Mount Baekdu, smiling as though he were saying hello. We were told that it was mandatory to line up and bow to the figure, and I thought how strangely familiar he had become, now that we had spent more than two weeks surrounded by his portraits and his words, hearing his name in every possible context, and for a moment, it seemed true that he was always with us.

The guide explained that there were two hundred rooms in total, that the gifts were divided up according to the years and months they had been received and the country of origin, and that the rooms held so many things it was impossible to see them all. So we would see only two rooms, which held presents from the United States and New Zealand. She took us down the corridor and tried one door, which was locked, then disappeared for a few minutes. When she returned, she told us that today the rooms she had intended to show us were locked, and that we would instead visit the other building. One of the teachers whispered that considering the admission fee had been fourteen dollars per person, it seemed almost ungracious that they would not even show us one of these special rooms. But we had no say in this matter and had to move swiftly outside.

Just across the way, the other building looked a little smaller but was identically set up. Again we put on the cloth booties and were searched, and the display of presents began in much the same way. Our tour began in the general room with gifts from South Korea, including 850 items from Kim Dae-joong, the former South Korean president known for his Sunshine Policy of greater economic and political cooperation with North Korea. The South Korean Ace Furniture Company, whose president hailed from the North, had given 350 pieces of top-quality furniture including desks, chairs, and armoires, which, the guide explained, was their entire output for five months. (This could not possibly have been true; the company was South Korea's leading furniture maker and surely produced more in that span of time.) There were also the familiar flashing numbers on a screen: 170 countries and a total of 59,864 presents. We were told that the number denoted only gifts for Kim Jong-il and was distinct from the first set of numbers in the other building. But at this point, so many numbers were jumbled inside my head that I did not much care about any of them.

We were then led along a corridor, again decorated with photos of wild animals, into a room where the presents were divided by countries. There was a silver tray and a gold watch from the U.S. House of Representatives, a blue flower vase from U.S. congressional delegates, and a pink crystal figure from the National Council of Christians. Here also were two familiar names: on April 1, 1992, Billy Graham had given the Great Leader a globe surmounted with white doves, and in 2006 Madeleine Albright had presented him with a Wilson basketball signed by Michael Jordan. The endless recitation of gifts was beginning to make me feel dizzy.

Finally we were brought to a room with a marble statue of Kim Jong-il sitting in an armchair in front of a wall illuminated to look like a sunrise, his face expressionless. I thought of the words that adorned the top of the IT building at PUST: LONG LIVE GENERAL KIM JONG-IL, THE SUN OF THE 21ST CENTURY. We had to bow here too. Our tour again ended without a look at any of the other rooms.

Mount Myohyang was beautiful, however. Nature did not lie, although it occurred to me that here even nature might, since we were being shown just one part of the famed mountain as we began hiking. The guide told us we were near Bohyunsa, the Buddhist temple where the famous monk Suhsan had gathered with his followers to counter the attack by the Japanese in the sixteenth century, although we would not be stopping there. Though the temple does exist, I saw no evidence that Buddhists had ever been to this mountain, only the enormous words THE LEGENDARY HERO, KIM JONG-IL carved into the rocky side of the mountain. Otherwise, the mountain was empty. Nearly anywhere else in the world, a mountain like this would be filled with families on a Saturday afternoon. Yet we saw only one group of schoolchildren the whole time we were there. They crowded around us and posed with us for pictures, but soon their teachers came down, stopped our picture taking, and took them away.

I fell into a chat with a few of the older teachers who were taking a break while the younger teachers climbed higher. One of them was in his seventies and originally from Pyongyang. He said that his father had been one of the richest men in the country before the war, and had owned a house and other properties where the Grand People's Study House now stood. Kim Il-sung had confiscated all private property right after the war, and had relocated families all over the country, much the way Mao did during the Cultural Revolution. Families were separated not only between South and North but also within the country. This explained why whenever I asked a North Korean "Where is your *bonjuk*?"—a customary question to ask a stranger in South Korea—the person answered that there was no such thing in North Korea. Instead, I learned, North Korea had an unofficial caste system called *songbun* in which citizens were divided into three main classes and some fifty subclasses, based on a person's political, social, and economic background, and although they pretended that such hierarchies did not exist, this affected their social mobility. The government had succeeded in wiping out the ancient clan system and replacing it with their own; many North Koreans no longer had the support of an extended family and had no one to rely on but their Great Leader. It was hardly surprising, then, that there were no noteworthy historical artifacts left on this famed mountain, since history itself was an obstacle in bolstering the myth of the Great Leader.

Another member of our group, a Korean-American woman

in her sixties, told me about her family's harrowing escape to the South during the war. She had been only eight months old when her mother decided to make her way south from Shinuju, the northwestern tip of North Korea. Her family had been one of the first Christian converts in the region, and her father had already gone south to start a church. So her mother packed up and began the journey with three children in tow, and at some point, she was told to give up the eight-month-old in case the baby cried and attracted the attention of the soldiers. But her mother did not give her up and miraculously made her way south and was reunited with her father. Decades later, during the 1990s, her eighty-some-year-old father returned to Shinuju with a humanitarian group. He pleaded with the authorities for a glimpse of his siblings, who lived within the city limits, and whom he had not seen in more than forty years. He was not allowed to visit them. Now ninety-six, he had asked her to make note of everything so that he might hear some details about his home before he died.

I thought about how, through all this, Mount Myohyang towered above, empty and stripped, one side carved to express allegiance to the Great Leader, a deformed remnant of what was once a great treasure, denied entirely to the people of South Korea, and perhaps denied to most people here as well.

Just then Mr. Han came over to inquire about my schedule, which seemed an odd thing to ask me while hiking. I told him that I usually went to bed before ten, sometimes as early as eight.

"Then you get up at five a.m.?" he asked.

This could have been an innocent guess, but it was so immediate, and I remembered writing an email to my lover saying that I got up at 5 a.m., and suddenly I was struck with paranoia.

Had I said anything that revealed more than I cared to in those emails?

I thought of other comments Mr. Han had made over the previous two weeks. For example, he would casually say, "Comrade Suki, I hear you and Comrade Katie are the most popular teachers, and the boys are just wild about you. Maybe your teaching is too 'free American style' and maybe I should go check out your class, ha ha ha." Or, "What's in your bag? I like you so much but you always hide things from me. Why do you hold on to your bag all the time like that? Is there a secret there you are hiding from me?" Each time he tossed off such a comment, my heart would sink. Of course I had a secret, many secrets, and I carried my bag everywhere with me because it held the USB stick that held my notes for this book, a copy of which I never saved on my hard drive, and I often worried that one day he would demand to search my bag and destroy the USB stick. So I copied the documents onto three USB sticks, hid two in my room, and carried one with me at all times. I also copied my documents onto my camera's SIM card. But even so, I was afraid that they would be discovered, and that I would lose them all.

On the drive back, as dusk fell, the minders got nervous. One of the older teachers had slipped and injured himself, and we were taking him to a hospital for foreigners in the diplomatic quarter in Pyongyang. The minders stopped at Hyangsan Hotel to see if they had any emergency care, but there was none. They seemed worried that we were behind schedule, and kept reminding each other that we should not be driving around at night. Someone asked if there was a city curfew and they said no, but it seemed that there must be an unofficial one. Between 6:00 and 7:40 p.m., the time it took us to reach Pyongyang, we again passed at least three groups of children sitting on the highway. They looked like they were between the ages of five and ten. It was dinnertime and the sight of unescorted children sitting on the pavement in the middle of a highway was unusual, but of course we could not ask the meaning of this. In the distance, I could see farmers tilling the earth despite the late hour. On a couple of occasions, I noticed formally dressed women walking alongside the highway, which seemed mysterious as there was nothing behind us and nothing they could be walking toward, and we had passed no buses or cars, and I knew there was no bus stop nearby, and it was rapidly getting dark.

There were no lights on in any of the houses we passed. It was possible that it was not dark enough to warrant turning the lights on, and yet . . . not one window during the entire drive revealed light. Either they had no electricity or there was a blackout, which was not uncommon in this country. But I had never experienced a scene so entirely devoid of noise. By "noise," I do not mean literal sound, but the noise of life, the evidence of life lived behind closed doors. I saw no running dogs or children, no chimney smoke, no flash of color from a TV set, and this greatly disturbed me, and yet what troubled me more was the fact that I did not know and would never know the truth of what I was seeing.

I suddenly recalled a Dutch movie I had seen called *The Vanishing*. A young woman vanishes at a rest stop on a highway, and her grief-stricken lover spends years trying to find out what happened to her. When he finally tracks down the man who might have abducted her, he is presented with a choice: *Do you want me to do to you what I did to her, or do you want to live the rest of your life without knowing? Those are your only two options.* You know, as he does, that the truth can only be horrible, but you cannot help wanting to know, and the lover chooses the knowing, and the movie ends when he wakes in a coffin, buried alive.

At the same time, it was impossible *not* to know what was happening in this country. The answer was right before my eyes. Small, dark, emaciated people with dead eyes. A landscape devoid of any organic signs of life. I remembered how Katie had whispered the word *slaves*. And when I saw my students marching, I thought of the word *soldiers*. There they were, every direction we turned: soldiers and slaves.

It turned out that the injured teacher needed three stitches. The hospital for foreigners charged him seventeen dollars, which was a lot of money there, and they did not use any anesthetic or offer him antibiotics. Even the school doctor had no medicine to offer. Instead, we were told to see if we had brought any suitable antibiotics, and he ended up taking the Cipro he had brought with him.

LATER THAT NIGHT, Sarah told me that she was so glad to finally see the mountains here. Many of her students had grown up in rural areas, so they often wrote about mountains, along with catching frogs and chasing dragonflies. She said that it sounded beautiful and carefree, but as she spoke, it dawned on me that what she said did not make sense. Her students' childhoods could not possibly have been so idyllic.

All her students had been born a few years before 1997, the worst period of the famine. North Korea had been on the brink of collapse. Even if they were from a privileged class, they could not have been shielded from the hunger and privation around them. So I was not sure how to make sense of the happy essays she described. Had they collectively been trained to say only good things about their childhoods? I wanted to believe their claims. I wanted to believe that some children had been utterly unaffected by the deadly famine, which seemed to have permanently stunted the people of North Korea emotionally and physically. It seemed unconscionable to wish for the ruling class to be spared the miseries of their countrymen, but I saw these young men daily, and it comforted me to know that these children, who had grown up to be such lovely, fine young men, might have escaped hardship.

It occurred to me then that none of my students had ever written about being raised in the mountains or chasing dragon-flies. Most of them were from Pyongyang, with powerful parents. Then I realized that Sarah taught sophomores and I taught freshmen. The sophomores were the first class at PUST and had enrolled a year ago, whereas my students had arrived only three months before, in April. From the beginning, I had been puzzled over how the counterparts decided who taught which class. It seemed that more care was being taken with the new students. Those of us teaching freshmen seemed to be more qualified to teach writing than the others, and we were assigned teaching assistants. Were the freshmen from an even higher social stratum than the sophomores, and if so, why had this fledgling university run by foreigners suddenly attracted these elitest of elite students?

Then that creeping knowledge of the whole setup came back to me. I realized that the decision to close the universities must have been made this past spring; otherwise, the sophomores would be of the same social class as the freshmen. Something had happened earlier in the year that made the regime close all the universities, and that made those who wielded power rush to pull their sons out of the schools they attended and enroll them at PUST. Something big was in the works.

10

I WOKE UP ONE MORNING IN MY THIRD WEEK THERE AND was no longer overwhelmed by my surroundings. I was now used to wrapping a sweatshirt around my waist to go jogging in case my shorts would be judged indecent. The Forever Tower and the white block of letters on red panels hailing Kim Jong-il as "the Sun of the 21st Century!" had become running markers for me. I ran the same path over and over, with the smoke stack always in view, and I knew the city of Pyongyang lay in that direction, even on a cloudy day. The inexplicably loud music booming from the outdoor speakers at 7 a.m. no longer bothered me, and the sight of the students marching now seemed oddly comforting. After dinner, when the students came out for gardening duty, dressed in sweats and sneakers, each one holding a bucket, it dawned on me that watching them dutifully pull up weeds, which had seemed alien just a few weeks ago, was now my evening ritual.

I must admit that during the time I spent with my students, I was happy at moments. Our life was simple, every day the same ritual, with little time for superfluous reflection. The fact that

I could never step outside the campus on my own, that I could never freely ask anyone a question, that I had no phone to call anybody, that I was not allowed even one unfiltered glimpse of the rest of the country—these things receded. With each day, I thought about the outside world less. It was not that I ceased missing it; rather, I began to accept that there was no point in thinking about it, since it was utterly inaccessible. Home lay far beyond this campus and country. Home was now an absurdly abstract thing, and that included my lover, although my longing for him did remain in some corner of my heart that still occasionally throbbed. But I learned to quiet even that, so I could be exactly what they wanted me to be: an English teacher in Pyongyang.

For the first time in my life, thinking was dangerous to my survival.

NOW BACK IN NEW YORK, I sometimes find myself yearning for that time when my old life was no longer relevant and I knew exactly what each day would bring. Those moments of nostalgia are fleeting, though. When I say my life in Pyongyang was simple, that was only true on the surface. By the third week, something had changed within me regarding my students. In those first few weeks, they seemed too good to be true. They were eager, polite, and hard working. "Teacher's paradise" (as some teachers called it) was not an exaggeration. No American students were ever this obedient. As a group, they rose in unison the minute I entered the classroom, not sitting down until I told them to do so. They shouted out each answer together, hung on my every word, and demanded more homework. I almost felt like a military sergeant rather than an English teacher. I had never been revered so absolutely. Sarah even said that she wanted to stay there permanently. Another Korean-American teacher exclaimed that if it were not for the portraits of Kim Il-sung and Kim Jong-il in the classroom, you could almost believe that these were South Korean students, although even they were not as well behaved.

He was deeply mistaken. I still adored them, and the sight of their faces warmed me instantly, and during the meals we shared, the conversation flew so effortlessly that we were often scolded by the Korean Chinese woman in charge of the cafeteria for being the last ones there. But I was growing increasingly disturbed by the ease with which they lied.

Once, a student asked me whether I liked flowers. "Yes," I answered, "but I don't have a garden back in New York, so I usually buy flowers from shops." The student immediately said, "Me too, until I came to PUST, I never planted flowers. I always bought them at supermarkets." I had never seen fresh flowers at any Pyongyang stores. Another time, a student got up from the table at lunch and said, "Oh well, off to a shop. We have to get ready for a birthday party, so we need to go buy some things." There was no shop on campus yet (PUST would open one later that semester), and Katie asked if he was allowed to go shopping outside the campus, at which point he pretended not to understand English and walked away.

On several occasions, I had to mark a student absent from a class or a meal. Each time, the whole class told me that the missing student had a stomachache, as though no other illness existed. After I began to pre-assign the students who would eat with me at each meal, I would sometimes find one replaced by another. One time, when I inquired about the whereabouts of the missing student, his two classmates answered immediately, in unison.

"Oh, he has a stomachache," one said, just as the other said, "Oh, he went to get a haircut."

"Which is it, is he getting a haircut or is he sick?" I asked.

"Oh, he went to get a haircut but got a stomachache," both answered, with no hesitation.

A few minutes later, I saw the allegedly sick student playing basketball, seemingly unaware that his classmates had covered for him so fervently. It dawned on me that it was entirely possible he had no idea. I realized that the whole group had noticed he was missing and immediately filled his place at my table and made up an excuse for his absence. There was something touching about such fraternity, but at the same time, the speed with which they lied was unnerving. It came too naturally to them—such as the moment when a student told me that he had cloned a rabbit as a fifth grader, or when another said that a scientist in his country had discovered a way to change blood type A to blood type B, or when the whole class insisted that playing basketball caused a person to grow taller. I was not sure if, having been told such lies as children, they could not differentiate between truth and lies, or whether it was a survival method they had mastered.

One student, whose English was nearly fluent and who handed in homework with nearly perfect grammar, claimed that he had never learned a word of English until just a few months before, when he arrived at PUST. Unlike his classmates, most of whom had had at least four years of English at middle school, he had studied Chinese as a second language and had to start from scratch. This sounded remarkable. Having learned English as a second language, I knew that it was virtually impossible for a twenty-year-old to become fluent in a foreign language in just three months' time.

On some mornings, the entire class looked unusually tired, but when I asked them what they had done the night before, they answered, "Nothing special." I wondered whether they had gotten in trouble during their Juche lessons. Sometimes they would announce as a group that they would not be attending the office hour that day, saying that there was a meeting.

The textbook theme for the third week was "honesty," so we decided to play Truth or Lie again. Among other things, we hoped it would encourage them to be more open. When we wrote a sentence on the board about a woman dating a man four years her junior, all the students immediately shouted out "Lie!" They said, "Impossible. Women don't date men who are younger." From this we concluded that it must be a taboo, at least among their peers. The idea of a beauty pageant was also completely new to them. For example, they had never heard of the Miss Korea pageant. I found this ironic, considering that until then I had seen only women employed as guides and traffic controllers, or servers at restaurants and hotels, and they were uniformly young and attractive. Also, the government itself reportedly maintained a group of beautiful young women known as *gippumjo* (Pleasure Brigade), whose sole responsibility was to pleasure and entertain Kim Jong-il and the party leaders. Required to be virgins, the women were said to be groomed for this role from a young age.

On the other hand, concepts such as "protest" and "student newspaper" did not seem to surprise them. From the way they responded, you would have thought that it was perfectly ordinary for them to gather for political protests, publish student newspapers, and say anything they wanted.

Then Katie wrote on the board "I love to visit the mountains in New York and ski."

"What is ski?" some of the students whispered to one another in Korean.

When Katie asked them how many of them knew what skiing was and whether people skied in North Korea, most of them nodded. A student, whom I later learned was the class secretary, raised his hand and said that he had gone skiing, but when I asked him where, he fell silent. Once Katie explained what skiing was, however, a few students shouted, "Lie!" It was not possible for Katie to be a skier, they said, since there was no snow in New York. They knew nothing about New York's climate, or even where New York was, but most noteworthy was the fact that they did not know about fake snow, so I doubted they knew what skiing was at all. And all of that would have been fine had they not so fervently pretended to know what they didn't.

But this is not to suggest that all of them lied at all times. Had they always been devious, I would have found it hard to love them. But they were not always devious, and our daily lives were almost merged together. From morning until sundown, I ate three meals with them, read their letters about their lives, watched them play Pictionary or basketball or soccer. Even though I was becoming disillusioned with their behavior, it was still very easy to love them, not only because we shared so much but also because I came from a world where we trusted more easily.

ONE EVENING I saw Lydia, a teacher from Mississippi in her fifties, in the corridor of the dormitory taking a photo from a third-floor window. As if making an excuse for taking the photo, she told me that she had barely any photos of her time in North Korea and wanted to be able to remember it. There were so few spots we were allowed to photograph, and the campus was one of them. The view from this window wasn't much: two main dormitory buildings adjacent to a courtyard, which was really just a patch of dry land with spotty grass. In the middle of it was a big rock, on which two students were perched doing homework. Lydia said that she often saw kids sitting on this rock studying, and that she wanted to remember this view.

She seemed quieter than usual that evening, so I asked her how she was finding her students. She seemed at a loss for words, but after thinking for a little while, she said that these students seemed so different from the South Korean students in her ESL classes back home. She had spent fourteen years as a missionary in Japan and a year and a half in South Korea, and had even adopted a Korean daughter, so she was no stranger to this part of the world, and yet she was puzzled by our boys.

Then she told me something that had happened the day before. She had touched the arm of a student to demonstrate the meaning of the phrase "He twisted my arm," and he had literally flinched. This mystified her, especially since the students were so physical with one another; we often saw them walking with arms linked or around each other's waists, or hand in hand. So she asked them why it was that they found the slightest physical affection from her so distasteful. When they would not answer, she posed it as a multiple-choice question. Was it because she was older, a woman, or a teacher? They told her it was all of the above and asked her not to do it again. I noticed that she had not offered them the option to say that it was because she was a foreigner. The students generally preferred Korean teachers. Many told me that they simply felt more comfortable with us. When I brought up that possibility, she said hesitantly, "I know . . . but I didn't ask that." She spoke with a Southern drawl that felt oddly familiar to me—more familiar even than the Korean accents of my students when they spoke English. Then she shook her head and said, "What bothers me is that . . . I just don't know who they are."

I had begun to feel the same way. When a student from Class 1 said, openly and unashamedly, that the unfortunate thing about losing the trivia game was that they had been caught cheating and should have cheated better, I wondered if it was possible that they had never been taught that lying was a bad thing. Perhaps they felt free to continue doing it as long as they could get away with it. Was it possible that they just did not know right from wrong?

When I thought of these things, I felt a tinge of dislike for my students, and I knew that if it kept growing, I would have no choice but to leave. This dislike was almost instinctive. In the same way that Lydia's students flinched at her touch, I began flinching internally at those who were more deceptive than others. Park Jun-ho, for example, would tell me elaborate stories about a student's absence, about how Jun Su-young was so sick that a car took him to a big hospital in Pyongyang, and he would shake his head and put his hand to his chest and say, "Teacher, today is just a bad day for our class. I just really hope he is okay." I tried my best not to show my feelings at those moments. These students were so quick at reading other people's expressions. They seemed almost trained at it. They could sense when tides turned because perhaps tides always turned, and no one spoke his mind, and so the only way to survive was to try to outdo one another at mind games.

There were clumsy lies too. The day I assigned the outline for a composition about honesty, about a quarter of them told me they had accidentally left their homework in the dormitory. When I asked them to go get it, they paused and said nothing before admitting that they had not done the assignment. One student said he had it in his notebook, but when I asked him to show it to me, he paused and finally admitted to not having done it.

Paranoia bred more paranoia. Without trust, relationships cannot grow, and my relationship with the students began to stagnate. Their lies kept me at a distance. I could not go further with them. On weekends I might see the whole class working the field or exercising in groups at 6 a.m., but if I asked them how their morning was, they would answer that they slept late, as late as 11 a.m., and felt very rested. Every single student said that he was anxiously awaiting the vacation so that he could see his parents and hang out with his friends. Although some of them had no idea where their friends were, they seemed to expect them to be back from whichever construction site they had been taken to.

Of course, they had been lied to themselves, all their lives. I thought about this the evening that Rachel pulled me aside and whispered: "Have you heard of Dangun?"

Dangun is the mythical founder of Korea, whose first kingdom is traced back to 2333 B.C. He was said to have been fathered when Hawnung, the son of the Lord of Heaven, breathed on a bear that turned into a woman. It appeared that Rachel's students had been taught that Dangun's remains had been excavated by Kim Il-sung in 1993, the year before his own death. (This was clearly meant to plant in people's minds the idea that he was predestined to rule Korea, and to legitimize his son, Kim Jong-il, who would come to power in 1994.) The students talked about their desire to visit the Dangun gravesite in a suburb of Pyongyang. Rachel found the students strangely gullible, yet it was she who roamed the ditch beside the teachers' dormitory, searching for the spot where the sacred bell from the first church of Pyongyang had "accidentally" been found on the PUST campus. We believe what we want to believe. If these sad people wanted so desperately to hold on to the myth of their Great Leader as the rightful heir to Dangun, who could blame them? The blame really lay with those who perpetuated these stories to control the masses.

And so I went from love to pity to repulsion and distrust, then back to empathy and love again, and these switches of feeling were confusing. I reminded myself that I did not come from a place where mind games were a prerequisite for survival to such an extreme degree, a place where the slightest act of rebellion could have unimaginable consequences.

Slowly, I became used to the expressions on their faces as they lied or said things they regretted, and I began to be able to tell which statements were true and which were not, which students never ever faltered, and which sometimes made slips. But there were some evenings when I did not want to play this guessing game, when my disappointment was so profound that I chose to sit with the students whose English was the poorest so that they would be less likely to lie to me.

This feeling was akin to heartbreak, and it took me a while to make sense of it—until one evening after dinner, looking at the students dotted across the schoolyard with their buckets, on gardening duty, which seemed to happen more frequently as we neared Victory Day, July 27, it occurred to me that it was all futile, the fantasy of Korean unity, the five thousand years of Korean identity, because the unified nation was broken, irreparably, in 1945 when a group of politicians drew a random line across the map, separating families who would die without ever meeting again, with all their sorrow and anger and regret unrequited, their bodies turning to earth, becoming part of this land. On that evening, as a sun the color of mournful pomegranate fell behind the Forever Tower, behind the smoke stack, behind this city, this school, behind the children of the elite who were now my children for a brief time, these lovely, lying children, I saw very clearly that there was no redemption here.

11

SUNDAY, JULY 24, WAS ELECTION DAY IN PYONGYANG, BUT for us it was a day of prayer. My fellow teachers had been asking for permission to visit one of the two churches in Pyongyang, and our destination was Bongsu Church. President Kim was with us that day and explained that it was not a real church but that we were to respect their desire to show us they had religious freedom, which they did not. The DPRK regime is known for repressing unauthorized religious activities with arrests and even executions.

From the bus, we could see that the mood was celebratory, the streets filled with people, with many of the women in brightly colored, billowing *hanbok* (Korean traditional dress). I saw a new slogan on a building: LET US ALL PARTICIPATE IN THE ELECTION AND SUPPORT THE REVOLUTION! Young children in school uniforms—white shirts, navy skirts or pants, red kerchiefs— sang loudly and marched in groups, waving plastic Kimjongilias and Kimilsungias and holding up a sign that read LET'S BUILD OUR SOCIALIST NATION TO FOLLOW OUR GREAT GENERAL KIM JONG-IL! They were gathered in long lines every few blocks or so, in front of big red signs that said "Voting Booth." We were told that the people were electing their city and county representatives, that the election happened every four years, and that anyone over the age of seventeen could vote.

There were even fewer cars on the street than usual, and President Kim told us that on Election Days, only the military was allowed to drive. Although we had been cleared for the trip, we were pulled over by a guard. Mr. Han seemed very upset and told him that the bus was full of foreigners, and that we were late for something important. Ten minutes later, we were permitted to drive. Usually the bus circled the same area, passing the Grand People's Study House, Juche Tower, Potong-gang Department Store, and the Koryo Hotel, which were all within a radius of a few blocks, but that day we took a different route. Along the way I saw women doing laundry in the murky waters of the Potonggang River, which ran through the heart of the city. Men fished from its banks. People were squatting and cutting grass or sweeping streets as usual. There was no lit-ter whatsoever. I also noticed a few bony women stooping over pools of water on the ground with buckets. They would pour earth into the water, let it soak up the water, then shovel the wet earth back into the buckets and dump it into a pile. This seemed to be Pyongyang's version of a storm drainage system. We drove past a big lily pond and saw someone fishing there as well. Perhaps those people were done voting.

The church was near a group of apartments that looked like a slum. The cement buildings were run-down and the first-floor windows had no glass, only metal guards. I glimpsed one man's face through the dark hole that was a window, and whatever was inside looked even darker. But before I could even reflect on it, our bus had zipped past and pulled up before a big, modern, nondescript building topped with a cross, reportedly built with donations from South Korean Christians. A man in a pastor's gown came down the front steps to welcome us. Although we were late because we had been stopped, the entire church had been expecting us and had waited to begin the service.

Inside, about a hundred parishioners and a choir sat in almost perfect silence on the pews. They were mostly women between the ages of thirty and fifty. As we entered they turned toward us and smiled in unison. They looked reasonably well off, although not as affluent as our students, and for a moment I wondered why those people were not at the voting booth. We were directed to front-row seats and given brand-new Bibles and hymn books in Korean and English. Each of us was also given a set of headphones and a device so that we could listen to the service with the aid of simultaneous translation. When you turned it on, a perky voice said, "Welcome to our church," as though it were an English conversation lesson. Next to the pastor was a projector screen on which we could see ourselves. I looked around to see who was filming us, but it was impossible to tell. Soon a woman in a shiny *hanbok* went up to the altar to recite a prayer—really more of a beseeching soliloquy about unification, the sorrow of the Korean people, and the evils of those who had separated us. It sounded as though she had performed it many times before.

The sermon was much the same. The pastor talked about the evils of the South Korean regime, which, backed by the American imperialists, kept Korea divided. This crime would be punished, he insisted, quoting Romans 6:23—"For the wages of sin is death . . ."—to underscore his point. At some point we all had to go to the front and sing to our North Korean Christian brothers and sisters, who put on happy and excited expressions as if on cue. We were encouraged to take photos throughout.

I kept looking at the faces of the pastor and parishioners, which revealed nothing. It was all theater, and I was part of it. They were pretending to be Christians, and we were pretending to believe them. I remembered that we had been instructed to pray secretly, with our eyes open, while we were at PUST. Here the situation was reversed: our group prayed openly and North Koreans performed what seemed to be a charade. Perhaps when they spoke of God they privately substituted the words "Kim Jong-il."

It was a relief to listen to the choir, which sang so fervently and beautifully that I wondered if they had been selected for their singing talent. This was not such a terrible duty, I thought. They could come here and daydream for an hour and sing. Their friends might even envy them such a cushy assignment.

Then they sang a tune that was oddly familiar to me. It had been my paternal grandmother's favorite hymn. She hummed it often, though she wasn't much of a Christian and only went to church when her panic attacks took a turn for the worse. Before the panic attacks, she had been an atheist, although, as with most Korean families, there were traces of Buddhism and Shamanism in our family's past.

My grandmother had married my grandfather at sixteen, borne three children and raised them, lived through the Japanese colonization, and nearly died of malnutrition during the Korean War. But she rarely talked about any of that. Instead she talked about the women—my grandfather's women, one of whom was a *giseng* (geisha) who moved in and took over the master bedroom. It was not clear whether this mistress was a real *giseng* or a common bar hostess, as these women inevitably came and went too quickly for my grandmother to learn their real identities, but this *giseng*, or fake *giseng*, would drink *jungjong* (sake) with my grandfather every night, and it was my

grandmother's duty to bring them trays of food. My grandmother always said that it was my grandfather's roving eyes that
caused her panic attacks.

It was after every doctor concluded that her illness was imag-
inary, including one who recommended that she try sucking on
mint candies as a remedy, that she visited the local priest and
turned toward Jesus. For her, Jesus was a way of dealing with
my grandfather's womanizing. When he was between women
and feeling remorseful, he would reluctantly take her to church,
always declaring that no one would see a Gwangsan Kim, a descendant of great Confucian scholars, carrying a Bible in public.
And so he would carefully wrap his wife's Bible in newspaper
before tucking it under his arm, and he would leave her at the
threshold of the church, never once crossing it himself.

It seemed unfathomable that life had led me to this unlikely
place, this fake North Korean church where I sat listening to a
fake choir with a group of real believers and stumbled on the
memory of my grandmother and her halfhearted Christianity.
But in that moment I realized that whether she had been a true
believer or not, church had offered her some comfort in her
tortured life, and I was grateful for that.

Soon we were ushered out and encouraged to take a Bible
and a hymn book with us as souvenirs. The parishioners smiled
and waved and sang, "Let's meet again," and the pastor stood
outside and posed for pictures with all of us. And we got on the
bus, all the parishioners still waving at us, and then we could
see them walking away all at once, quickly disappearing into
Pyongyang's streets as though they had dispensed with their
morning duty.

That afternoon, some teachers were shown an election
booth. They were urged to take photos, and the standard pretty
female guide explained how votes were cast. According to her,

there were two candidates' names on the ballot, and Pyongyang citizens chose one of them, just as they might in any other free country. One of the teachers, however, who taught English to the counterparts said that those in her class had let slip that there was only one candidate, handpicked by the government, so Election Day really meant that you showed up and picked that candidate. Did this mean the government had set up a fake election just for us? Beyond the church and the election booth and the people lined up to vote, what else was there for our eyes only? Did the lights in the windows go dark as soon we drove past them?

At dinner that night, my students asked, as usual, what we had done that day. Since we were not supposed to talk about Jesus with them, I asked what they had done. They all answered that they had voted in downtown Pyongyang. This was the first election in which they had been able to vote, and they found it very exciting, they said. The school did not have enough vans to transport all 270 students into the city, and I knew they were never allowed out anyway, so I asked them how they had traveled to the voting station. They walked, they told me. I could not believe what I was hearing, but I pressed on. It was about ten minutes to Pyongyang by car, so I casually asked how long it had taken them to walk there. On this, their answers varied. Some said thirty minutes; others said one hour. What time had they left? Some said 8 a.m.; others said 9. However, we had left at 9 that morning, and we had seen no trace of them.

THE NEXT DAY, at the staff meeting, we were told we had to reimburse PUST for gas and for the meals for our minders and driver. It was a modest amount, five or ten dollars for each of our outings, but considering that we were teaching for free and had spent our own money, or that of a sponsoring church, to fly there, it seemed strange that we were expected to pay to be guarded.

Then we were told that the Arirang Mass Games, a major festival that celebrates the DPRK each August, would cost each of us as much as $400 if we wanted to go. The school recommended that we purchase the mid-range tickets for $225. I had seen the games during one of my previous visits and was taken aback by the price. Once you got over the novelty of seeing tens of thousands of children forming the petals of Kimjongilias or Kimilsungias or a hammer and sickle, you couldn't help but imagine the countless hours they must have been forced to rehearse. A few other teachers seemed shocked at the price but agreed to buy tickets since they did not know when they would return. This was always the case with North Korea. It was like the bad boyfriend whose presence could never be depended on, so you always had to seize the opportunity to spend time with him when he made himself available.

The next piece of news was delivered by Dr. Joseph, who looked almost embarrassed as he asked everyone for donations to feed the students. According to him, "the others"—the counterparts, I assumed—kept urging him to make a personal donation of $500 or more for "a meal with plenty of meat in it." I suspected that the meat was not for the students but to satisfy the greedy demands of the counterparts. One of these men often liked to repeat, "Oh, you're Comrade Kim Suki. You caused us much trouble. You have no idea what a headache it was for me to get your visa. After all I went through for you, maybe you should thank *me*." I felt quite awkward the first time he said this but laughed along with him, pretending that it was a joke.

This kind of extortionary behavior was typical in transactions with North Korea. During the New York Philharmonic's visit, I had met a number of South Korean journalists who were rather jaded by North Korea and uniformly said that to understand the DPRK, you needed to follow the money. The funding for PUST came from individual donors around the world, as well as from the South Korean Ministry of Unification, with no contribution that I knew of from North Korea. Apparently, the rest of the world was feeding and educating the children of their leaders. On a micro level, there were the frequent requests for small sums of money that we had gotten used to. The counterparts wanted to be fed, and we were expected to accommodate them.

The last bit of news was slightly alarming. Dr. Joseph told us that, according to the counterparts, some of our students would not be going home for the summer break. Only *some* students would go home, Dr. Joseph said. Some of the richest ones, most likely. I could already guess who among my students would be chosen. The differences among them were obvious. A few used smooth white sheets of paper, the kind we were used to back home, for their homework, but most used the rough, brownish paper that was the norm. The white-paper users were often the same boys who owned electronic dictionaries, had glowing complexions, and spoke better English.

It turned out that the students' entire year was meticulously mapped out. During breaks, they either stayed on campus doing extra work or worked at some sort of collective farm. None of it was their choice. Dr. Joseph clarified that there was no such thing as a vacation in the DPRK. Sarah confirmed this. The theme of the reading she had to teach that week happened to be "vacation," and she had realized that the vacation here was different from our idea of vacation. There was time set aside for recreation, such as playing sports, but there was no such thing as a prolonged holiday. All students had six days of school per week, and on Sundays many had duties to perform. This schedule did not change much during their vacation, since they either attended schools for Juche meetings or Daily Life Unity critiques, and the rest of the time, they were ordered to work at collective farms. This was a country where no one was allowed free time.

Every one of my students had told me he was going home for the month of August. Unless they were pretending, it seemed they knew as little as we did.

12

THE DAYS LEADING UP TO THE END OF THE SUMMER SEMES-
ter were a jumble. There was much picture taking and sporting
competition, as though the incessant activities would distract us
from our approaching goodbye. I was torn between sadness and
the desire to escape this place. I had been invited back to teach
during the fall semester, and I had said yes, but I was honestly
not sure if I could go through with it again.

After lunch on July 26, Ruth and I were called to President
Kim's office and told that we would be attending the ceremony
for the 58th Anniversary of the Great Victory at the Pyongyang
Indoor Stadium. This was a state event, hosted by the Workers' Party and the Pyongyang People's Committee, on the eve
of Victory Day. Among the invitees were a small group of the
PUST senior staff; we would be the only teachers. Joan later
told me that she had been working with President Kim for
nearly a decade, since the idea of PUST was first conceived, but
had never been invited since she was a "white face." We were
chosen, she said, because we were both returning in the fall and
because we were of Korean heritage.

When we arrived, it was dead quiet inside the stadium, even though all twenty thousand seats were occupied. Half the attendees were army personnel, the other half citizens in gray summer suits, a sort of civilian uniform for Party members. I saw no non-Korean faces. The stage was decorated with the words ONE HUNDRED WAR, ONE HUNDRED WIN! 58TH ANNIVERSARY OF VICTORY 727, and on either side of it were similar slogans. On stage, three rows of chairs faced the audience.

Soon about a hundred men came out wearing army uniforms, the same ones my students wore to guard the Kimilsungism Study Hall, and everyone in the audience rose and clapped as the men took their seats on the stage. Many of them were porky, with rotund bellies and generous jowls, and their jackets were covered with shiny gold medals. There were two women among them, one wearing a white pantsuit, the other a *hanbok*. It seems likely that one of them was Kim Kyung-hui, sister of Kim Jong-il and wife of Jang Sung-taek, then the second most powerful man in North Korea.*

One of the men walked to the podium and began reading an address that was at times unintelligible because of the terrible speakers.† It was mainly about the glorious achievements of Kim Il-sung, and the heroic way he had fended off the attacks of the American imperialists and won the war. Curse words directed at the United States and South Korea were scattered throughout the speech. The speaker said that Lee Myung-bak, then the president of South Korea, was driving the entire peninsula into the greedy hands of America, and that if this continued,

---

* Kim Jong-un had Jang executed for treason in December 2013. At the time of this writing, Kim Kyung-hui's whereabouts are unknown.
† I later learned that this was Ri Yong-ho, the Vice Marshal of the Korean People's Army, who was removed from his post by Kim Jong-un in July 2012. He has not been seen in public since, and it is believed that he was either sent to a political prison camp or executed.

Seoul would turn into a "sea of blood" filled with "death and corpses." The event was being taped and televised, and we were periodically told by our minders to applaud. The man ended his speech with the words "Long live our Great Leader Kim Il-sung! Long live our Great General Kim Jong-il! Long live our Workers' Party!" Then we all rose to our feet and shouted the words together.

When we returned to school, around 5:30, I sat alone in my office and was puzzled to hear what sounded like bits and pieces of the very same speech. Although the sound was garbled, I was able to trace it to the open window of one of the bigger classrooms around the corner. I pretended to use the bathroom and tiptoed over to that corner. Through the window I could see the students watching the taped speech on TV as a part of their special afternoon meeting.

At about 6:45, I sat in the cafeteria and watched my class walk in. They wore dark expressions and avoided our eyes. Some of them literally cringed at the sight of us. I should have felt hurt, but I understood. I had seen and heard the speech. It could only have been deeply confusing to be exhorted to prepare for a war against the American imperialists and then have to turn around and face us. They were like soldiers during wartime, preparing for death and destruction, while we bounced around, asking "What's your plan for the summer break?" or "Do you have a girlfriend?" Tonight, when they saw us, I knew that I had become the enemy, South Korean and American, the very target they had been taught to shoot and kill.

So I sat there and waited, and as I expected, no one wanted to take a seat at my table, until finally one of the class monitors joined me. He took on the burden of eating with me for the sake of his classmates, who did not want to. From his face, it was impossible to detect anything. When I asked why they were late for dinner and what they had done in their afternoon meeting, he simply shrugged.

"We watched TV," he said.

THE NEXT MORNING we had Sports Day, and clearly their mood had lifted. Every school across the nation performed this ritual twice a year, and so the students were familiar with the routines and cheers. Everyone, including teachers, participated, and the entire student body was divided into two teams, one with blue baseball caps and the other with white. The students had been looking forward to it for weeks, but after days of torrential showers, they were very worried that it might be rained out. Thankfully, the weather had cleared.

I could not help being reminded of my childhood in South Korea. We also waited all year for Sports Day, like American high school girls counting the days until prom. We were also divided into a blue team and a white team, and we played similar games, including three-legged races and tug of war, and had similar cheering competitions. The only differences were that we were elementary school children, and the time was the late 1970s. But I was not good at team sports and felt intimidated by the competitive spirit that seized my classmates. I remember moping around and waiting for my mother to appear with my lunch box containing her homemade *kimbap*. Every mother brought *kimbap* on Sports Day, and they all looked different, some very elaborate, with curlicue carrots and flower-shaped cucumbers, and it was as though the mothers were also in competition.

On Sports Day at PUST, I dutifully participated in the games, and I clapped and cheered for my students' team. If it had been a movie, perhaps that little girl from South Korea

would have found some peace, but there were only fleeting moments of connection—during a race where a student and I had
to run with a ball wedged between our heads; when all the
students and teachers danced in a circle, hand in hand. But
soon it was all over, and I returned to my dormitory while my
students returned to their gardening duty, pulling up weeds all
afternoon, even when the rain began to pour, on this Victory
Day when, according to them, Kim Il-sung had risked his life
to save them all.

LATER THAT AFTERNOON, there was the Victory 727 celebration
at the People's Palace of Culture. Again, only teachers of Korean
origin were invited. When we arrived, we noticed many shiny
cars, including Land Rovers and Mercedes Benz 300s, all of
them black like every other car I had seen in Pyongyang. I wondered if some of the attendees were my students' parents. Every
time I saw people in power, I asked myself the same question. I
looked upon those people as the cause of North Korea's ongoing
demise, and yet I loved their children.

As at the ceremony the evening before, the audience was
made up of army officials and formally dressed civilians. About
ten Workers' Party leaders were seated in the orchestra center
seats reserved for VIPs. I saw about twenty non-Koreans in one
corner of the room, including two men who wore army uniforms and spoke Russian, a woman in a head wrap, and a black
man in a traditional looking kaftan.

The opening act was performed by the Samjiyon Band of
the Mansudae Art Troupe, the country's most renowned group
of male and female musicians. Wearing fluffy, sequined, strap-
less gowns in pink, red, and white, the women onstage looked
to me like Las Vegas showgirls, although the program said many

of them had been awarded medals by Kim Jong-il and Kim Il-sung. The backdrop was an abstract neon-colored projection that reminded me of the default screen saver on a new laptop. On the ceiling, I could see about fifty pink and red balloons as well as a tiny rotating disco ball.

After the opening, the women danced to the music of "The Song of National Defense" and "To a Decisive Battle," and the soloist, a solemn-looking man in black tie, burst into "The Song of the Assassin," the theme of which was hunting. As we listened, it became clear that the objective of that hunting was to get the heads of the "Yankee *nom*," which means, roughly, "Yankee bastard." The refrain, over and over, was "Hunting American *nom*s." The word the performers used for Americans' heads was not *mauri* but *daegari,* which is used only to refer to animals.

Each time I visited the DPRK, I was shocked anew by their bastardization of the Korean language. Curses had taken root not only in their conversation and speeches but in their written language. They were everywhere—in poems, newspapers, in official Workers' Party speeches, even in the lyrics of songs performed on this most hallowed day. It was like finding the words *fuck* and *shit* in a presidential speech or on the front page of the *New York Times*. Their spoken language was equally crude, no matter the occasion. For example, during the previous day's speech, Lee Myung-bak and his administration were referred to as *nom* and *paetguhri-dul* (that bastard and his thugs). I was relieved that I did not hear my students speak Korean often enough to know whether they had inherited this legacy.

Yet I would sometimes hear expressions that warmed my heart—archaic, innocent-sounding words that made me feel as though the entire country were a small village undisturbed by time. Instead of the prosaic *soohwa*, meaning sign language,

North Koreans said "finger talk," and instead of "developing photos" they said "images waking up," which I found lovely and poetic.

Next, a group of about twenty girls between the ages of eight and ten sang about their love of the motherland, smiling adorably. They followed that up with a perky song about the greatness of their Great Leader, and the three in front shook something open, unfurling the DPRK flag, which they raised over their heads with theatrical affection. Then, suddenly and in the same sweet voices, they broke into a refrain about the "burning hatred in our hearts," and I had to close my eyes to escape the concert hall, the relentless slogans, the brutal words coming from angelic mouths.

The show went on and on. At one point a man delivered a monologue in which he lashed out against South Korea. Everything the Lee Myung-bak administration did was the opposite of good, he said, sternly warning Lee to stop if he did not want to be killed. His closing words were "Ready, aim, fire," followed by a simulated gunshot by the orchestra, at which the audience broke into applause.

The last performer was a woman at the side podium wearing a *hanbok*, using her hand to make a "sand picture" that was projected on a giant screen. Deftly rearranging the sand, the woman made a picture of a figure wearing a chef's toque, and the audience applauded. She transformed this into what looked like a pig with suckling piglets. Then some sort of bird. Then perhaps a revolutionary youth, although I was, by then, cocking my head along with the rest of the audience, trying to guess. On the ceiling, the disco ball continued rotating.

13

WHEN ARE YOU LEAVING?

It was the last day of the summer session, and my students kept coming up to me, asking the same thing over and over, the way children do. I told them that all the teachers were going to meet at 6:30 a.m. to leave for the airport.

"Teacher, we come and see you off," they said, repeatedly.

All of us knew they could not do that, as it would mean deviating from the schedule. Even though our dormitory buildings were next to each other, they could not just roll out of bed and come outside to say goodbye. Yet they kept promising. *Teacher, we see you off tomorrow morning.* One student must have said it five times.

I liked believing that they very much wanted to, and that they repeated it so many times in order to show me that, but knowing that it was impossible filled me with sadness. There was no mercy here. I knew that, and yet each time it was confirmed I found myself surprised all over again.

On the last evening, the students were for the first time given permission to join us after dinner in the cafeteria, where we sang and performed skits. It lasted about half an hour, and after the first twenty minutes, a few of the counterparts showed up. Their presence meant time was running out, and the students became visibly tense. Some of the boys made eye contact with me and did not look away; that was all they could do. When nothing can be expressed openly, you become quite good at interpreting silence. And I read theirs as they read mine.

For days, they had been teaching me a song. It was the least nationalistic song I had heard there, and when I told them I loved it, they were delighted and offered to teach it to me. Together, we translated the lyrics:

> *Dandelions blooming on the hills of my hometown,*
> *Those times when I played flying a white kite,*
> *Ah, that blue sky I saw as a child,*
> *Why didn't I know then that was the pride of my motherland?*

That evening I sang it with them, in English, then in Korean. It was the only way I could show them that I loved them and would miss them dearly. When I began crying, which I could no longer help, some of them whispered, *Teacher, smile please.* I kept hearing those words: *Teacher, smile please.* I wondered what they would say if they could speak freely, and this wondering made me cry more, and I worried that the counterparts would notice and would not like it.

The last thing we were allowed to do together was pose for group photos. For the sake of efficiency, the teachers were seated in a single row, and each class of students took turns standing behind them, forming three rows. After a class had been photographed, the students in that group were to shake hands with the teachers and make room for the next group, then return to their dorm immediately. I heard my class calling out "Sophomores first!" because they knew that the students who had their photos taken last would get to be with the teachers the longest. One very tall student stood behind me during the photo session, and no matter how much the teacher taking the photo demanded that he move to the back row, he would not budge. When I turned around and met his eyes, he mumbled, "Thank you and goodbye, Teacher," and I realized he had stuck to his spot just to tell me that. When the photographer told him yet again to move, I nodded, my eyes on his, hoping he knew I understood him, and it was only then that he moved. Later the teacher who took the photos told me that all the students wanted to stand close to their teachers. Being physically near them was the most they could do to show their love.

I was as speechless as my students. I could not say, as I shook hands with each of them, *Leave this wretched place. Leave your wretched Great Leader. Leave it, or shake it all up. Please do something.* Instead I cried and cried, and I smiled. And each student met my eyes and smiled in return. And that was our goodbye. Some still said, "We see you off tomorrow, Teacher." I wanted them to claim their own actions by saying "I" instead of "we," but here there was no "I." Even "we" did not exist without the permission of their Great Leader. As they stood in their units and marched back to their dormitories that evening, they bellowed out the song I had come to know best, as if to remind us and themselves to whom they really belonged:

Without you, there is no us.

That night, I looked out my window at the student dormitory, but it was completely dark, as though they had all instantly fallen asleep at the same time. But we had been together for a month by then, so even buried in that darkness, behind those opaque windows, each one was special and known to me.

The next morning, at 6:30 a.m., standing outside the faculty dormitory with the other teachers waiting for the bus, I looked for my students, even though I knew they would not show up. Still, I clung to the hope that some exception would be made. Then I saw them marching toward the cafeteria, singing at the top of their voices. The distance between us was at most a hundred yards, but they never once turned to look in our direction. We boarded our bus and were told that we would be stopping at the IT building, where classes were usually held, because the chief counterpart wanted to say goodbye to us.

At 7 a.m., we were parked in front of the IT building when we saw a few students coming down the road. They had finished breakfast and were apparently walking to classes, though we wondered who could be teaching them. Someone joked that the students would probably have Juche boot camp to counteract the influence of their brief Western education. Then I noticed that some of the students were craning their necks, looking for the faces of their teachers, and when they spotted us through the bus windows, smiles dawned on their faces, and some waved. But they could not stop walking, since a voice inside the IT building was shouting for them to come in, which they did, although many of them walked extra slowly, their faces still turned toward us. And even after they went inside, some of the boys stood at the window of the building, squinting to make out their teachers.

That was how we parted, our gazes locked, the students watching from behind glass as we were driven to freedom.

PART TWO

The Sun of the 21st Century

14

Reunions are rarely what we imagine them to be. When I got back to New York, the man in Brooklyn and I went through all the phases of lovers: anticipation, doubts, resistance. "Let me look at you," he said when we met at a sushi place on Smith Street. He seemed lost for words, except to note with concern that I looked thinner. Perhaps it was a compliment, but having just come from North Korea, "thinner" no longer sounded flattering. He seemed like a stranger to me that first night, as I must have to him. He had no idea what I had been through, and I did not try to explain.

Instead, I retreated. He preferred texting to calling, but on those occasions when he did phone, I would inevitably let the call go to voice mail. I was not acting aloof, as lovers sometimes do. I just felt unable to face him after such a long absence. Separation had cost us. We were who we were despite the separation, and because of the separation. It was neither simple nor easy.

For that matter, neither was New York. The free world I had so longed for, with its intoxicating lights and abundance, overwhelmed me, the way the dawning of spring stops me each year. The sheer suddenness of the sun feels like an intrusion, and I spend most of those months indoors. I am wary of the outpouring of so much life all at once, and I become tentative, like a child learning to walk and see and feel. August passed that way, and I felt a bit more comfortable in my skin as September rolled around. Yet by then it was time to pack and return for the fall semester. I did not *have* to return, but I did. There was still too much I did not understand but this time, I would be there until the end of December. I did not know if I would be able to endure it.

LATE SEPTEMBER IN Pyongyang was cold compared to New York. I was nervous, not sure whether the bond between my students and me had survived our time apart. During the summer, they had let their guards down somewhat, but now I was again a foreigner, bearing traces of the outside world. Perhaps we would have to test the waters all over again. But when the students came into the classroom on my first day and I saw the pure delight in their faces, my heart melted. Some of them could not even meet my eyes from shyness and excitement. I noticed small details—that some looked frailer, that one now had a slight limp, and I couldn't wait to talk to them.

At lunch, I asked a few students what they had done over the summer vacation and was bombarded with tales of leisure time filled with activities with friends. Park Jun-ho said he had gone swimming for three to four hours at a time at the gymnasium at least three times a week. Han Jae-shik said that he had gone Rollerblading at the gymnasium and seen the Arirang Games with friends a couple of times. Kim Tae-hyun said that he had thrown a birthday party in August at a restaurant in the Chongryon Hotel.

"Seventy students came!" he said with smiling eyes. "Only twelve from my former university, and the rest from PUST. It was a good time!" I wondered who his parents were that they were able to throw him such a lavish party, and I also remembered how easily my students lied.

Jae-shik explained that parties outside PUST were different, that they could do more than just sing.

"At a birthday party, there would be food the birthday boy's mother would make," he said. "There would be some drinks."

"Alcohol?" I asked.

His only answer was a smug smile.

Jun-ho chimed in: "There were these girls there, but Tae-hyun would not let me near them. He was so protective of his younger sisters that I only got to speak to a couple of them!" He gestured with his arms spread open, mimicking his friend furiously guarding the young women.

"I don't know what he is talking about," Jae-shik said, rolling his eyes. "Tae-hyun has only one sister!"

"Oh yes, but all the other cute girls were the friends of Tae-hyun's sister!" Jun-ho countered.

Jae-shik exclaimed, "I only saw three girls there!"

"Because they were not interested in you!" Jun-ho said, chuckling. "But I saw seven. The girls were all saying about me, 'What a charming guy!'"

Finally, one of the students from the adjacent table leaned over and said: "Change the topic please. This guy," pointing at Jun-ho, "is too interested in the younger sisters of his classmates! Always going on and on about younger sister younger sister!"

While they were sparring about girls, I remembered what Dr. Joseph had said: that some of the students would be sent to do manual labor in August. It seemed at least these students had avoided it. They looked unfazed, luminous, as though they had never lifted a finger in the sun.

At dinner that night, I found out that some others had not been so lucky. One student told me that he had been sent to work at a construction site for ten days, from six a.m. until six p.m. He said it matter-of-factly, explaining that they were building an extension for the Korean History Museum. He had felt alone there, he said, since most of his friends had been building an extension for Kim Hyung-jik University. The other two at the table remained silent. When I asked whether they too had been sent to a construction site, they shook their heads and said that honor was only for those living in Pyongyang's central district but they lived in a suburb, and to assist their Great General and their powerful and prosperous nation, it was imperative that university students contribute in "building buildings."

The next day, I saw a student whom I had been very fond of, who was no longer in either of my two groups. For the fall semester, I was still assigned to Classes 1 and 4, but the students had been shuffled around according to their grades; some students had been moved to higher levels, others dropped to lower ones. I called the student over to join me for a meal. He broke into a shy smile but kept saying that he was embarrassed, and I realized that he meant he wanted others to come sit with us. Of course, I had forgotten that they could never be one on one with us, so when I saw another familiar face, I called the student over to join us, and my student relaxed visibly.

The talk was mostly about basketball, which he loved but could not play anymore because his new group preferred soccer. At first, I wondered why he could not just play with his old friends, but then I remembered that that was the way things went here. Each group was like an army platoon, and a student who changed groups did not just move his belongings to a new room; he did everything with the new group. They had lived this way all their lives and did not question it, but, sitting across from one of my loveliest students, I suddenly found it hard to swallow, and I put my spoon down. He looked at me innocently and asked, "Professor, are you not hungry?"

THIS SEMESTER, I was asked to teach the counterparts—the people who read and approved all our teaching materials—as well as the students. I jumped at the opportunity. There were thirteen men, mostly in their forties and fifties, and two women in their thirties. One said that he had worked for the Department of Communication and Information. I had no idea what that was, but I knew not to ask further. Others were professors of computer science, agriculture, and engineering, and the two women said that they were secretaries. I recognized some from the cafeteria, but I had never seen most of them before.

Where had all the other teachers gone if every university in the country had been closed? With no students to teach, were they at construction sites too? Why were these men chosen to be sent to PUST? Though many of them read English well, they all wanted to improve their spoken English and said that they were very happy for this chance to converse with a fluent speaker. Some days I had the uneasy feeling that I might be teaching the very people who were monitoring our emails, that I was training them so that they could spy better.

Spying was not the only thing I worried about. I dreaded bumping into some of the minders or the counterparts because they could be unpleasant, but darkness fell so early at that time of year that I had no choice but to go running during the day, between classes. On one such afternoon I saw Mr. Hong getting out of the school van. He was one of the men I tried to avoid, since he had a habit of making spiteful comments with an oily smile. Today was no exception.

"Comrade Kim Suki does whatever she feels like, no matter where," he said. My running must have struck him as either too American or too leisurely, or both. "The more I see Comrade Kim Suki, the more I'm certain that she's not the right material for the DPRK. She doesn't know how to control students to get them to excel and respect her as well as fear her, all at once. Please don't feel offended by anything I say. I only want to help you."

His style of criticism—indirect, using the third person—was not unfamiliar to me. I had interviewed many defectors in the past, and it was surprising how many of them readily bashed the people around them, often behind their backs. I wondered if their behavior stemmed from the lifelong indoctrination of weekly critiques, from the constant spying on their fellow citizens.

Mr. Hong shook his head and continued, clicking his tongue, "Really a long road ahead for Comrade Kim Suki. I taught at Kim Chaek University for ten years, and I am part of the National Education Committee that grants people PhDs and Masters, all thanks to the solicitude of our Great Leader, and I could declare with certainty that she has no clue about teaching!"

I was now getting a bit worried that this might be a roundabout way of terminating my employment there, so I asked, "Did my students say something to you? Is the school unhappy with my teaching? Is my class not good?" We were speaking in Korean, and for "not good" I used the Korean word *byulro*, which could also be translated as "not all that."

"*Byulro*? What kind of a word is that?" He looked away, feigning boredom. For a moment, I thought perhaps that particular word did not exist in the North.

"Do you not understand this word?" I asked him.

"*Byulro*? *Byulro*? I don't understand, Comrade Kim Suki! *You* are *byulro*!"

I realized then that he knew exactly what the word meant and was just playing games.

He wasn't done yet: "But students do like her very much. When I see Comrade Kim Suki casting her feminine glance over her students in the cafeteria, I wonder if her students are all captivated by her feminine charm. They must lose sleep at night thinking about their teacher. They are young virile boys after all."

I was feeling increasingly uncomfortable, though his behavior did not surprise me. The minders sometimes said things that bordered on sexual harassment. Luckily, Mr. Hong's cell phone (counterparts and minders always carried them) rang, and I walked away.

Immediately I went to see Beth, who told me that as a "white face," which was how she and Joan often referred to themselves, she never got such treatment. Mary, who was a Korean Chinese woman in her late thirties, told me that perhaps I should try to wear more conservative clothing, although I failed to see how much more dour I could look. In trying to pass for a missionary, I generally wore long skirts, high-necked blouses, and cardigans in lukewarm shades of beige and brown. I also spoke to Abigail, a Korean-American teacher in her fifties with a long history of dealing with North Koreans.

"Oh, the minders and the counterparts do it all the time," she said. "They are unbelievably repressed. They can't do anything. So they get all worked up and harass women verbally to take out their frustration. Even ones in high positions you'd never expect to do such a thing will suddenly say things that back home would be considered harassment. Besides, these guys do it also to get bribes. That was a form of blackmail. They whine about everything. Every visa process, they will claim difficulties every step. What he was angling for was extra cash. You just have to be polite but firm. Smile and say: 'In my country if you say such a thing, you could go to jail.' That will shut them up!"

Abigail was more matronly and was there with her husband, though, and I was not sure the same approach would work for me. Suddenly the prospect of living in the same building and eating three meals a day with the very men who watched me and reported on me and harassed me felt insufferable.

Later that evening, I spoke to Ruth, who confirmed my feelings. She was a Korean New Zealander, thirty and single, and had taught at YUST for years. She had had similar encounters and now she knew better. To avoid being alone in public, she always teamed up with another teacher, even at meals, and she took care to walk back to the dormitory in a group. Although her Korean was excellent (her mother had made her memorize a page from the Bible in Korean each day), when the counterparts spoke to her in Korean, she pretended her Korean was not good enough. She also made sure the counterparts knew that she had no spare money so that they would not pressure her for bribes. As for my running, she did not understand why that should be a problem.

"Just run during nap time," she said, shrugging.

"What nap time? You mean like *siesta*?"

She burst out laughing and said, "You didn't know about it? It's between twelve and two! Have you ever seen anyone walking around then? They all nap because You-Know-Who told them to!"

The campus was extremely quiet during those hours, but I had always assumed that the students were preparing for afternoon classes or attending extra Juche lessons. According to Ruth, some of the Korean Chinese workers—the cleaners and some administrative staff—had complained about not being able to get work done during the "damned nap time," which applied to every North Korean on campus, both the students and the counterparts. The nap time was confirmed by my students. They all went back to the dormitory and slept, it turned out. Some told me the naps were specific to PUST, and that they had never heard of a nap time before they arrived there.

Whatever the case, from that day on, I ran unmolested through that dead quiet campus, where everyone was fast asleep, as directed by their Great Leader.

THE GLOOMY FACES at the next staff meeting told me that something bad had happened. One of the summer missionary teachers had written a blog post about her experience at PUST in the *Washington Post*. They would not show it to us, or even tell us what she had written, and it was too risky for us to visit the website. All we knew was that President Kim was very upset and said that they intended to screen teachers more carefully.

"I told every teacher that they shouldn't talk to the press, and that if they were approached, they had to send everything my way first," Joan said, somewhat defensively.

"Did the summer staff sign the same agreement we signed last winter?" asked a British teacher who had been at the school since it opened.

"No, but I did tell them to be discreet!" Joan replied.

Another teacher added, "She wanted to return here next summer, and even bring her husband, and now I guess not."

They all nodded, agreeing to be extra careful from then on. It was eerie to see how quickly imposed censorship led to self-censorship. I was afraid they would make me sign some sort of agreement, and I instinctively tightened my grip around my key chain, to which I had attached two USB sticks. I knew I would eventually tell the world what I had seen there and that this would cause my colleagues much anguish, the thought of which was upsetting. I could only hope that they would forgive me by turning to the Bible and their Lord who, according to them, created everything, including me and my eventual, inevitable betrayal.

15

In October, I learned that Steve Jobs had died and that Qaddafi had been killed in Libya. Newspapers around the world were buzzing about the Arab Spring, about a new order in which civil discontent could no longer be so easily suppressed. In the DPRK, however, life continued exactly as it had for the past sixty-some years, with no news that did not concern the Great Leader.

Lessons also continued much as they had during the summer, but because of the more demanding fall curriculum there was no time for activity hours or a weekly personal letter, so I could not be as creative. A new system of team teaching had been introduced to ensure that we kept each other in check, just as the students did with each other. This was a different thing altogether from my arrangement with Katie, who had been a TA and followed my lead. Katie had not returned for the fall semester, and neither had Sarah. Now I had to check every lesson with Martha, the other team teacher—a twenty-four-year-old Brit who taught Classes 2 and 3—and I felt the small freedom I had in teaching evaporate.

Still, using the excuse of teaching students the difference between casual and formal language, I came up with a lesson involving a job application letter, and it was approved. I hoped to find out more about how employment decisions were made there, and also to show them that we *chose* our jobs outside. The assignment was to write a letter applying for a dream job. Many simply followed the example on the board, which was a letter applying for a job as a translator. Only a few came up with their own job possibilities. One wrote a letter to Manchester United asking for a position, offering to provide a résumé, as though this was a reasonable way to prove one's worth to a professional soccer team. Others said they wanted to apply to the NBA but did not want to ask a Western person for a job, so I told them that they could give the person they were addressing a Korean name. Another student told me that he wanted to ask Bill Gates for a job but had no address for him. I told him just to make up an address for the moment, but since he had never seen a foreign address, he was still baffled. Without access to the Internet, even simple tasks caused them great stress.

Almost no one understood the fundamental idea behind writing such a letter. They would write sentences such as "I have no job and would like a job" or "I am bored and want a job." The entire concept of making oneself marketable in the eyes of a prospective employer did not exist.

Since this was a lesson on comparing formal and informal, I insisted to Martha that I needed to check up on their informal letter-writing skills. Then I asked them to write me a personal letter to remind me who they were. The resulting letters were far more emotional than I had expected. Many filled both sides of the page. Instead of writing their names at the end, some described themselves and asked me to guess who they were, and one of them signed his letter with "Shy boy (only in English)."

Another tried to be funny and wrote, "My brain is bad, and my appearance is ugly. My head looks like a pumpkin and my body looks like a potato. Now can you name who I am?" Yet another wrote, "Dear Professor, considering your elegant manner, we think you must have a charming guy, how on earth find this guy." They talked about Sports Day and the spelling bee and missing Katie. One of them mentioned how touched he had been when gardening duty lasted longer than usual one evening, and Katie and I waited for them so we could all have dinner together. Another wrote, "In the summer semester, you were our good professor, but you were also like our familiar sister. We regretted not to see you off when you left for the airport." Yet another wrote, "During the vacation, I missed your catchword, 'gentleman,' and it used to make us amazed but we could read your mind that you wanted us to be gentle in life."

Many recalled the last evening of the summer semester when I sang their country's song with them. One wrote, "Your singing struck a deep impression on us because you sang this song happily, and sadly, and your eyes were drained in tears. If you thought about the days you spent with us, you would have been happy and if you thought about separating from us, you would have been sad." Most of them had remained stone-faced then, but another wrote, "On that day, teacher, you cried, and of course we cried in our minds too." This might be as far as I could go in reaching them, I thought.

Or maybe I could go further. Since technology in North Korea was so dated and they were exposed to so little of it, I wanted them to see what was out there. I could have starred in a commercial for Apple the way I made sure to always keep my brand-new MacBook open on the lectern during lessons. I also pulled out my Kindle whenever I could. I kept thinking of the ways to make them aware of the world of modern technology.

For our next writing exercise, I decided to use obituaries of Steve Jobs to teach them about the art of biography. The catch was that I had to run the material by my team teacher before getting it approved by the counterparts.

Martha came into my office, holding up the printout of the nine obituaries I had selected, shaking her head. "Most of these won't work. We'd have to delete all the interesting parts. In this Cuban blogger one, for example, about how she came from a repressed society and felt personally touched by Steve Jobs, we'd have to cut out her discussion of politics. And this article about the Chinese reaction is no good. The Chinese are laying down flowers at his memorial tribute as though he were Mao. The counterparts will never go for that."

Martha was a good Christian girl and firmly believed in rules, but she was also young, so I put my foot down. "Why don't we just cut a paragraph or two?"

So we sat in my office, butchering perfectly well-written articles. In the end we narrowed it down to three: CNN, *Forbes,* MTV. The one that worried Martha was the obituary from the MTV website, which listed devices the students had never seen, like iPods and iPads. "These mean nothing to them," Martha insisted. Although the counterparts approved the lesson, none of the students, some of whom were computer science majors, had ever heard of Steve Jobs. They showed little interest, not even when I told them he had helped mastermind the machine they saw sitting in front of me.

It seemed odd that they had all heard of Bill Gates but drew a blank on Mark Zuckerberg and Steve Jobs. The only two English-language writers I ever heard them mention were Sidney Sheldon and Margaret Mitchell. Several students told me they had read *"Disappeared with the Wind"* and quoted passages from it. In 2002, I had visited Kim Il-sung University, and students there had told me the same thing. Perhaps it was the conflict between North and South, in which the North wins, that appealed to them. "Do you know the words to 'Aloha Hawaii'?" the two youngest counterparts in my class, both in their late thirties, asked, referring to the "very famous" American pop song. When I told them that I did not, they were surprised. I later looked it up and discovered that in 1973 there had been a concert and album by Elvis Presley called *Aloha from Hawaii*. What washed ashore or found its way into North Korea had a random feeling to it; there seemed to be no pattern, no rhyme or reason to what aspects of Western culture—whether an icon like Michael Jordan or the detritus of the culture—might be allowed in.

THIS SEMESTER ALREADY felt different. The students were used to me now, and we were all less cautious. Many of them now told me openly that they were not allowed cell phones at PUST; however, a few sometimes borrowed them from campus workers to call home. They had very powerful parents, so it made sense that they could wield some influence with the workers. Although these parents were not allowed on campus, they could, on rare occasions, stop at the gate to see their children briefly or drop off things. One day, a student could not make it to lunch with me as scheduled. Later, he explained that his mother had come to the gate with rice cake and roast chicken because it was his birthday. He was an only child, and she wept during their twenty-minute meeting, so he told her, "If you keep crying, I am going to go back inside." He was laughing as he said this before his friends, but his eyes watered.

The students asked me the meaning of the word *exclusive*, so I gave as an example a very well-known Pyongyang restaurant,

Okryu-gwan. One student brightened and told me that his friend from middle school was a waitress there. She had not passed the university exam, so she had been assigned a waitress job. I asked if she gave him extra *naengmyun*, and he said never, but that she served him fast. Clearly, even residents experienced long waits at restaurants, just as visitors did. In any case, the class all shook their heads at my example and said, "No, that is not exclusive, that is popular!" Then they said perhaps I meant the Koryo Hotel restaurant. At Okryu-gwan, they explained, they paid for a meal with a government-issued food ration ticket. At Koryo Hotel, however, they were expected to pay with money, which excluded some customers.

"Are the same number of ration tickets given to everyone?" I asked.

They answered yes, although some added that the number of ration tickets depended on the person's loyalty to the party. This ration ticket versus cash system was confusing. I knew that the State distributed some things for free while others had to be paid for, but I could never get an answer as to where they got money.

One student surprised me by giving Samsung as an example of an exclusive label or company. They were not supposed to praise anything South Korean, and moreover, Samsung was not as big a presence there as Hyundai, whose founder, Jung Ju-yong, hailed from North Korea and had once led a hundred trucks containing 1,001 cows across the DMZ (demilitarized zone) into the North, among other inter-Korean projects.

Another change was that they now asked things about America. At dinner, one student cautiously asked, "In America, among college students, is it a secret to have a girlfriend?" I said, "No, it's pretty natural for us, but I come from a different kind of society. What about here? Is it a secret?" He nodded, but another student shook his head. They were hesitant, yet it was a step forward that they trusted me enough to ask such a thing.

Since they liked sports, I decided to give them a short article to read on why baseball and basketball were more TV-friendly than soccer in the United States, and the counterparts approved it. The author's main argument was that soccer was less well suited to commercial breaks, which made networks less enthusiastic about airing soccer matches. There was no such thing as a commercial in the DPRK, so I explained that a commercial was a very brief movie made by a company to sell a product. I used as an example one of the few locally produced products, a bottled spring water called Shinduk Saemul.

"Okay," I said. "During a basketball game, let's say there's an interruption for a commercial featuring Michael Jordan." They smiled at this reference. Then I pretended to be Michael Jordan dribbling a ball and dunking it, turning around, wiping sweat off his forehead, taking a sip from the bottle of Shinduk Saemul, and saying, "Wow, Shinduk Saemul *is* the best!" They all burst out laughing, and I explained that that would be a typical commercial in my country. I told them that if the company that made Shinduk Saemul were owned by a person, rather than a government, the company would "target" the basketball audience by hiring Michael Jordan and paying the television station for airtime. The company's goal was for viewers around the world to watch the commercial and want to drink the same water Michael Jordan drinks and buy it. They liked the notion of a famous American basketball star drinking their water, and, amazingly, they seemed to understand the general concept of marketing. Their curiosity grew.

"How many TV channels do you have in America?" a student asked at dinner one night.

"A lot," I said.

"A hundred?" A hundred television channels was like a joke to them when they only had three government channels, so he was probably just guessing wildly. But in fact my cable TV provider offered nearly a thousand channels.

"More," I said, shrugging. "We have about thirty free channels, but hundreds of ones through cable TV, which we pay for. These are very specific. There are movie channels, cartoon channels, news channels, sports channels. For example, children's programming might be divided into cartoons and live-action shows, but there might also be different channels with cartoons for three-year-olds, five-year-olds, and ten-year-olds. Same for sports. There are channels that show only basketball, golf, baseball, American football, and more, throughout the day."

Some gawked at me, and some just lowered their gazes. I could not tell if they believed me, but my detailed answer seemed to bother them. I was being bolder than ever, but by that time I trusted them not to report me. I also knew that I could somehow connect it to the lesson on TV commercials if I were questioned by counterparts. For weeks afterward, several students asked me the same question about the number of TV channels in America, and my answer always had the same effect: a look of disbelief and something else I could not quite grasp—something between envy and self-doubt. I was not boasting about American television, since much of it was junk, but I wanted them to see that we had choices, many choices, and that what their leaders had told them about them being powerful and prosperous was pure fantasy. They were behind, farther behind than almost everyone else in the world, and if they wanted to truly become a powerful and prosperous nation that produced much more than spring water, it was important for them to rise up.

But I could not tell them any of this, so instead I kept repeating that we had a *choice* of hundreds of television channels.

Another time, they talked about exchange programs, and one student said that his roommate wanted to go to Stuttgart, Germany. I told them I had been there and they asked when.

"Oh, when I was living in London many years ago. Germany is close to England. Europe is small. For example, it only takes two hours and fifteen minutes by train to get from London to Paris."

"What about the sea?" the student asked, shocked.

I explained that a tunnel had been built and that it was a high-speed train.

"How many kilometers is it between London and Paris?" he asked.

I did not know the exact number, so I told him that I would get back to him. A few days later, I told the student that I had looked it up on the Internet and that the distance was 340.55 kilometers. This knowledge seemed to bother him. Perhaps he now realized that my Internet was different from his intranet, and I wondered if he would deduce that the transportation system in his country remained decades behind, and that his world was designed to restrict movement.

Even the counterparts had little knowledge of time and distance beyond their daily commute. During one of our lessons I asked them about their morning schedules, and it turned out most of them left their houses in Pyongyang around 6:30 a.m. in order to arrive at PUST by 8:00. Then I asked how long it took to get from Pyongyang to Wonsan, one of their major cities. It was like asking a group of American teachers how many hours it takes to go from New York City to Washington, D.C. One answered three hours. Another said eight. Another said fourteen. When I asked why their answers were so vastly different, they remained silent. I could not tell if this was due to their lack of English, to embarrassment over their inefficient transportation system, to ignorance, or if it was because so few of them had ever been to Wonsan. One answered as if he were speaking on behalf of the class, "I do not like trains. I drive there. So I do not know the time it takes from Pyongyang to Wonsan." Concepts like *jet lag* and *frequent flyer miles* confounded them. It seemed that these middle-aged men were as clueless as the undergraduates.

I recalled how Mrs. Johnson, the fortysomething Korean wife of an American teacher, had remarked that teaching these North Koreans was "a waste of time" and that her nine-year-old daughter knew more about computers than the computer majors there. Of course, the DPRK purposely infantilized its citizens, making everyone helpless and powerless so that they depended on the state.

WITH MIDTERMS APPROACHING, the students were in a small panic. Their grades were so important to them. Some told me that they studied during nap time instead of sleeping and one stayed up so late memorizing vocabulary that he suffered nose-bleeds from stress. This was a system where hierarchy was everything. I learned that even the morning roll call was in order of their class rank. Many of the students came from their local Middle School Number 1, and some of their parents worked at

Hospital Number 1 and lived in District Number 1. Each person's value was clearly marked in numbers.

In other ways, their world was not so different from ours. Although they did not travel freely, the elites there moved in a small circle. Many of the students had known each other since they were young. One student proudly told me that he had gone to Pyongyang Eastern District Middle School Number 1, the second best school in the whole country, right after Pyongyang Middle School Number 1, the school their Great Leader had attended. Seven other students from Class 1 had gone there too. The school offered a class on Mao and had an exchange program with China's Beijing Middle School Number 5, where they had an entire course dedicated to Kim Il-sung. The parents of the more privileged students all seemed to be either core members of the Party or prominent doctors. Many of their fathers had been abroad for work, to China or Libya or Russia. Their mothers usually did not work. If their siblings were old enough, they attended one of the well-known Pyongyang universities. Many of my students were only children, though.

Those who were not from Pyongyang—who were instead from other cities such as Hamhung, Saryun, Nampo—had different stories. Their parents were often local doctors or scientists, and their siblings were in the army. Some admitted that they had no idea how long their brothers or sisters would serve—perhaps nine or ten years. As far as I knew, the mandatory service was ten years for men and seven years for women, but it seemed to vary. One of them said that his older brother had been in the army for five and a half years and was stationed in the northernmost corner of the country. I replied that it must be very cold there, and he nodded and said he missed him very much. His brother had been allowed to come home only once. This, in a country the size of Pennsylvania! These students seemed to have ended up at PUST on the basis of academic merit. Their more modest upbringing was visible in their suits, their shoes, their bags, their pens, which were never quite as nice or fancy as those of the Pyongyang students.

Yet there were a few exceptions—non-Pyongyang students who seemed like the wealthiest of all. Some of the border regions had recently benefited from illegal trades with China, and I suspected the parents of these students might have bought their children access to PUST. These class differences seemed positively capitalist, yet another crack in North Korea's facade.

The more I learned about their system, the more I saw that their obsession with grades sprang from more than a zeal for academic excellence. They believed that grades and rankings determined virtually their entire futures. For example, they did not apply to colleges. They took college entrance exams during their junior and senior years of high school, and then their regional governments decided which colleges they would attend. There were no interviews. But it was not all determined by grades. Their family backgrounds, or their *songbun*, played a crucial part in determining which colleges they were assigned to. According to President Kim, there was a long waiting list for next year's undergraduates at PUST because every Party leader in this country wanted his son here instead of at a construction site. Corruption was everywhere. Their grades weren't the only thing that would save them, but they were the only thing under their control.

It was the same with their careers. Jobs, like college, were decided for them by the government. My students insisted that this was a fair practice. Their government based its decision on three things: the person's ability, as indicated by his grades; the reports made about him by his friends and teachers; and, finally, his loyalty to the Party. I wanted to know more details about the last criterion, but questions about their political party were forbidden.

Finally, I asked, "So the job application letter I assigned you never gets written in your country?" They all answered, "Exactly, we do not write such letters." Later, a student asked me whether Americans wrote such letters. I told him yes, and that I myself had written such a letter to get my first job out of college. He asked what happens after that, and I explained that we get called for an interview if we are chosen as a candidate for a job. He seemed mystified. "Then what happens at these interviews?" The only interview they had ever had was here at PUST, in order to evaluate their proficiency in English. I knew that writing such a letter was something they most likely would never have to do, and now I regretted giving them the assignment. Was I unnecessarily upsetting them by suggesting what existed beyond their borders?

AS HOPELESS AS it seemed at times, teaching them never felt to me like "a waste of time." The students *were* becoming more aware about the world beyond theirs. One of them asked me the date for International Youth Day. He said that they did not celebrate the day, but a few foreign teachers had taught him about it last semester and he could not recall whether it was November 11 or 12. It turned out to be August 12, according to Google, which I relied on almost as much as they relied on books written by the Great Leader. When I told him the next day, he was elated.

Another repeated a riddle he had heard somewhere: "The man that made it didn't want it. The man that built it didn't need it. The man that used it didn't know it." He said that he just could not figure it out. "A coffin," I told him the next day. He then wrote to me in his letter, "Frankly, I did not know that an answer to this riddle would be on the Internet, and on the occasion of that answer, I realized how useful the Internet was."

At dinner one night, I took a risk and told the students that I was able to call home. Some teachers had begun using Skype to call their families, although most of us shied away from it, not wanting to expose our families to those who were listening in. The students seemed either confused or uninterested, but I kept going.

"Have you heard of Skype?" I said casually.

They shook their heads.

"It's a program on the Internet, and we use it to make phone calls anywhere in the world."

"Is it free?" one asked.

I said yes, and that seemed to impress them. Yet they looked confused, and they did not ask any more questions about it, although I kept dropping the word *Skype* over the next few weeks.

When I told them that Katie, who was now working in the Middle East, had emailed to say hello to them, Kim Tae-hyun immediately asked, "You can be in touch with Miss Katie from here?"

"Sure," I said casually. He did not ask anything more and seemed deep in thought.

"When did she say hello?" another student asked.

"Just yesterday," I said. The whole table became quiet.

This semester, a library had been set up on the third floor of the cafeteria building. One area consisted of the stacks, with books that had mostly been donated by South Korean organizations. Almost none of them contained pictures, though a few inevitably slipped by. For example, there were some South Korean architecture magazines, which had a few pages of advertisements for condos, showing famous actors and fancy high-rises. One student told Ruth that he had seen a picture of South Korea in a book at the library. She asked him what he thought of it, and he answered, "Bright." There were computer stations and a study area with large tables. None of the computers there were connected to the Internet.

There was also a small room with about ten computers, in front of which a female guard stood watch. The door to it was closed, but there were windows so we could see in. The teachers said that soon some of the graduate students would be taught about the Internet there. (The grad students were a small group of men in their mid-twenties, studying English, computer science, and economics. I rarely saw them except when we stood in line at the cafeteria.) This was a major development, and we all anxiously waited for further news.

16

That October, it rained a lot. The same rain fell here as anywhere else, and that seemed wondrous to me, and I remembered the monsoon in Seoul, and for the first time I even missed it. Often I stood by my window and watched the rain for hours because it was like a whiff of home. The sameness of every day under a constant watch had begun to take its toll again. A feeling of hopelessness saturated me and could not be washed away. My thoughts were the only thing I could claim as my own, and they circled in my head all day long until I wrote them down. But words were not enough.

I missed my lover. I carried my longing for him everywhere. It was like an illness and at times had nothing to do with him. Missing him was my only reminder of life in New York and the girl I used to be. I missed that girl, in jeans, which Kim Jong-il had banned, rather than my dreary missionary schoolteacher outfits, and with a glass of wine in downtown Manhattan instead of asleep at 8 p.m. just because it was dark outside and we weren't allowed to go anywhere, and those still awake were either the students on guard duty or the other teachers reading their Bibles. In that world, I needed a lover, no matter how abstract, and that need drove me crazy some nights. I wrote him feverish emails that I did not send. Besides, he wrote me back so infrequently that he could not be considered a lover in any worldly sense.

The few times he did write me, he seemed to have misunderstood my coded emails. I had warned him before leaving that our correspondence would be monitored, but he kept forgetting and would write that he was befuddled by what I had written, as though he expected me to explain myself. One time I included a word he had often used about feeling low: *anhedonia*. I was afraid to use the word *depressed* because I feared a screener of my emails would conclude that I was saying negative things about the place, so I wrote that I "had" anhedonia and I misspelled it on purpose so that the minder would not be able to look it up. But my lover did not understand and simply wrote back with the corrected spelling of the word.

Sometimes he would talk about the difficulties of being in New York, which I knew, or used to know, but those "difficulties" now seemed unreal. One time he wrote that he was hung over and couldn't concentrate, and that he was going to miss his deadline. Those were the woes of the free world, the angst of an artist, and he had no idea how luxurious it sounded from where I was sitting. Another time, he sent me the draft of an article he had written, with a title and his full name, even though I had told him never to say anything that might reveal him to be a writer. But I knew there was no way for him to feel the paranoia of the world I was occupying. And so I longed to hear from him, and yet I was relieved when he did not write for a stretch of time.

Besides, writing emails was a long and laborious process. I did not know exactly how they monitored our emails, but I was worried that being online made it easier for those in charge to sift through my other emails, or even access my hard drive. So I always composed emails off-line, in a Word document, which I read over and over to detect anything that might get me in trouble. Then I would go online, copy and paste the text into an email, and press "Send," only to find that the electricity was out. Often, this was how my weekend passed, writing and rewriting short emails, then waiting for a connection to send them. But there wasn't much to write about anyway. Every day was more or less the mirror of the day before.

With each day, my concerns became smaller. I looked up the amount of protein in canned fish, since that was my main source of nutrition some days. The cafeteria food consisted mostly of marinated vegetables, and I hardly touched the meat, which was served very rarely. I was not much of a meat eater and was also suspicious that it might be dog meat, which had been served once during the summer. I snacked on nuts and dried fruits that I had brought with me from New York, and I bought extra eggs during my grocery outings and boiled them in my electric kettle. I had never been a health freak, but there I was acutely aware that I could not afford to get sick. Luckily, Pyongyang Shop in the diplomatic compound carried several kinds of canned sprats from Latvia, and the price dropped as the expiration dates drew near.

This semester, in addition to the stores at the diplomatic compound and Potonggang Department Store, we were allowed to shop at Tongil (Unification) Market, a block-long cement building full of tiny stalls selling vegetables, meat, fruit, clothing, household equipment, and electrical appliances. The exchange rate fluctuated from week to week (in the summer it had been 2,500 won to a dollar, but now it was 3,500 won to a dollar), as did the food prices. For example, the price of eggs, which were sold in tens, in a makeshift straw carton, kept changing, from three dollars to two dollars, then back to three. Fresh fruits were so expensive that I did not see how people there could afford them. Plastic hangers that might cost ninety-nine cents for ten at a discount store in the U.S. were priced at a dollar each. An ancient-looking Chinese-made flip phone cost eighty dollars. Virtually every product that was not fresh was made in China.

At the market, the sellers were all women, dressed in turquoise uniforms. The customers wore bulky coats and looked like peasants. No one appeared to notice the presence of foreigners, since this place seemed to have become a mandatory tour stop. Once, a couple of the saleswomen asked me where I was from, and when I told them that I had grown up in the South, they said that they had assumed as much from my Seoul accent, which they found beautiful. That was the first time I realized that some ordinary North Koreans liked South Koreans, or maybe even found us glamorous. It was the same with the students. Although we weren't allowed to speak Korean with them, some of them had heard me speak the language with the minders, and had remarked that they found my accent very attractive. This surprised me, since their government spoke of South Korea with such venom; and yet there was warmth on a personal level.

THE ONLY OTHER time we got to see the city during the week was on an outing to the Seventh Pyongyang Autumn International Trade Fair. Inside a big building called Three Revolution Exhibition, booths were set up on two levels, with an enormous poster of Kim Il-sung and red banners with quotations by Kim Jong-il. The booths had a seemingly random selection of products for sale, including laptops, sewing machines, solar panels, pantyhose, body lotion, straw containers, and vitamins. Although it was billed as an international fair to show the "flourishing trade" between the DPRK and seventeen other countries, including Italy, Germany, and Switzerland, almost all the booths I saw belonged to Chinese companies, with only a handful representing local concerns, such as Chosun Computer Center.

After a look around each booth, which took less than thirty minutes, Ruth and I got bored and walked out of the exhibition hall. We had one hour before we had to meet everyone at the bus. Our minders were still inside with the group, and they were not watching us because they knew that there was nowhere for us to go except for the blocked-off area outside, manned by guards. So we walked to an area at the side of the building where about fifty or sixty people were sitting on plastic chairs around plastic tables, and a couple of food trucks were selling lamb kabobs, *naengmyun*, instant ramen, and other food. We splurged and treated ourselves to a bag of Singaporean potato chips and cans of instant coffee.

"To suddenly make our own choices . . . I don't know what to choose!" exclaimed Ruth, settling on lamb.

I ordered a cup of instant ramen, which turned out to be Chinese and tasted of some foreign spice. We South Koreans grow up on packaged ramen the way American children grow up eating peanut butter sandwiches, and even a child is able to tell the flavorful ones from the bad. Ours were usually spicier and heartier, but here, any ramen available out in the open was Chinese. I never came across North Korean ramen.

It was a chilly but sunny afternoon, and there were many people eating outside. About half of them looked Chinese or Korean Chinese, groups that seemed to account for the majority of foreigners in Pyongyang, but the rest were local. The only thing that distinguished the Pyongyang citizens from the Chinese were the Great Leader pins on their chests. Many of them were eating *naengmyun* with beer, a combination that was popular mainly during hot summers in South Korea, not in the late fall. None of them were as well kept as our students, but then no one ever looked like our students. Still, these people had ruddy cheeks and did not look as famished as most people I saw outside the bus windows or even in the market.

The more I saw North Korea, the more I realized how similar it looked to the parts of China that I had seen. On my way home from the summer semester, I had stopped in Seoul and given a North Korean cookbook to my sister's Korean Chinese housekeeper. As she looked through the photographs of dishes, she exclaimed, "Oh, this is our food! It's Chinese! I feel homesick just looking at these pictures." For South Koreans, however, many of the dishes in the book were foreign. On the streets of Pyongyang, the people looked Chinese to me. They wore clothes imported from China. Women's hair was inevitably permed and pinned with sparkling barrettes the way I had seen women style their hair in China. Kim Il-sung lay embalmed in Kumsusan Palace much the way Mao lay in the Mausoleum of Mao Zedong. The scene before me could have been a small Chinese colony.

Perhaps the similarities were not all that surprising. For more than sixty years, North Korea's closest ally, apart from the Soviet Union, had been China. While South Koreans became consumed by American influences to the point that its youth adopted American names and mannerisms and looks, and its young women dyed their hair blond or red and turned to plastic surgery to Westernize their features, North Koreans took up the aesthetics of China. Culturally and visually, the nation seemed to have grown to resemble China. And this made me wonder: If North Koreans were to see Seoul today, would it look American to their eyes? Sixty-some years ago, the super-powers had artificially divided Korea, and this Chinese Korea was the legacy of that division.

Sitting there, I felt increasingly uncomfortable. When I vis-ited either of the two Koreas I always imagined that I was trav-eling back to my roots and would discover new truths about my past. Now it occurred to me that the past I was seeking had for many years been buried under and overtaken by American and Chinese influences. The Korea of my imagination existed only in paintings, history books, the memories of older generations, and in the remnants that I glimpsed, every now and then, like shards of glass poking out from the buried past.

"WE ARE GOING outside tomorrow!" Ryu Jung-min blurted out during lunch. It appeared that he could not control his excite-ment, since the students rarely volunteered information. I asked him where they were going, and he answered, "We don't know. But we are going outside!" Another student added, "Yes, maybe for one hour, we don't know. But it is our first time since we came to PUST." They said that they had been told it was part of their studies, and that maybe they would be taken to a con-struction site in Pyongyang. Not to work, just to have a look, they insisted.

At dinner, Choi Min-jun confirmed that it was true. He had no idea where they were going either. When I said that perhaps his parents might walk by and see him while he was in Pyong-yang, his eyes widened. "But Professor, our parents don't know we go!"

At breakfast the next morning the students were dressed

in their usual dark jackets and ties. They were leaving at nine o'clock, they said, yet they still did not know where they were going, or even how they would get there. On my way back to the dormitory, I saw two of the senior teachers talking quietly. They were discussing how afraid the graduate students were of being drafted to do construction work, so I asked about that day's trip and my students' mention of going to a construction site to watch, not work.

"What is there to watch at a construction site?" one of the teachers asked. "If you are called to those places, you do the labor, you don't watch. In any case, the kitchen was ordered to pack two hundred lunches."

All day long, I worried about my students. I imagined them being driven to a construction site and told to do manual labor, and I was afraid that it would become a regular occurrence. Maybe they would be required to work the field every weekend instead of playing basketball or pacing the walkway, memorizing the English vocabulary on their MP3 players. Would these days of studying English and writing letters in English soon become the stuff of fantasy?

I went for a run later than usual that day, and I was circling the campus at about five p.m. when I saw two double-decker buses coming toward the IT building. I had never seen the buses before, so perhaps the school had borrowed them. The students were back! The sense of relief I felt was enormous. Even if they had spent the day lifting heavy objects, at least they had been allowed to come back to school before sundown, with enough time to shower before dinner. I turned down the volume on my iPod and scrutinized the faces in the bus windows. From far away, it was impossible to see much, but they were still wearing their suits, which suggested that they had not been doing manual labor. What had they done for the past eight hours?

The answer, when it came, was strange. At dinner, they told me that they had gone to Pyongyang Central Zoo and Mangyongdae, the birthplace of Kim Il-sung. I looked for signs of contradiction in their faces but found none. It had been a sunny day, but their faces were not sunbaked, and they did not look nearly as exhausted as they would have if they had spent the day in a construction field. The odd thing, of course, was the fact that they had suddenly been given this trip. This was midterm time, and all other university students across the country were doing labor. But these students were taken to a zoo and the birthplace of their Eternal President. Not only that, the guide at Mangyongdae had explained things to them in English, they told me, and they understood everything since they had been there many times in the past.

I wondered if there was some reason why two hundred North Korean students who looked better than any of their peers needed to be present at Mangyongdae on this particular day. Perhaps there were important foreign visitors, and the regime, famous for positioning people in the right place at the right time, needed these students as a backdrop. The students said that people had stared at them as they were being given the guide's explanation in English, but they did not know who these "people" were.

For the next couple of days, the students could not stop talking about the animals and about how spectacular and big the zoo was. One student told me about a dog climbing on the back of a goat and how funny that was. They seemed greatly impressed by the "animal tricks." Another said that nearby was the Daesung Amusement Park where he had gone as a child and would certainly return someday with his children. They talked about the lions and tigers and asked if I had ever been to a zoo myself.

The last time I had been anywhere near wild animals had been on safari in South Africa. I had gone there in 2010 to cover the World Cup, when North Korea's Chollima team had qualified for the first time in forty-four years. But I did not tell my students that, or how their team faced Portugal, the opposing team, all alone in a stadium packed with more than sixty thousand Portuguese fans and just seventy North Korean laborers shipped in from Namibia. Seeing the World Cup in person would have sounded unreal to them, and besides, they did not like the topic. North Koreans still seemed to feel great shame over their team's loss, despite the fact that in the world's eyes it had been an admirable effort. But for them failure of any degree was not tolerated.

Instead, I told them that I did not much care for zoos. This was true. As a little girl, when my parents took me to the Changgyeongwon Zoo in Seoul, I would look at tigers, giraffes, and penguins and think how claustrophobic they must feel, stuck in small cages and tanks all day; how humiliating it must be to be peered at, objectified.

"Why don't you like zoos?" the students asked, wide-eyed.

"I don't like to see things trapped."

We had just learned the word *trapped*. They all nodded with apparent understanding.

"You mean, like in a prison?"

"Yes, I want things to be free. I would like to set those animals free if I could."

As I said the words, I realized that I was becoming more passionate on this point than I should have allowed myself to be. Yet I knew that the very reason they kept talking about their day at the zoo was the same reason we teachers jumped at the chance to go to the grocery store in Pyongyang once a week, even if there was nothing we needed to buy. I could not imagine a group of American college students enjoying a zoo as much as they had.

Whenever the conversation got awkward, there was always a student who broke the ice. "You know Bae Young-taek?" Park Jun-ho asked. "Well, our bus passed right by his apartment! Young-taek was so sad. He kept staring at the window to see if anyone might be there by chance. His family had no idea we were passing it!"

Another student said that they had taken a group photo at Mangyongdae, and this photo would be given to every parent individually. Copies would first be handed to the parents of each class monitor, and those parents would in turn send the photos to each household. All this seemed so strange. There must have been a reason why this trip had suddenly been arranged, and why the evidence of it was being delivered to each student's family.

After dinner I took the enclosed walkway back to my room. I no longer walked outside in the dark alone since there had been reports of rabid dogs on the loose, biting workers. The walkway was like an unlit tunnel, and I had to use a flashlight to find my way. I thought about emailing my lover about the dogs, since almost every other topic was taboo, but then I imagined him in Brooklyn, where the tree-lined streets had "curb your dog" signs everywhere and people hired walkers and daycare services for their dogs, and it seemed absurd. Instead, I buried myself under blankets, and for a moment, it felt as though I were inside a zoo and had become one of the animals in cages, while the wild dogs roamed freely.

17

RUTH, MEANWHILE, BEGAN INTRODUCING THE USE OF forks and knives, which she had brought with her from China. We all used spoons and chopsticks there, and no one thought twice about it. However, she explained to the students that it was time they became "international men." At the beginning of each meal, she would politely say to those students at her table, "Welcome to our restaurant. I'm sorry but I have to confiscate your spoons and chopsticks and give you these instead."

Most of them had never used forks and knives, and they were at a loss as to what to do with them. There was rarely any meat to cut with a knife, and they were accustomed to using spoons to scoop up rice. Watching Ruth with the students was a bit like watching Henry Higgins and Eliza Doolittle from *Pygmalion*. Some could not stop giggling; others were confused and embarrassed. One later joked, "A meal with Professor Ruth is not a meal but a class. We must use these forks and knives while focusing on speaking and listening in English. Too many things to do at once. It makes our heads ache!"

·   ·   ·

THE TOPIC OF the current reading from the textbook was love. I had to teach a short story on love titled "Love Under the Nazis," about impossible love during wartime. As I reviewed vocabulary such as "Nazi" and "concentration camp," I wondered whether they had any inkling that their Great Leader was considered one of the worst dictators of the modern era, almost on par with Hitler or Stalin. In the morning, Martha handed me a sheet that read, "Love _ kind. Love _ patient . . ." with blanks to fill in for the verbs—a grammar exercise that had been approved by the counterparts. I glanced at it quickly.

"Isn't this some cheesy song from the eighties?" I asked. There were moments like these when I let my guard down and forgot where I was.

"This is straight from the Bible!" Martha said, dumb-founded.

I immediately covered with "I know, but it's also from a song!" I was lucky that she was too young to remember the eighties, because she looked at me earnestly and asked, "Which song?" I suspected the counterparts had not realized the quotes were from the Bible when they approved them; this was a risky move on the part of Martha, who had come up with the idea of doing this exercise. We all had an agenda.

Martha then told me that she had tried to make her students write about love but it wasn't really possible. "All my students kill off everyone in their stories. They're obsessed with death. I don't know if it's their culture or if they're just being boys." Theirs was a culture where any place of work was referred to as *juntoojang,* or "battlefield." Everywhere around the city I saw this word, even on the back door of a big restaurant, and when I asked a student about it later, he explained, "That would mean an area where the restaurant workers prepare meals." Even the word *monitor*, which in South Korea was *banjang*, was translated there as *suhdaejang,* which means "platoon leader." A classroom was not a classroom but a platoon. They marched in groups, singing songs about war. Their culture was saturated with messages about killing South Koreans and Americans and references to horrifically gruesome acts, and it seemed as though they spewed those messages back out unthinkingly, perhaps in the same way that young Americans mimic behavior they see in violent movies and video games. There was really no point in holding a discussion about different kinds of love, since they all agreed that the only real love was the love of the motherland.

"Can you love someone from an enemy country?" I asked.

"No!" they shouted out.

"Can you be friends with someone from an enemy country?"

"No!" they shouted out again.

"What about me?" I asked them later, during a meal. It was not fair to put them on the spot, but I was curious. One answered, "You are different because you are our teacher."

THE INTRODUCTION OF forks and knives was not working out. "Some days here I feel really cranky," said Ruth while we were in line for teachers and graduate students at the cafeteria. At breakfast, she told me, a student from Class 2 had refused to use a fork and knife. Then another refused as well. She explained to them that she was preparing them for the day when they would have to have a meal with a foreigner in a foreign place where there would be no chopsticks. But they responded that they did not care about becoming international men. It was just not important to them. They would not budge. Finally she told them,

"If you don't respect others, they won't respect you." Now she was afraid that her next group at lunch would also refuse.

I had just heard U.S. defense secretary Leon Panetta on CNN Asia, expressing pretty much the same sentiment about North Korea. In anticipation of the impending talks in Geneva between officials from the United States and North Korea, Panetta had given a press conference where he said that North Korea's nuclear proliferation was "reckless and provocative," and that its actions could "only lead to the possibility of escalation and confrontation." In a small way, the same drama was being played out here in this corner of the Rang Rang district of Pyongyang, where the future leaders of North Korea felt bossed around by foreign teachers and refused to play along. Martha shook her head and said, "This just tells me how deep the divide is between them and us."

The Class 3 students also refused to use forks and knives. Ruth came to my office afterward and said that she felt discouraged. The refusal was clearly made as a group, so she thought perhaps the boys had brought up the matter with the counterparts during the more recent Daily Life Unity critique.

"It's the divide," Martha said again.

WITH THE MIDTERMS approaching, I went in search of chocolate during one grocery outing. We were allowed to give the students such treats if there was a specific occasion for it, and if we gave the same thing to everyone. Unfortunately, there were not many options when it came to one hundred individually wrapped small pieces of chocolate, given that I could not shop around. Many products on the shelves were of dubious quality—either expired, almost expired, or from countries I had never associated with the product, like Latvian cookies.

I did see Swiss chocolates, but they were preposterously expensive, and another teacher pointed out that it would be like giving fine wine to a nondrinker, since these students did not know good chocolate from bad. I had never missed Hershey's Kisses or miniature Snickers bars as badly as I did then.

While looking for chocolate, I was reminded of my father. His family had lived in Seoul during the war, and they fled when the bombs fell, just as my mother's family had. They weren't lucky enough to make it onto a vehicle, according to my father, although this use of the word *lucky* would make my mother unusually quiet. If only they had walked instead, she probably thought, then her brother would have been spared. My father instead would become lost in memory. He often talked about a certain American soldier who gave him chocolate. "Chocolate was like gold, better than gold, diamonds. I'll never forget what it tasted like." He remembered the smiling soldier throwing him a tiny piece, which he caught. He was six years old. The memory was dear to him, so lucid against the vague panorama of three years of dire war. What he recalled was kindness, but I cringed at the description. I had grown up seeing too many movies with heroic Americans saving poor Asian children, and I did not like the thought of my father on the receiving end.

Yet here I was, decades later, an American buying chocolate for North Korean boys. The only suitable ones were bite-sized Malaysian milk chocolates, and they tasted like watered-down, artificially sweetened caramels—I could not finish even one. Mary said, "They're all like that, less cocoa content, but I'm from China, we're used to it." The students seemed to like them, though, and this eased the tension of exam day.

Two classes, fifty students in total, took the exam together, and between first and second period, when the next set of two classes came to take it, the teachers had to make sure that the groups did not speak to one another, since cheating was not uncommon. Afterward, I asked the students how they thought they had done. Several said they found the reading comprehension section difficult but the texts fun, especially the one about blue jeans. They were referring to a short article about Levi Strauss and how he had begun producing jeans to serve miners during the Gold Rush. This was the exact reading that had worried Mary, although the exam had been approved by the counterparts.

One student said, "I had no idea that blue jeans were originally made for miners, but one thing I never could understand . . . why are torn jeans fashionable?" There had been no mention of torn jeans in the text, and I doubted any foreign visitor to Pyongyang would wear them. He had to have seen them somewhere, most likely on a forbidden DVD. To some degree, I had the same question he did: why do we tear perfectly good fabric to look stylish? However, analyzing trends in Western fashion would have required a lot of other information, which I was not allowed to give. So instead, I tried to explain the idea of casual dress in Western culture through the example of baseball caps, which many Americans wore but which they never did (except on Sports Day, when the teachers lent them caps). He answered, "That is different from us. We do not wear those caps because we think they are not elegant."

GIVEN HOW FIERCELY competitive the students were, the day after an exam was a hard day for the teachers. We were bombarded with questions about the exam. If students discovered they had made mistakes, they became utterly dejected. To accommodate their incessant questions, Ruth decided to hold an extra afternoon session where she brought a projector and gave a PowerPoint presentation explaining exactly how she had graded the oral exam. After the special session, Ruth showed up in my office, outraged. She had tried hard to explain her methods, but the students got so angry about their low marks, they walked out as a group before she had even finished.

"It's just so rude," she said. "I can teach English all I want to them, but how is it supposed to work if they totally lack any social skills, and won't learn any?"

She leaned back further in the chair, upset. I offered her dried apricots, which were precious to me in this land where fruit, even dried, was a novelty. She popped one in her mouth and said, looking seriously troubled, "They say that they want to learn English, but they don't like us. Their attitude is like 'Just give us the English we need but don't step over this way.' But you can't expect everything when you give nothing."

That was the inherent contradiction. This was a nation backed into a corner. They did not want to open up, and yet they had no choice but to move toward engagement if they wanted to survive. They had built the entire foundation of their country on isolationism and wanting to kill Americans and South Koreans, yet they needed to learn English and feed their children with foreign money.

PANICKED ABOUT GRADES, the students came to see me in pairs, and soon my office was packed. They said they found it hard to improve their reading grades because the textbook was not only confusing but very dull. Their textbooks were outdated—PUST had such profound faith in Chinese education that they only allowed tests and textbooks that had been approved in China, and those were often old. For example, one of the readings from the textbook was a piece called "Judge by Appearance," which described a woman trying to pay for something with a two-dollar check, and a cashier who did not bother to ask for her ID because she was dressed like a beggar but instead kicked her out. Such texts required a footnote from me. I told the students that most people no longer purchased things with a personal check but with a credit card. Back in the summer, Katie had shown them her credit card and told them that she paid for things with it, and they claimed to have understood, but then they said that she must be using her IP address.

Also, their North Korean dictionary was so unreliable that they thought the word *guy* meant "bastard." One student told me that they had been very upset with an American professor who taught them over the summer and started nearly every sentence with "you guys." Often students used words or expressions that were British or obsolete. They would say, "I was watching TV, and it was fun and I shouted hip hip hurrah!" or "Professor, it is raining like cats and dogs outside," or they would toss out a word like *portage*. I had to look some of these words up in the dictionary on my Kindle, which I still used as often as possible, hoping they would ask about it. No one had said anything yet, but they looked at it with curiosity. One afternoon, two students showed up in my office with a question about the word *blockbuster*. Their dictionary defined it as a type of bomb. Does the phrase *blockbuster movie* mean a film about a bomb or just a war film? they asked. When I explained that the most common definition of the word was "a commercial success," their faces brightened. "Like *The Lion King*?" Along with *March of the Penguins*, it was the only other American film they admitted having seen. I wanted to tell them that there were a massive number of blockbuster films, some of which I was certain that they would prefer.

Another time, a student came to me to ask about some

phrases in their textbook having to do with air travel. "What is economy class?" he asked. "Do they give classes on an airplane about the economy?" I tried to explain the concept of class, which existed there as well under the unofficial caste system of *songbun*, though North Koreans pretended it did not. Still, the idea of paying for different levels of comfort was difficult to explain.

Once a student asked me the meaning of *biological parent*. My students found the idea of adoption bizarre. They did not understand why anyone would take on a child who was a stranger and claim him as theirs. When I explained that some people could not have children or felt that adoption was preferable to having a biological child since the world had so many orphans who needed parents, the student immediately responded, "How sad it is then for a baby! Just because the parent is too poor and give the baby to the orphanage, a rich American would buy the baby." I suspected that perhaps they had been taught negative propaganda about Americans adopting babies from China.

Many students were confused by the idea of *women's studies*. Some guessed that it was a major where girls were taught how to cook and put on makeup. After they learned that it had to do with women's rights, they said that in their country such a major was not necessary. According to them, equal rights for women had been formalized in 1946, when Kim Il-sung announced that women made up "one wheel of a wagon in socialist revolution and construction." This referred to DPRK propaganda about women as one of the driving forces of its nation building.

Another time, they told me that only women wore jewelry, and only after graduating from university. "Why only women? What about men?" I asked. "Don't they wear wedding rings?" They said no. They seemed aghast at the idea that any decent man would be seen wearing rings.

"Do American men wear jewelry?" they asked. "Even ear-rings?"

"Some, I guess, mostly young men though."

Their eyes widened. One student said, "There are some strange things about America that I would never understand, like this adoption of buying a baby and men wearing jewelry!"

Then they asked, "What about hip-hop and techno?" There was a mention of it in their conversation textbook, which was not as outdated as the others, and they could not make sense of it. I was not sure how to explain hip-hop to young men who had heard only—or at least professed to have heard only—songs about their Great Leader. I said that it was a sort of music that young people liked, but also more than that—an attitude that expressed itself in many aspects of youth culture, including fashion and language. But even I was dissatisfied with that explanation, and finally I said maybe it was the sort of thing you just had to experience. Then one of them nodded and said, "Yes, we never really understand until we see it."

But no phrase puzzled them more than *Social Security deduction*. They understood the meaning of the word *deduction*, but the rest was a mystery. They were also confused by taxes, which I felt safer discussing now that it was related to a lesson. So I explained that Americans' taxes are deducted from their pay and used to fund programs that benefit the disadvantaged, including those who are poor, disabled, or retired. Since their argument for the superiority of their society was that everything in North Korea was free, my explanation confused them. Yet they now trusted me enough to know that I would not lie to them. I explained that Social Security was exactly what it sounded like: guaranteeing security for members of society, and that you could almost think of it as a socialist aspect of capitalism. Everyone in the nation contributed to it, but each person's contribution was based on his income. They nodded, but I was not sure how much they understood. And it was nearly impossible to make them understand words like *passport* and *insurance*, which also popped up in the textbook.

How was I to explain the entire world to them, this unfathomably diverse world brimming with possibilities, where Arab youths were turning their rotten regimes inside out using the power of social media, where everyone except them was connected through the Internet, where the death of Steve Jobs could move a nation as stoic as China? From there, this world seemed completely inaccessible, and yet vague hints of it were everywhere, even in the pages of this outdated English textbook once approved in China.

Then one of them said, "All this is interesting, all about being international. But some of us don't want to be international. Like what happened with Professor Ruth."

He was referring to the incident with Ruth and Classes 2 and 3. He said that he had asked some of his friends in Class 4, who had also refused, "Why did you make Professor Ruth nervous and upset?" But he confessed that he too found using forks and knives cumbersome. "With Korean food, it is very difficult," he said. I asked him if being asked to try it once seemed disrespectful to his Korean identity, and he replied no. Two of my former students who now belonged to Class 2 brought it up over a meal as well, saying that they felt embarrassed at the way a few classmates had reacted. Some of them had felt offended, and some had not, and before they knew it, the matter had gotten out of control. Class 2, as a group, decided against using forks and knives, and the other classes followed. "Professor Ruth just gave up!" another one who had been offended shouted. It was one of the very rare times when I had seen individual students protest anything, and it was a relief to hear individual voices, to

see them disagree with one another, as well as with an authority figure. Still, they all had refused to use forks and knives,
because they did everything as a group.

A FEW DAYS later, Ruth told me that she had not just given up.
A counterpart had stopped by her office and suggested that she
stop pushing her students to use forks and knives. "The thing
is, I had their permission from the beginning," Ruth insisted
indignantly. "They okayed it. I had to submit the plan to them,
and they approved. I never would've done such a thing without
getting permission first. The school is lenient. It's the students
who are more conservative." She seemed hurt, and for a while,
the forks and knives incident continued to be the talk of the
campus.

18

THE DÉJÀ VU OF EVERY DAY EXTENDED TO OUR RARE OUT-
ings. The teachers were taken on the same organized trips in the
fall as in the summer—to a mountain, a church, and a couple
of major national sites. The trip I was most looking forward to
was the one to Kaesung, the capital of ancient Korea. It was located only five miles from the DMZ and the JSA (Joint Security
Area), which I had never seen from this side. For the teachers
who served as our liaison with the counterparts, getting a trip
approved was a complicated process that involved applying for
travel passes for not only the visitors but also the vehicles, and it
usually took several weeks. The trip had caused much conten-
tion between the minders and the missionaries. On Saturdays,
the minders had Daily Life Unity critiques, and besides, the
DMZ was under the control of South Korea, and not open to
tours from the North Korean side. However, Sundays were also
out, since the teachers had religious services. Ultimately, the
trip was rescheduled for a Friday when most of us had classes to
teach and could not go.

Instead of Kaesung, we were taken on our only overnight

trip, this time to the Kumgang-san (Mount Kumgang) Tourist Region, an inter-Korean project that, since 1998, had been developed and operated with South Korean money for South Korean tourists, though they had not had access to it since 2008, when a South Korean housewife was randomly shot dead by a North Korean soldier.

Due to poor road conditions, the trip took eight hours each way. Along the way, we saw a number of trucks and buses stopped at the side of the road, gray fumes rising from their engines. This sight was so frequent that I began counting the breakdowns, stopping at ten. When our bus also broke down about an hour outside Pyongyang, someone whispered that it must be the bad fuel sold there.

A replacement bus was dispatched, and after about an hour we were on our way. The view along the highway was the same as on our other trips. After five or ten minutes of driving with nothing but farmland on either side, I would see, far in the distance, a group of identical houses, a bigger building with a Great Leader portrait that looked like a school, and a tall tower with the slogan OUR GREAT LEADER KIM IL-SUNG IS ETERNALLY WITH US. This same grouping of buildings appeared over and over, as though identically copied. At one point, I saw a building with the same sign as the Kimilsungism Study Hall on campus. PUST, I realized, was just another version of these villages.

Suddenly, as we passed the city of Wonsan, the sea appeared and my heart leapt. Here it was, the Eastern Sea of Korea, looking utterly unspoiled, so different from the crowded and overdeveloped South Korean side, which was so close, only a couple of hours south of us by car. This coastline had no hotels, no condos, no beach bars, no commercial logos, nothing but itself, and we all sighed in unison. It was beautiful, yet eerie, since it seemed no one was allowed on it, either on the beach or in the water. I did not know how else to interpret the absolute emptiness.

We drove another two hours to the Mount Kumgang Tourist Region, which was like a ghost town since South Korean tourists no longer visited. There were some Chinese and Korean Chinese tourists but not many. That evening, the electricity was out everywhere, and we were told that the only place serving dinner was the restaurant next to the hotel. On each table were small plates full of tiny pink and white pieces of raw meat for barbecue. It turned out to be black pig, but it looked like something at a market that was about to be thrown out. The soup was lukewarm and smelled strongly of fish.

I was seated with President Kim's secretary, a Korean Chinese woman from Beijing. Her family originally hailed from North Korea, and she still had relatives here. "People here used to be wealthier than us in China," she said, remembering the seventies and eighties, when the Soviet Union still existed and the North Korean economy was much better. "When we were little, my mother would visit her parents and bring back so many things from here—clothing and appliances, anything at all. Now it's the opposite. We find it hard to keep in touch with our relatives here because they always ask for money." I had heard similar complaints from other Korean Chinese people with relatives in the North. All of them inevitably said the same thing: they had no choice but to give their relatives whatever they needed because they were family.

After the meal, some of the teachers grew lively and stood up to sing. First there was a rendition of "Amazing Grace." Then a Korean-American teacher got up and said, "I don't usually sing songs like this, but today I'll sing Choi Jin-hui's song. Mr. Ri, you must know this song, everyone knows Choi Jin-hui here, no?" Choi Jin-hui is a South Korean singer popular among the older generation. Mr. Ri gave no reply and walked out, which mystified most of us. Then another teacher got up and sang "Woorinun," a folksy South Korean song. The other minder, Mr. Han, and the two North Korean drivers walked out. Then one of the older teachers explained that North Koreans could be punished for listening to South Korean songs. "Now we know what we must do if we need to get rid of them!" another teacher said.

The next morning, we all started hiking up Manmulsang Hill, but I had an attack of vertigo and turned around, and then waited for the others in the outdoor parking lot. Our two drivers waited with me, along with two other drivers whose Chinese groups had also gone hiking with guides. When I pulled out my laptop, which I carried with me everywhere, they gathered around me to look at it but quickly lost interest and sat down on the pavement, where the other drivers played poker while listening to what must have been a black-market CD of Simon & Garfunkel at top volume. It struck me as strange that they chose such iconic 1960s American music, especially since they could be punished for playing it. For a little while, as I sat on a bench with my laptop with "Bridge Over Troubled Water" blasting in the background, it seemed an autumn day like any other. But the bench, I noticed, had a sign that read "A long bench our Great Leader Kim Il-sung personally used. 1973.8.19," so I immediately stood up and looked around for a rock to sit on. Then I noticed that all the rocks were inscribed with Great Leader quotations (there are reportedly about four thousand such inscriptions in this mountain range). Just then, we saw people descending the hill. The drivers immediately switched to North Korean music, and just as quickly the spell was broken.

On the way back, once we passed Wonsan, the landscape

was again barren. Again, I saw people squatting on the highway, moving only when the bus got close. Sometimes two or three sat talking, and sometimes it was a larger group, sitting in a circle and eating. These scenes did not make sense to me as they were sitting either on the shoulder or on the road in the middle of nowhere, until it dawned on me: This was their café, their public square. The stretch of empty highway closest to where they lived was the only place where they saw evidence of the outside world. They sat on the pavement to feel connected.

THE OTHER TRIP we took was to the tombs belonging to Dangun, the mythical founder of Korea, and King Dongmyeong, the founder of Koguryo, the ancient kingdom that existed in what is now North Korea. It was a bit odd to be taken to the burial places of these ancient kings when we were ceaselessly told that the Great Leaders were their kings. Once Martha had devised a lesson using a news item about the British royal wedding. (In the DPRK, according to my students, a wedding was usually just a dinner at home with neighbors; there was no wedding dress or exchange of rings.) The students had never heard of either William or Kate, so I explained that Britain had a queen and asked which countries still had a king. They answered, "Japan!" and "Cambodia!" and "Korea!" I asked where their king was, since the Korean monarchy had ended in 1910, and they all shouted out "Kumsusan Palace!," where Kim Il-sung lay embalmed, looking eerily alive.

But it turned out that Kumsusan Palace was not the only resting place of a king in North Korea, and now we were on our way to the other one. Once out of the city limits, we were stopped twice at checkpoints. I recognized the empty road as the same one we took to the apple farm.

"I used to live near here, and when I was fifteen I was rounded up for the construction of Kim Il-sung University," said an old Korean man who sat next to me on the bus. Those who were originally from the North often broke into such confessions to whoever would listen. When the Korean War began, this man had been seventeen, the very age my uncle was when he disappeared. He was the only son among four children, and the family decided that he should head south first, and that they would follow soon after. So he fled alone, but before his family could join him, the border closed. In the 1980s he found a way to visit Pyongyang and was able to meet with his parents twice; each time, he was allowed to spend just one night at their home. Now everyone in his family was dead except for one sister, and their visits were restricted to a few hours at a restaurant at the Koryo Hotel. But those visits cost too much. He had to pay money to the North Korean officials who approved and arranged the meeting, to the minder and the driver, and then to his family members since everyone here was needy.

I asked if he felt at home here, especially since some neighborhoods had probably not changed at all. "No, not at all," he said, shaking his head. "This is all foreign to me. PUST is so near where my family lives, but I can't keep in touch with them. I'm not allowed to even call them. I can't go visit any of my old places since we can't move around freely. And I've given so much to this land, and I can't help but feel resentful." The whispers became heated, and I glanced at the front of the bus in case the minders could hear us. We were arriving at the tombs, and I did not speak with him again.

The remains of both Dangun and King Dongmyeong had been excavated, and the tombs had been built by Kim Il-sung in 1993. The Dangun tomb was a large pile of cement bricks shaped vaguely like a flat-topped pyramid. There were no visitors, only the guide and a guard at the tomb. The focus of the tour guide's speech was, as always, the Great Leader. Surrounded by bare hills, this tomb of the son of a bear from thousands of years ago seemed unreal, like a mirage.

King Dongmyeong's tomb looked remarkably similar. Another immaculate grave with no one about. Inside a nearby stone structure, which served as a small museum, there were rather modern, manga-like paintings on the wall, which were said to have been excavated, though they bore no resemblance to Koguryo-era art.

Next to the tomb was a small Buddhist temple, also rebuilt in 1993. A lone monk greeted us at the gate as though he had been expecting us all afternoon. Unlike the gray ones often seen in South Korea, his thin red robe looked Tibetan. The Worship Hall had a golden Buddha in it, and the monk went inside to light candles. Like the church we had been taken to in Pyongyang, the temple had the feeling of a stage set, except here there were no worshippers. Most of the missionaries refused to enter.

A border existed here too. Perhaps here was our greatest fear, the fear of the other.

19

With the arrival of November, the wind at night turned thorny, with ice in it. At PUST, they did not turn on the heat in the dormitories until well into winter, so I covered myself with layers of thermal underwear, fleece tops, and a down coat to stay warm. In the evenings, I would bury myself under a double layer of blankets and force myself to go to sleep early because it was too cold to be awake. The rabid dogs that had bitten four workers had been put down with rat poison and, according to Ruth, the North Korean staff had eaten them. Now that the dogs were gone, I wanted to walk alone outside again, but the evenings were so cold that we all took the enclosed walkway. On some nights, when the footsteps of the students echoed down the long, dark corridors, I felt almost as though I were in a Harry Potter movie, in some gloomy passage of Hogwarts castle.

But when I looked across the courtyard at the six students on guard duty each night, I felt like a spoiled American. In this weather, guard duty meant standing for hours in below-freezing temperatures. In their khaki uniforms and parkas, the students on duty would come to dinner a bit earlier than the others. They were unwaveringly somber and rarely met my eyes. It was as if they were about to go to battle. Sometimes I tried to talk to them, but often they looked too serious and ate silently. I could not decide if they were simply depressed about having to stand outside all night in the Siberian cold, or if they saw this as a holy mission and felt unable to converse with me because they suddenly viewed me as an American imperialist. When they did speak to me, it was just to say that yes, it was cold outside, just a little bit, but it did not bother them. Then they would hurry off together.

Of course the female guards must have suffered too, but these were my students, and I did not want them to freeze in front of an empty building. At times, I wanted to shake them and say, "The man is dead! He died in 1994, and you don't have to stand outside all night for him!"

Although they probably did not know it, we shared a Confucian heritage, and I wondered if this was their version of an ancestor worship ritual. If it was, it had become so single-mindedly devoted to their Great Leader that it was no longer recognizable as a remnant of Confucianism. Besides, they were raised to believe that they could be attacked at any moment and must be ready to defend themselves against invasion. There I was, a spy of sorts, hoping not to plant bombs but to plant ideas. They had their mission, guarding a shrine to their only ancestor, and I had mine.

AS THE CHILL deepened, the electricity went out nearly every day. I would get ready to put the kettle on for my morning coffee only to find that there was no power. Or just as I was brushing my teeth before bed, the bathroom would turn pitch dark.

I had brought three flashlights with me, a miniature one that I attached to my key ring so that I could find my way back to my room at night, and two bigger ones that I kept by my bed and in my office.

When the lights went out, darkness fell so abruptly and completely that I could almost touch it. Sitting with a group of students in my office, I would be going over the differences between a past participle and a past perfect participle, and suddenly the room would go dark. Immediately I would reach for my flashlight, and we would continue, using the flashlight like a candle, because this was the way of things. There were many evenings when I would stand in the corridor with a flashlight so that the students could find their way to the cafeteria for dinner. The unpredictability of the outages made lesson planning difficult. We all shared one printer and one photocopier. When the power went out, we could not use either one, and sometimes we had to change the lesson at the last minute. Yet there were moments when the blackouts felt like an adventure, because I was a visitor and I knew such inconvenience was only temporary.

One evening, while we were walking back from dinner, a student shouted, "The light's come back on!" in Korean, and we all felt pleased that we would be returning to brightly lit rooms. Then he asked me how to say it in English, so I did an impromptu lesson on different phrases: "The light's back on," "The light's gone out again," and "The light's come back." They liked learning practical phrases they could use every day.

"Do the lights go out like this in New York, too?" one of them asked.

"No, never like this," I responded, shaking my head.

A few of them laughed awkwardly, and I wondered if my

answer had sounded callous. I tried to recall in which year the last big blackout had been, and I thought maybe I should tell them about it. But then I realized that it might strike them as even stranger that my entire city had made such a big fuss over a blackout when such outages were a daily occurrence for them. So I kept quiet, and one of them asked, "But since you pay rent in your country, do you also have to pay for electricity?" I expected this. Whenever the teachers pointed out anything that made life outside sound better than in North Korea, they inevitably brought up the solicitude of the Great Leader, under whose reign everything was free. So I just answered, "Yes, true, we have to pay for electricity, but I know that it's free in your country." I did not point out that this free electricity did not flow equally in all parts of the country. They seemed relieved and looked at me with something akin to pity, and said proudly, "Yes, it is free for us." In that moment, I felt relieved that they took comfort in their superiority, no matter how illusory.

Many of them asked me often if it was as cold in New York as it was there, and I would answer, "Yes, about the same. But it feels a bit colder here." They seemed puzzled that I found it so excruciatingly cold when I came from a place that also had harsh winters, but I could not tell them that it did not feel as cold in New York because heat, for the most part, was plentiful there.

When the electricity was working, I would turn on the TV to ward off loneliness. Ruth had attached a metal hanger to my TV to serve as an antenna, so on some nights I was able to tune in the local channels: Chosun Central TV, Korean Educational and Cultural Network (KECN), and Mansudae TV. But KECN was said to be on for just a couple of hours each day and was never available when I tried it, and neither was Mansudae TV, a weekend-only network that was only for Pyongyang citizens. So in reality there was just one functioning channel, which came on at around 5 p.m., shutting down at 11 p.m.

At seven o'clock, there was a news program for twenty-five minutes, almost exclusively about Kim Jong-il. There was no live film, just old photographs of him visiting factories, and the newscaster would read, verbatim, whatever he had supposedly said on those occasions. Next there was a thirty-minute music program, in which the lyrics scrolled across the screen karaoke style. The songs had titles like "Defend the Headquarters of Revolution," which described the North Korean people as "bombs and bullets." Then there was a slot for a drama or film, followed by another news program on the more recent movements of Kim Jong-il. This was the news that my students had mentioned watching each night. There were, of course, no commercials, but the news was sometimes interrupted by Kim Jong-il quotations that filled the screen. Another music program followed; one night it featured a group of men playing the accordion to a song about Kim Jong-il. After that came a peculiar segment called "The Report by the Unification and Peace Committee." Every night the broadcaster delivered a soliloquy berating South Korea and the United States, using oddly colloquial expressions like "freaking out" and "cut the crap."

In some ways, watching their news felt more like listening to a radio drama or an audiobook. There was not much live action; instead the anchor would speak in a melodramatic tone, like a stage actor overplaying his role, describing the movements of the Great Leader in such intricate detail that Kim Jong-il became extremely vivid in listeners' minds. This singular obsession with his every movement, from the way he laughed to the exact angle of his gaze, was because only one topic existed.

There was only so much you could say about one man who was probably sick in bed, so they filled the time by dissecting every last aspect of his life.

The only international news item not involving the Great Leader that I recall was a mention of the flood in Thailand, which featured photos of the devastated areas and of people being swept up by water. The rest of the time, the commentators exhausted every glorifying adjective to describe Kim Jong-il, who was "so great" and "very great" and "the greatest." The message was, of course, the same in their newspaper, *Rodong Sinmun*, as well as in the students' Juche class. I once saw a student's notebook in which one page was entitled "The Great Achievement of Our Great General."

At one point, the students' favorite topic of conversation was a Chinese drama based on a 1936 Russian novel by Nikolai Ostrovsky called *How the Steel Was Tempered*. It aired from 8:30 to 9:30 on some nights. There was one television on each floor of their dormitory, and at least sixty of the hundred freshmen gathered in front of one of them. It was like a party, they said. Steel was a metaphor for the character of the hero, and the show had very good morals, they told me. Since Russia and China were their allies, they said, they understood their culture better and vice versa. For example, when the North Korean film *The Flower Girl* was shown in China, they had heard that all the streets were empty because every Chinese was home watching it. I did not have the heart to tell them that what was currently popular in China was no longer an old North Korean film but glitzy South Korean soap operas featuring stunning plastic-surgery-enhanced actors. Released in 1972, *The Flower Girl* was about the persecution of poor peasants under the Japanese occupation. It was based on an opera supposedly written by their

Eternal President Kim Il-sung, and starred then seventeen-year-old Hong Yung-hui, who became known as one of Kim Jong-il's mistresses. I had once tried watching the film and had found it too slow and dated.

I promised to try watching their favorite drama so that we could discuss it over meals. But I had already tried the last one, *The Age of Steel*, and found it dull, so I asked if this one was better. Most said yes, but one told me, "Well, we do not have anything else." This was the first time any of them had admitted such a lack.

I HAD NOW been back for more than a month, and the sense of being watched at all times was draining. I felt as though I was being buried alive, like sand was being poured into my face. I began to feel a nausea, almost like seasickness, from the sameness of each day. To fight it off, I took up basketball on those rare afternoons when there was some sun despite the cold. I had brought a soccer ball and a basketball from New York to give to my students, since I had noticed in the summer that the ones they were using were tattered and getting flat. We were supposed to hand such gifts over to the counterparts, who would distribute them to the students at the right time. But I was afraid that the counterparts might keep them. Back home, I had printed out fifty copies of a set of the best photos of my students from the summer and, upon returning, I had submitted them to the counterparts to be given to the students. Although a few students thanked me for them, they mostly avoided the topic, so I was not convinced that they had been allowed to keep the photos. Because of that, I had been looking for weeks for an opportunity to give them the balls directly. One afternoon, when

I saw both classes on the court, I ran to my room, grabbed the new balls, and came back out. Then I casually handed them to the monitors and said, "Hey, do you want these? I bought them for me, but I don't have much time to play." It was as simple as that, and they used those balls for the rest of the semester.

Sometimes I played with them, but most times I took a ball from the teachers' supplies and dribbled alone during their nap time or on weekends. The court was right beneath their dormitory, and often I saw smiling faces pressed to the windows when I played. They loved to count the rare occasions when I made a shot. It soon became a favorite topic at meals. One would say, "Professor, you are getting better. Before it was one out of fifty, now it is more like one out of ten. Yesterday I saw you got thirty-two in out of a hundred and sixty-four tries!" Another would say, playfully, "You are improving, Professor. But you could be better. You teach me English, I teach you basketball!"

On some days, though, it was simply too cold, or the court was too wet to play, since the drainage system at school was almost as bad as the one in downtown Pyongyang, and there were pools of water everywhere. Those empty, bleak days felt longer. It was now dark by 4:30 p.m., and the concrete campus, already so dreary, became even more so. The early winter light was relentlessly gray, and I dreaded the weekends. Although I saw the students at meals, I had no classes to teach, and the only things to look forward to were the trips to the stores on Saturdays and the Sunday services.

"Even inside the market, everyone's watching us," Mary warned me. "You don't know who will report you, so don't do anything that will get us in trouble."

Despite her warnings, Mary herself had been buying small rice cakes and passing them out to homeless kids who roamed the market and picked pockets. She would walk fast and slip food into their hands and keep on walking so that no one would notice. I worried about her getting reported.

On weekend nights, I felt even more helpless. I longed for phone calls, an outing to a movie, a restaurant, the little things I took for granted in the outside world. I moped about the campus, and sometimes peeked into Ruth's room. The fat Bible usually sat on her table, along with an open notebook in which she had copied out passages and underlined phrases. That was how most of the missionaries passed the time: rereading the Bible, gathering together in the evenings to share their thoughts about scripture. Not all teachers attended these Bible studies, since there were factions among the missionaries, so my absence was tolerated. Looking at Ruth, I thought that she seemed comforted.

One night, while we were walking back from dinner, a student asked, "Do you live alone in New York?" I was not sure whether anyone lived alone in the DPRK, but I said yes. Then another asked, "So what happens to your apartment while you are here?" I told them that my friend was living in it. "What about the rent?" he asked. "How do you pay it while you are here?" I replied that I had arranged to make the payments through the Internet, and they nodded, as usual. They presumably thought that our Internet was their intranet, but perhaps some were now beginning to realize that there was a real difference between the two.

Another student asked me what part of New York I came from and if I had encountered many gangs there. He was the third student who had asked about gangs in New York that week. I asked him where he had heard about such gangs, and he said that his conversation textbook mentioned the film *Gangs of New York*. Another random phrase they liked to repeat was

"The Big Apple." Then another asked, "How about Brooklyn?" To him it was just a strange word he had picked up from his textbook, but Brooklyn was where my lover lived and I was suddenly overwhelmed by missing him. I paused. I was midway between the cafeteria and the dormitory. In the distance was the smoke stack and the fumes rising from its tower. I could see the glimmer of the Pyongyang cityscape. I was very far from Brooklyn.

20

"DO YOU HAVE A BUDDY?" MRS. DAVIS ASKED ME. SHE WAS married to the doctor at the clinic, and both were Korean-American missionaries in their early fifties. I had stopped by to visit Ri Sang-woo, who had been sick with flu for a few days.

"Here, you need a buddy," she said. For a married couple, it was easy to keep each other in check, she said, but for single people, one false step could be hazardous. "Watch everything you do or say because they are watching your every step like a hawk," she continued. "They are afraid there might be a spy among us." I knew I was a spy of sorts, but could there be someone else?

Then she told me that for the past year, no matter where she and her husband were in the evening, the minders tracked them down instantly if there was a medical emergency. They might be sitting in a teachers' room, and the intercampus phone would ring, revealing it to be a minder. In China, during the nineties, when they worked for YUST, even their friends' email accounts had been hacked, and North Korea often resorted to the same tricks as the Chinese, so before this posting, they had asked all their friends back home to set up new email addresses meant only for correspondence with them.

Mrs. Johnson told me something similar. Back in the spring, she had asked one of the minders to get her a box of Shin ramen from Tongil Market. Because Shin ramen was a South Korean product, officially banned, this was something of an under-the-table transaction. (At the PUST shop, the teachers who helped out had to cut out the labels on clothing donated by South Korean churches before giving them to students.) But minders sometimes offered to get you things that were hard to find, and it was understood that there would be a markup, a fee for the minder. The fact is, you could buy Shin ramen on the black market, with Chinese packaging, about as easily as you can buy marijuana in downtown New York. Samyang ramen, another South Korean brand, was also easy to find because it was often included in packages from humanitarian groups and found its way onto the market. Shin ramen, however, was the favored brand. One of my students proudly said that his favorite food was ramen, but not just any ramen, only Shin ramen. It seemed that there was some sort of cachet associated with Shin ramen because it was South Korea's most popular kind.

In any case, when the minder came back with a box for Mrs. Johnson, he shortchanged her, either by mistake or on purpose, and Mrs. Johnson discussed it with Mrs. Davis on the phone, and within minutes there was a knock on her door, and there stood the minder, upset at being accused of dishonesty. He had overheard their entire phone conversation.

Mrs. Davis and Mrs. Johnson were kind women who often offered me helpful advice, partly because they were afraid that I might get sick of PUST and not return. There was a shortage of teachers. For some of them, the constant surveillance made it impossible to be there. A teacher from Hong Kong, a retired businessman who taught economics to graduate students, said that he would not be returning in the spring. He had met President Kim by chance at his church and had been recruited, but he had not been told much ahead of time, and had had no idea that he would not be able to move about freely. He asked when my return flight was, and when I told him December 20, he exclaimed, "Lucky you. Mine is December 21." He said he was counting the days until he could go home. He had been to villages in China where as many as ten people slept in one room, where three brothers only owned two pairs of pants and took turns wearing them, yet this was the worst place he had ever experienced. I asked him why.

"There's no freedom," he sighed. "They are watching us constantly. I know they are recording everything we say and keeping files on us, and I feel really bad all the time. I just don't feel comfortable here. It's not about the terrible food and the material lack of everything. It's the basic humanity. It's missing here."

All of us had become paranoid, for good reason. But human beings are resilient, and also forgetful. I wonder if at times I willed myself to forget so that I could keep going, and whether my students did the same. On several occasions, I left one of my USB sticks lying on my desk in the dormitory and only later remembered and panicked. I was becoming careless. I had been there more than a month, and after a month even a prison feels like home at times.

INSIDE THE CLINIC, I saw Kim Yong-suk sitting by Ri Sang-woo, who was hooked up to an IV bag, with an English textbook open at his side. The buddy system among the students was remarkably tight. Buddies seemed to spend all their time together.

They sat together, ate together, and, at times, held hands, either while walking or sitting in a class. When one student sprained his ankle, he limped a little and did not need a crutch, yet his buddy was always by his side to support him, wherever he went. So it was Yong-suk who brought every meal from the cafeteria to the clinic for Sang-woo and spent all but his class time at his bedside, helping him with the schoolwork he was missing. He even spent nights on an air mattress next to Sang-woo.

I was both impressed and disturbed by the buddy system. I noticed that with the shuffling of classes from summer to fall, most of the pairings changed as well, and students were never seen with their former buddies again. Yong-suk had been Hwang Jae-mun's buddy during the summer, but now, despite the fact that they were in the same class, Yong-suk was devoted only to Sang-woo. There was perhaps nothing unusual about friendships shifting at the beginning of a new semester, but in this case buddies were paired by the school, through designated seats and room assignments. Their loyalty to each other seemed boundless, and that made their ability to shift alliances overnight seem oddly heartless. Also, the ease with which they followed orders to immediately become someone's best friend struck me as unnatural.

Yet, not all buddies were so enamored with each other. For some, it seemed just a duty, and they did the minimum. They were there for each other when one got sick or needed help with a menial task, and they sat together in class and at meals. But otherwise, they did not hang on to each other all the time. Not all held hands or laughed together constantly. And a few of my students who had been switched to a new class made an effort to sit with their former classmates, even though it was technically against the rules. Even here, there was such a thing as chemistry.

Perhaps their communal life staved off loneliness, but it had its downside. There was no privacy, and the constant together-ness made it easier for illnesses to spread. Since there was never enough heat, many of them came down with colds or the flu, and that often meant that their buddies got sick too. But they were young, and they seemed to recover quickly.

Ri Sang-woo sat up and smiled with delight when he saw me. Under the fluorescent light, the room looked big and empty, with several air mattresses on the floor and a single table against the wall. It was a bleak place, and I was glad that he had his buddy with him. Next to his bed was a big container of Imperial Powdered Milk from South Korea, which I knew was either prohibited or expensive. I also noticed a carton of bottles of apple-flavored seltzer water, sold in the campus shop.

"What's all that?" I asked, and Sang-woo blushed.

"My classmates brought them. They have been so nice."

Judging from the number of seltzer bottles, it seemed that almost every classmate had bought him one. This was unusual. The students were given a modest amount of credit by PUST, with which they bought school supplies and snacks from the campus shop. This credit system was similar to the food ration ticket system. When they ran out of credit, their parents appar-ently sent them extra money. It seemed extravagant for every student to give Sang-woo a bottle of seltzer; they had not done the same when another student was ill a few weeks earlier. It was possible that Sang-woo was just more popular. His spoken English was better than that of almost everyone else in the class. At about five foot eleven, he was tall, which was greatly envied there, and he excelled in his studies as well as in basketball. Perhaps most important, he was from a very powerful family. I knew as much from details in his letters, from our conversa-tions, and from the fact that his father had been abroad.

He was the crème de la crème among students, but when I saw him lying there in his nylon sweats, most likely imported from China, I wished I could scoop him up and take him shopping at a gigantic American mall. It was absurd to think that material goods would fix anything, but at that moment, I hated seeing him wearing those pathetic sweats, clinging to a can of powdered milk. My wishes were quite simple. I wanted nice warm clothes and fresh milk for my students, and I wanted the lights to come back on when it went dark, or at least enough flashlights and batteries for all of them. I wanted enough heat to ward off the cold, better food for these boys who were still growing. There were times when satisfying their basic needs— light, heat, nutritious food—seemed as important as giving them freedom.

AS I WAS coming back from shooting baskets one afternoon, Ruth's door opened a crack and she waved me into her room. I should have just said hello and kept walking, but I think I wanted company. I kept forgetting that I was not one of them.

"It's about Sunday!" she said, so brightly that for a moment I thought there must be a trip coming up, but in fact she meant the previous one. "I saw you taking communion, and I don't think you should."

She asked me if I took communion at my church back home. This made me nervous. I said no, preparing for the worst. She reflected a moment, and then said, "If you don't believe in taking a part of Jesus's body into you, you shouldn't receive the bread. I'm only saying this out of a concern for you because harm will come to you if you take it and you're not a believer. I know it sounds like a superstition, but it's not."

Then she began telling me that she knew I cared for my

students, but maybe my reason for being there was different from hers, which was solely to bring the Lord to this land. The Lord has his ways and his designs for these people, she told me, and it was her job to wake them up to be ready for his grace.

"Because, Suki, this life here is temporary. They will be received by Him in heaven."

I knew that I should keep quiet and leave before she went any further, but in that moment I felt an incredible wave of anger. I felt she was delegitimizing the suffering of the people of North Korea. Weeks of keeping silent had finally become too much for me, and I lost control.

"So are you saying that it's okay for North Koreans to rot in gulags because in your estimation it isn't real?" Ruth seemed taken aback, but I continued. "I think this 'temporary' life of yours being a schoolteacher in a nice dormitory for a semester before you get back home to New Zealand is a different kind of 'temporary' life than the lives of these people, who are basically slaves to their regime. If the eternal life waiting for them in heaven is so amazing, should the millions who are suffering here just commit mass suicide? Why don't you go check out a gulag and then dare to tell me that it's temporary?"

Almost as soon as I spoke the words, I regretted them. I knew that I had been unnecessarily harsh, but the chasm between us felt like an abyss.

Ruth looked at me with pity and shook her head. She started to say something, but I told her I was tired and walked away. I felt such deep rage that I needed to be alone to calm down. The exchange depressed me so much that I could not sleep all night.

The following Sunday, I skipped the service and spent the time crying in my room. Then I tried to compose an email to my lover, but there was nothing I could freely write about that would interest him. Our lives were drifting apart. He wrote that he was missing me, but that he was also busy. There were gallery openings, movie screenings, and dinner parties. I thought again of telling him about the rabid dogs, about how the staff had killed and eaten them, but I worried that he would only be upset by that, and that whoever was monitoring my email would not like it. I was not especially worried that they would disapprove of the part about eating dogs, since that was normal there, but I was afraid it would sound like I was complaining about my working conditions.

I wanted to tell him that Ruth had confronted me about my faith, that my cover was blown, that it was possible the missionaries rather than the North Koreans would kick me out. I wanted to tell him about my immense fear and loneliness, but I did not see how I could explain it all. I thought of comparing myself to the Little Mermaid in Hans Christian Andersen's story. She had traded her voice for a pair of legs; I had traded my voice to be there. But I doubted he would be able to decipher what I meant. Finally it dawned on me that my longing for him and missing him simply did not matter. So long as I was there, he was no longer relevant. Love could not save me.

21

In the second week of November, sacks and sacks of garlic and cabbages were delivered on a truck at lunchtime, and several classes were called outside to unload them. They brought the garlic into the cafeteria, and for two consecutive days students and faculty spent more than an hour peeling them. That was how I learned that this was the week of *kimjang*.

In both North and South Korea, in the late fall, most families make enough kimchi to last through the winter. This tradition originated more than a thousand years ago, when vegetables were not readily available year round. When I was a child, the *kimjang* season was always festive. The women in my neighborhood got busy suddenly, buying the ingredients—cabbage, radishes, chili peppers, scallions, garlic, ginger, marinated baby shrimps, and anchovies. Then they gathered together to wash the cabbages and radishes, salt them, and make barrels and barrels of kimchi. It was a time of laughter, gossip, and good feelings all around. I would hover around my mother, waiting for a bite of freshly made kimchi dripping chili liquid. That piercing taste of crispy cabbage and raw seasoning was etched in my memory as the first sign of winter. The finished kimchi would be stored in earthenware pots and kept outside to ferment slowly. The increasingly pungent-tasting kimchi kept us strong through the snowy nights of the long, hard Korean winter.

I had not thought about *kimjang* in a long time. When we moved to America, my mother worked seven days a week and made kimchi less and less, so we got by on the store-bought kind. Besides, with most vegetables available fresh year round, there was no reason to make so much kimchi at once, never mind the fact that we had no garden or balcony to put out the pots. Yet, there I was in Pyongyang, peeling garlic for *kimjang* with hundreds of young North Korean men who rolled up their sleeves and obliged without hesitation, cheerfully sharing their memories of *kimjang* at their own houses.

One said he always helped his mother by carrying buckets of water up the stairs: "It takes a lot of water to wash one hundred fifty kilos of cabbage." That suggested there was no fresh water at his house, despite the fact that his family was part of the elite. Another chimed in that his family was small, just he and his parents, so they only needed eighty kilos.

Then they asked me how many kilos my government delivered to my house for *kimjang.* I could not bring myself to tell them that *kimjang* was a disappearing tradition for the modern generation, and that the city of New York did not distribute a ration of cabbages to each household, so I just said that my mother no longer did *kimjang.* They seemed confused and asked how my family then obtained kimchi during the winter. I explained that America was big and the weather varied from region to region, and that all kinds of foods were available during the winter because we traded with many other countries. I used their country's trade with China as an example, which helped them to understand.

I confessed that I too was confused, about their way of doing *kimjang*. What about peppers and radishes and scallions, since each family, presumably, had its own unique recipe, with slightly different ingredients? A student explained that the rations varied. This year, for example, the harvest had been bad and there was not enough cabbage for families, so some people bought whatever extra was necessary. This was the second time a student had admitted to a lack of anything.

I was also surprised to learn of the connection between *kimjang* and auto accidents. According to the students, there were so many trucks transporting cabbages in November that their government considered it a dangerous month, with a much greater risk of traffic accidents. (May was also considered a dangerous month, with a greatly increased risk of drowning.) I found the idea of collisions with cabbage-bearing trucks unlikely considering how few cars there were, even in the streets of Pyongyang.

On the second day of garlic peeling, I woke up to the news of the Penn State riots. On CNN Asia, there was live coverage of American students toppling a media van to show their anger about the firing of a coach who had failed to investigate another coach accused of raping young boys. The scandal was the headline of the international segment, and the anchor repeatedly emphasized the importance of college football, and the money it generated, in American culture. "Almost a billion in profits!" he said, implicitly shaming a culture that cared more about money than stopping child abuse. The network's finger-wagging seemed the real point of their excessive coverage of this particular, sensational story, since there was far more urgent news in the rest of the world. In Italy, Berlusconi was stepping down after seventeen years; the Greek prime minister had just resigned; and Libya was in disarray after Qaddafi's death. Yet filling the screen were shots of drunken American college students wielding beer bottles and brandishing fists in solidarity with their football team.

It seemed surreal to walk into the cafeteria later and face these North Korean college students about the same age, joyfully peeling garlic, talking of their guilt at not being able to help their mothers this year. A few got up and swept the garlic peels from the floor. Others sorted through the peels to see whether any garlic cloves had accidentally been tossed out. Even when the kitchen staff came out and told them to stop peeling and get ready for classes, many kept on working, politely insisting that it was easier and faster when everyone helped.

MY COUNTERPART CLASS had been canceled that week, but at lunch I saw a few of them in track suits instead of the usual jackets and ties. I asked where they had been, and one answered that they had been working at a teachers' cooperative farm so that they could get enough cabbages for their family's *kimjang.* He seemed embarrassed, so I asked casually, "Was it fun to work with your colleagues?" He shook his head and said, "So so," which was his way of saying "Not at all." These were proud men and they seemed ashamed to admit to doing manual work. Among them were the former deans of Kim Chaek University and Kim Il-sung University, and a new addition who had been an English professor at the former, whose spoken English was so close to perfect that I wondered why he wasn't teaching the students himself, and what he might be doing in my class. Another of the counterparts said, "Not fun. Too much work. I lifted and carried things. It is easier for women, but not good for men."

Theirs was a chauvinistic culture. One student told me that he had lived in a dormitory at his previous university, and the one difference from PUST was that there were girls. Then he admitted that there had been only two in his class since it had been a science college and girls weren't good at science. However, he said he used to give them his shirts and they were very pleased. I imagined this to be either a joke or a gesture of flirtation, but he explained, "So they could wash them! It is difficult to be at PUST since here I have to wash not only my shirt, but jackets and pants too. At home, my mother and my sister washed them."

Later that afternoon, I dropped by the library and looked in the window of the Internet room. Sitting in front of the computers were second-year graduate students, as well as a counterpart from my class who had previously been a dean. They seemed to be learning how to conduct a Google search. I went inside to say hello to the former dean. He had just looked up a computer term, which yielded more than 600,000 hits. A graduate student was explaining that that was the number of results. The former dean did not seem to understand what the number signified, so the student repeated it. "More than 600,000?" he said, amazed. I wondered if the counterpart was there to keep an eye on what the students were looking up.

The graduate students were under strict orders not to reveal anything about the Internet, including their access to it. One senior professor said that one of her graduate students complained of a chronic headache, but she believed that it was ideological confusion and suggested that Mrs. Davis secretly pray for the student at the clinic while putting her hand on his temple and taking his temperature. However, we were not certain how much of the Internet the graduate students were actually allowed to access. Our dean of the computer department said that he thought their access must be quite limited since they kept coming to him with the simplest questions about their research papers.

Outside the room, my undergraduate students were either at the reading desks or using the regular computer stations that had no Internet access. Several of them came up to me to say that the homework that I had just assigned, a paragraph detailing their family's *kimjang*, was too difficult since kimchi making was for women, not men. There were many words they did not know, and they were stuck on descriptions. The assignment would have been easy if they could have done an Internet search, but that was not an option.

There were only a few applications on the regular computers: the Longman Dictionary, the Cambridge Learner's Dictionary, the Oxford Dictionary, an encyclopedia in Korean, and a document called *Juche*. I sat down in front of a computer, opened the most recent program, and saw the words "Kim Jong-il and Kim Il-sung Juche Study." Mary, another Reading and Writing professor, had gotten approval to upload about sixty classic novels such as *The Great Gatsby, Wuthering Heights, War and Peace,* and *Robinson Crusoe*. But the students said that they did not read them because they were difficult and seemed too old. Other than these materials, there was not much else.

Yet the students seemed to like computers. They did not use the computers to type their essays; they did not know how to touch type, and since there was no printer, typing was of no use anyway. Mostly, they just used dictionaries, although they found them difficult and preferred using their Korean dictionaries. The sight of the country's best students of science and technology staring blankly at screens was so pathetic that I was seized by a pang of anger, mixed with sadness, and soon left the room.

I HAD BEGUN to notice a pattern in my relationship with the students: The moment I felt that we had made progress and relaxed a little, they inevitably backtracked. This seemed similar to the behavior of the notoriously unpredictable (and ironically quite predictable) North Korean regime, which often lashed out against South Korea just when inter-Korean relations seemed to improve. So I was not surprised when suddenly our conversations mirrored previous ones, as though the students had been told what to say and when.

"I could have gone to Singapore but I love our country and chose to stay here," said one of the class monitors at dinner. This was the fifth consecutive meal at which a student had told me such a thing. Each time a student told me that he had passed tests that would have allowed him to study abroad but had turned down the opportunity because he preferred studying there. Two students cited Beijing's Tsinghua University as the school to which they had been accepted and claimed that their government had offered to foot the bill for their tuition and their room and board, but they had declined and come to PUST. Two other students mentioned that they had the opportunity to go to Germany but chose not to.

Often, the topics were contrived. Suddenly they would introduce a subject as though they had a list to cover during meals, with the phrase "How about we change the topic?" This helped them when conversations went in a direction that made them feel nervous, such as when the talk of exchange programs led a student to ask how many countries I had visited.

During the summer, I had avoided this topic, and even in October I was careful to say very little. But by November I was becoming increasingly reckless, and truthful, so I told them roughly the number of countries I had visited and went further by saying how lovely some of the European cities were, and how I hoped they would have the chance to see the world. Then I got carried away and added, "Oh, of course Asian cities are beautiful too, like Kyoto." I stopped myself, remembering Japan was their enemy.

After a pause, one student asked me: "What about our city? Do you find our city beautiful?"

The question made me pause in return. I did not find Pyongyang beautiful. It was a monotone, bleak city, filled with concrete buildings and people dressed in rags who looked starved. But it was not Pyongyang's physical attributes that made it so ugly in my eyes. It was what it stood for. It was the most horrible city in the world to me, and every time I saw it in the distance, on the horizon, outside the van window, I felt disheartened. Pyongyang was the Xanadu of North Korea—the city the rest of the country slaved to feed. It was a greedy, bloodsucking monster, and sometimes I wished it would just go up in smoke. Yet it was also the city to which my uncle might have been taken at seventeen, alone, the city my grandmother dreamed of until her dying day. It was the home of my students, the city of hope for all North Koreans. All they ever wanted was to get here, where electricity came on, and cars and trams and buses ran, and civilization could be glimpsed. Sitting across from my young students, who looked at me with such expectant faces, waiting for me to declare that their Pyongyang was indeed the most beautiful, I felt I had no choice but to lie a little. So I said, "Well, some parts." I knew that my answer was disappointing, and this was heartbreaking, but I saw no alternative, and as always a student at the table piped up, "So how about we change the topic?"

I compensated for my unsatisfactory response by dropping the fact that I had recently spent a year at Ewha Womans University, an all-girl school in Seoul. Usually, when I mentioned Seoul, they did not ask anything about it, except possibly, "So you were born there?" It was clearly a taboo topic. But the allure of an all-girl university on the other side of the border seemed to pique their interest, though they shyly lowered their gazes. Ewha was something like Wellesley, but of course that comparison would have meant nothing to them, so I simply told them it was famous in South Korea, and that the students were fine girls from good families. They all looked at me as though they wanted me to continue. Finally one student asked, timidly, "Were they pretty?"

I nodded and said, "Yes, the prettiest girls from Seoul, as handsome as my gentlemen from Pyongyang."

This did not make up for hurting their feelings earlier, but it made them all break into giggles. One asked, "Do they have a monitor too?" The idea was so preposterous that I had to stop myself from laughing. I could not tell them that at South Korean universities there were no monitors, and certainly no platoon leaders, and that students did not march to classes or the cafeteria. So I just answered, "Well, most of them don't live on campus. Ewha girls just come and go individually, so no monitor."

NOW THAT WE were heading straight into winter, gardening duty became harder because the ground was often muddy, and then frozen. When I expressed concern about them having to work despite the weather conditions, a student matter-of-factly said they had boots, so it was not a problem. He told me that all of them had grown up tending to trees and plants. All DPRK citizens planted trees in October, which was "tree planting" month, and all Pyongyang citizens were ordered to do gardening work throughout the winter. *Gardening* was just a fancy word for manual labor that often included digging and hauling water. Now it made sense why, on our weekly grocery run through the city, I always saw people in scarves and gloves tending to the grass and bushes on the streets and riverbanks. My student recalled carrying buckets of water when he was as young as five. He said it so proudly that I realized he considered it a patriotic act. Besides, he added, gardening duty lasted only three or four hours, which allowed them to squeeze in some sports time, but cleaning floors or toilets took longer and left no extra time. So they preferred gardening duties.

That week, the students spent three hours digging a hole in the freezing cold. The previous week, it had been four hours. The students continued to assure me that the work was good for them, but some now admitted how tired they were. One said he had never labored this hard before coming to PUST.

On nights when the winds howled outside the window, I thought of the students out there on guard duty all night. None of them had the kind of heavy-duty coats that would have protected them properly. Their Great Leaders were always compared to the sun—Kim Il-sung's birthday was Sun's Day and Kim Jong-il was called "the Sun of the 21st century"—but there was no warmth from that sun. I finally brought up my concern about the cold at dinner one night, and they explained, reluctantly at first.

"It is very difficult for us . . . yes . . . but we are so happy to do it because it is a great honor that will help our Party and build a powerful and prosperous nation."

Each student at the table nodded, so I asked if they had ever done this before getting to PUST.

"Yes, we did this at our former universities too."

I then asked what about before university.

"Yes, since we were thirteen or fourteen. Everyone in our country grew up doing it."

The frequency of guard duty depended on a man's professional position, but they all performed this duty throughout their lives. Women, too, though they did not have to continue doing it once they gave birth.

As I had suspected, such duty existed in every one of the villages I had seen alongside the roads on our field trips. Those shrine-like buildings, known as Kimilsungism Study Halls, existed in every hamlet of their country, like churches or McDonald's all over the world.

22

Essay was a much-dreaded word among my students that fall. They were very stressed about having to write one, since it would be as important as exams in calculating their final grade. They were supposed to come up with their own topic and hand in a thesis and outline. When I asked them how it was going, they would sigh and say, "Disaster."

I emphasized the importance of essays since, as scientists, they would one day have to write papers to prove their theories. But in reality, nothing was ever proven in their world, since everything was at the whim of the Great Leader. Their writing skills were as stunted as their research skills. Writing inevitably consisted of an endless repetition of his achievements, none of which was ever verified, since they lacked the concept of backing up a claim with evidence. A quick look at the articles in the daily paper revealed the exact same tone from start to finish, with neither progression nor pacing. There was no beginning and no end.

So the basic three- or five-paragraph essay—with a thesis, an introduction, a body paragraph with supporting details, and a conclusion—was entirely foreign to them. The idea they had the most difficulty comprehending was the introduction. I would tell them that it was like waving hello. How do you say hello in an interesting way, so that the reader is "hooked"? I offered many different examples, but still they would show up during office hours, shaking their heads and asking, "So this *hook* . . . what is it?"

ONE MORNING, THEY shouted, "We beat Japan!" in unison as I walked into the classroom. Their national team, Chollima, had just beaten Japan's Samurai Blue team for the World Cup qualifying match. The match had taken place at Kim Il-sung Stadium and had been televised live.

Here, the rage against Japan remained as vivid as when Japan had colonized Korea more than half a century before. The students were exuberant, proudly telling me about Jong Tae-se, their national team's striker, and another one of their players who had been scouted by Manchester United. They did not acknowledge the fact that Jong was in fact a third-generation Zainichi Korean, a term used for ethnic Koreans born, raised, and living in Japan whose loyalty lies with North Korea. In their eyes, Zainichi Koreans were Japanese, their sworn enemy, and yet at opportune moments they considered them North Koreans.* I knew better than to comment on that.

"How exciting!" I said brightly. "Wouldn't it be great if Chollima makes it to Brazil for the World Cup?" They all nodded, smiling.

---

* The most famous Zainichi Korean is Ko Yong-hui, who died in 2004. One of several consorts of Kim Jong-il and the mother of Kim Jong-un, her low-class birth, or *songbun* status, has been whitewashed and she is known as the "Mother of Great Songun Korea."

It was not until later that day that I looked on the Internet and learned that North Korea had already been knocked out, and the results had been announced some time ago. The match against Japan had to be played simply because it was a game owed. Either the students would not admit this, or they did not know the truth. Not only that, I learned that the game had not actually been televised live. Rather, it had been broadcast as soon as it ended, when the regime could be certain that their team had won. One student told me that it was very boring to watch only winning games. Moreover, no matter how hard I searched online, there was no mention of a North Korean footballer playing for Manchester United. As always, their government had sown misinformation, and my students' claims lacked any basis in reality, so I could hardly expect them to back up their theses.

YET NOW THAT the graduate students had begun using the Internet—for about three or four hours a day, they told me—my students had become aware that they were missing out on something. At meals, I took out my laptop to show them the photos I had taken on Sports Day. They liked looking at photos of themselves and always wanted me to zoom in on their faces. "Okay, most handsome!" a cheeky student might declare. "You can print that one!" I changed my screen saver to a shot of the Manhattan skyline so that they would inadvertently get a glimpse of it. Sometimes I would open up a cute program called Photo Booth and take pictures of us sitting together while tiny pink hearts scrolled across the screen. "What are they? Why are those small pink things moving like that?" they would exclaim and then burst out laughing. Maybe it was because they had been taught since birth that they were soldiers that I liked to see them express simple joy.

They had also begun to express their admiration more openly. "I never saw a computer so thin!" said one student, regarding my laptop. Another said that he had never heard of a Mac until now and asked if it was the same as Windows. I reminded them about our previous lesson on obituaries and Steve Jobs. Some also remarked that my dictionary was unusual, to which I responded that a Kindle was not a dictionary but an electronic device that could contain thousands of books, the way an electronic dictionary holds thousands of words.

A student told me that he was very curious about my computer because his major was information technology. At his former university, he had been in charge of the intranet, and he hoped that after graduation he would be assigned to work for Chosun Computer Center. He added that he would have learned "hacking" in his junior year had he not been transferred to PUST. When I asked him if there was an actual course on hacking, he told me a story about a notoriously smart second-year student at his former university. One day the student hacked into the government system and improved all his grades. Government officials found out but decided that since the student was so brilliant, they would let him keep the high grades. The moral of this story seemed to be that hacking is a crime, but permissible if done well.

The student then asked if my MacBook connected to the Internet. I had recently been asked by another student if I could connect to the Internet using my iPod, which they had seen me listening to while running. They did not understand that it was not enough to have a device capable of connecting to the Internet; you had to have access to a signal. I explained it as well as I could and added that I could connect to the Internet with any computer, virtually anywhere, including parks and cafés, except in his country. I knew I should not be talking about this, but I could not keep silent.

Soon, one by one, my students began asking questions.

"Did you watch movies on the Internet today?"

"How long could you watch movies for?"

"How many movies can you watch?"

"Well, imagine infinity," I said, struggling to explain. "The Internet is a little like infinity. There are hundreds of thousands of websites that can be visited, tens of thousands of movies to choose from." They nodded, but then again, they always nodded.

One of my most sophisticated students, Song Seung-jin, asked me if I could help him find information about alcohol. He wanted to write about its advantages and disadvantages, but he had never drunk alcohol and did not know how to go about researching it. He was a son of a doctor who had been surrounded by medical information all his life, with the ambition of becoming a doctor himself, and yet he did not have a clue as to the effects of alcohol. What he was suggesting, I realized, was that I look it up for him on the Internet.

This vacuum of information was becoming an inconvenience the students could no longer ignore because they lived with us, who had the knowledge they lacked, who expected them to know some of it for the papers we assigned and the conversations we had at mealtimes. We, the products of Western culture, were reminders that this vacuum was a real obstacle to learning.

But misinformation and lack of information were not the only problems in teaching them how to write an essay. In their storytelling, a conclusion was always predetermined. For example, we had organized a competition, just like in the summer, for which the students were supposed to come up with brief, original skits, and Ruth, who was advising some of them, poked her head into my office one afternoon with a question. I had avoided her for some time now, but I was relieved that, apparently, my cover had not really been blown, since she assumed that I was Christian, but just not as devout as her.

"Do they sell organs in America?" she asked.

I shook my head and said, "No, that's illegal."

She explained that one of her students had an idea for a skit about a man who is horrified by organ buying and selling in America, and amazed when he comes to North Korea and finds out that hospitals are free, due to the solicitude of the Great Leader.

Class 4 performed a skit about a group of firemen rescuing a couple caught in a fire, before breaking into a song about the Great Leader. The winning skit was about a landowner's brutality against farmers, and was set during the era before the Korean liberation, which, the narrator explained, had been heroically conducted by their Eternal President Kim Il-sung. At the end, the whole cast again burst into a song about their gratitude to the Workers' Party. The exact reason why they suddenly thanked their Party was unclear, but all of the skits ended, regardless of plot, with a song of gratitude to either their Leader or their Party.

INSTEAD OF A lesson on sources, which was not possible here, I asked that they read a simple essay from 1997 that quoted President Bill Clinton on how important it was to make all schools wired. I got it approved by the counterparts because it related to our current textbook theme of college education. I hoped that they would grasp how behind they were. I also gave them four recent articles—from the *Princeton Review,* the *New York Times,* the *Financial Times,* and *Harvard Magazine*—that mentioned Mark

Zuckerberg, Facebook, and Twitter. None of the pieces evoked a response. Not even the sentence about Zuckerberg earning $100 billion from something he dreamed up in his college dorm seemed to interest them. It was possible that they viewed the reading as lies. Or perhaps the capitalist angle repelled them.

The next day, several students stopped by during office hours. They all wanted to change their essay topics. Curiously, the new topics they proposed all had to do with the ills of American society. One said he wanted to write about corporal punishment in American and Japanese middle schools. Another wanted to argue that the American government's policy of deciding a baby's future based on IQ tests should be forbidden. A third student wanted to write about the evils of allowing people to own guns so freely, in America. A fourth student said biofuel was toxic and America was the biggest producer of it. A fifth wanted to change his topic to divorce. There was no divorce in the DPRK, but in America the rate was more than 50 percent, and divorce led to crime and mental illness, according to him. "So what happens when people are unhappy here after being married for a while?" I asked. The student looked at me blankly. Still another student wanted to write about how McDonald's was horrible. The same student then asked me, "So what kind of food does McDonald's make?"

One student asked me which country produced the most computer hackers; he had been taught that it was America. This question stumped me, especially since I had just seen a news item on CNN Asia about cybercrime by North Korea. Instead, I told him that computer crimes could be committed anywhere, by anyone, even a visitor, so it would be hard to pinpoint one country as the source.

When their thesis sentences came in, I saw that one student had written: "Despite the harmful effect of nuclear weapons, some countries such as the United States keep developing nuclear weapons." It seemed he had no idea that North Korea's development and testing of nuclear weapons was an international concern. Another wrote that starvation was an impossible problem to solve, especially in Africa, and especially since even rich countries, such as England and America, had starvation problems. Another chose the topic of money and how it made some societies do unethical things.

One thing was clear. Their collective decision to switch their essay topics to condemn America seemed to have been compelled by the articles about Zuckerberg. What I had intended as inspirational, they must have viewed as boasting and felt slighted. The nationalism that had been instilled in them for so many generations had produced a citizenry whose ego was so fragile that they refused to acknowledge the rest of the world.

My efforts to expand their awareness kept backfiring. The paragraph about *kimjang* I had assigned led to a pile of preachy, self-righteous tirades. Almost half the students claimed that kimchi was the most famous food in the world, and that all other nations were envious of it. One student wrote that the American government had named it the official food of the 1996 Atlanta Olympics. When I questioned him, he said everyone knew this fact, and that he could even prove it since his Korean textbook said so. A quick Internet search revealed that a Japanese manufacturer had claimed that kimchi was a Japanese dish and proposed it as an official Olympic food, but had been denied. Somehow this news item had been relayed to them in twisted form and was now treated as general knowledge.

To correct my students on each bit of misinformation was taxing and sometimes meant straying into dangerous territory. Martha said, "No way. Don't touch that. If their book said it was true, you can't tell them that it's a lie."

Sometimes they would ask why I never ate much white rice. They piled their trays with huge heaps of it at every meal, whereas I always put just a little on my tray. I explained that I liked white rice but did not care for it all the time. They asked what kinds of food I ate other than rice and *naengmyun*, their national dish. I couldn't exactly go on about fresh fruit smoothies and eggs Benedict, so I named two Western dishes I knew they had heard of: spaghetti and hot dogs. I knew that North Koreans enjoyed their own version of sausage because I had seen them lining up for it at the International Trade Fair. One of the students then wrote in his *kimjang* homework, "Those Koreans who prefer hot dogs and spaghetti over kimchi bring shame on their motherland by forgetting the superiority of kimchi." Nothing, it seemed, could break through their belligerent isolation; moreover, this attitude left no room for any argument, since all roads led to just one conclusion. I returned the paper to him with a comment: "Why is it not possible to like both spaghetti and kimchi?"

Despite the failure of her forks and knives experiment, and though it was not encouraged, Ruth still wanted to educate the students about Western culture. She downloaded a song called "Around the World" by a techno duo called Daft Punk and songs by the hip-hop band Roots so that they would experience different types of music. The counterparts approved this since it related to the textbook, but all the students hated the songs. The only thing they did not hate, though they did not seem to like it much either, was rock 'n' roll, inspired by the Beatles' "Yesterday." Later, a few students told me, "This hip-hop is only words, and techno is only beats. Boring!" Another shook his head and agreed: "Disgusting!" The others chimed in, "It is like our song, 'Yanji Bomb,' about the bomb our Eternal President Kim Il-sung used against Japanese Imperialists. It is all words too, but that was done a long time ago. A very old song. So we are ahead of Americans!"

AFTER SEVERAL LESSONS on the essay, a student said to me at dinner, "A strange thing happened during our social science class this afternoon."

They never volunteered information about their Juche class, so I listened intently.

The student continued, "We had to write an essay!" He explained that they normally wrote short compositions in Korean and he had never thought of them as essays before, but now he did, and it made him feel strange.

"What was so strange?" I asked.

"I don't know," he said, pausing thoughtfully. "I looked at it as an essay, and I realized that it was different now. Writing in English and writing in Korean are so different, but then it is also the same, and I kept thinking of the essay structure as I was writing it, and it made me feel strange."

I did not question him further, but I thought I understood. It must have been deeply confusing to approach his writing on Juche like an essay. In his country there was no proof, no checks and balances—unless, of course, they wanted to prove that the Great Leader had single-handedly written hundreds of operas and thousands of books and saved the nation and done a miraculous number of things. Their entire system was designed not to be questioned, and to squash critical thinking. So the form of an essay, in which a thesis had to be proven, was antithetical to their entire system. The writer of an essay acknowledges the arguments opposing his thesis and refutes them. Here, opposition was not an option.

I stared across at him and felt a familiar sick feeling. Perhaps this was only the beginning. The questions they would have. The questions they should be asking. The questions they would realize they had not been asking because they did not imagine they could, or because asking meant that they could no longer exist in their system.

23

THANKSGIVING WAS COMING, AND THE NEWS AT HOME, according to CNN Asia, was the rising candidacy of Herman Cain, followed by accusations of sexual harassment. One of the headlines read: "God told me to run for President." This was familiar to me. When I asked the other teachers why they had come to PUST, each of them had a similar answer. "God brought me here." When I asked how much longer they would be here, many answered, "For however long God wants me here. He knows everything. He will decide."

This reminded me of Ruth's claim that the Lord has his designs, and that the sufferings of North Koreans were a temporary stage on the way to heaven. Gulags, then, served a purpose in the name of Jesus, much the way my students were taught to follow their Great Leader despite the famine, or rather *because* of the famine, which was reinterpreted as a form of martyrdom necessary to the building of a "powerful and prosperous nation." Thus, the Arduous March became a rite of passage that helped unite them against an outside world that demonized them.

I returned to the Sunday service although Ruth had told me not to participate in communion, which took place only occasionally, for some reason. Afterward, at lunch, a student asked, "What did you do this morning?" I stumbled for a moment and answered, "Well, a teachers' meeting." My breath felt caught.

"You have meetings on Sundays too?" Their eyes widened. "Where? In the dormitory?"

Everything on campus was visible from all angles and, just as we wondered what went on when they as a group were not visible for a few hours, they must have wondered the same about us. I answered, as truthfully as I could, that we sometimes met to discuss small details like the teachers' trips, and how much to pay and who was going. They nodded, although they did not seem convinced.

The temperature was dropping every day. On some days, my fingers were too numb to hold the chalk while teaching. We all wore winter coats all the time, even in the classrooms. I still had to wear a skirt, so I doubled up on tights. Now that it was almost Thanksgiving time back home, I was even more homesick, though I had grown up celebrating Chuseok, the Korean Harvest Day, not Thanksgiving, and I did not eat turkey. At some meals, the students tried to distract me with funny stories, almost as if they could sense my spirit sinking.

One evening, Chang Min-su, a bumbling student from one of my groups, told me about his older sister's impending wedding. She was twenty-seven and worked at the swimming pool at Changgangwon. She had met her fiancé in college, and he also worked there. An amateur boxer, he was a very nice man but with a "terrible appearance," which Min-su proceeded to describe in minute detail: the man was short and fat; his nose was so big that it took up his entire face; his mouth was positioned too low, at the bottom of his chin; and his eyes were slivers, set too far apart. Worst of all, his eyebrows were so faint that they were virtually missing. The first time he saw him, Min-su said, he was appalled because he had never seen a man with missing eyebrows. This man would wait for Min-su's sister in front of their house every morning; his sister was very pretty since she had had plastic surgery on her eyes and nose.

So far, several students had mentioned that plastic surgery was not uncommon, and one of the older professors who had worked with North Koreans for a long time told me that the local women described plastic surgery as a sort of reward that their government granted some women to enhance their looks. On previous visits, I had often noticed women in Pyongyang who looked as though they had had double-eyelid surgery, the most common cosmetic surgery in South Korea.

Another student, Park Se-hoon, then burst into a story about his girlfriend. During the summer, they had all insisted that they had none, but the barriers between us were breaking down. He said that he had had a girlfriend at his former university, who was very sad when he left for PUST, but now he had a new girlfriend, supposedly thanks to the homework paper I had assigned on "how to successfully get a girl." He had remembered the lesson, and during the vacation, he had met a girl at the Grand People's Study House, where they saw each other every day. The other students laughed and said he was joking, but he was emphatic. She was pretty and a student at Pyongyang's Foreign Language University, and she was enamored with him because his English was better than hers, and because she found him very handsome. I told him that I was impressed that he had been able to find a girlfriend in the short time he had at home. The other students began laughing hysterically and said, "This guy is very talented in girl catching!"

It was Hong Mun-sup's birthday that day, and the students planned to gather at 7:30 p.m. in one of the dorm rooms to celebrate. Everyone, with the exception of the six on duty, would take turns singing a song for Mun-sup, and then they would all gather in a TV room and watch their Chinese drama. I asked Mun-sup what his mother usually gave him for his birthday, and he said teddy bears. He had about ten of them. Another student, Kim Yong-suk, said that his parents gave him a watch for each birthday; however he was very forgetful and had managed to lose every single one. Finally, his father stopped buying them. On his last birthday, his father said, "I would rather give a dog a watch than you!" He then said that his mother had bought dog meat from the market and made him his favorite meal, dog-meat soup. Another said that his mother gave him filleted cat meat to put on his skin to ease sore muscles. They were thrilled by gross descriptions. They knew I did not care much for meat, and they watched me to see if I would turn queasy at the details, until finally I said, "Okay, enough, I get it!" At this, everyone at the table would burst out laughing.

Then, out of nowhere, Chang Min-su asked, "Are Americans racist?" He said he had read a mention of it in a textbook and worried that perhaps white Americans treated me badly since I did not look like them. I paused, not due to my usual fear about getting anyone in trouble, but because it was a complicated question. He was genuinely curious, and I had a lot to say on the topic. However, before I could answer, he continued, "What about dark people?" He meant African-Americans. They had never seen any ethnicity but their own until they arrived at PUST, where there were white teachers but no black teachers, so it was a very abstract concept for them. I was impressed that he would wonder about such a thing after spending a relatively short time with foreign teachers, but Mun-sup quickly hushed him. "Boring! Please change the topic. That has nothing to do with our lives."

It was always like this; immediately the discussion was dropped. But scraps of new information stayed with them, partly because they were young, but also because so little happened to them. For example, a student asked, "Is J. K. Rowling a famous writer?"

Then another: "Is Hogwarts a nice place?"

And another: "Quidditch *does* sound fun!"

It sounded as though they had read the book or seen the movies, but of course neither was possible. Apparently the story had been mentioned ever so briefly in one of their textbooks from the previous spring, but they remembered it vividly. I began to fantasize about showing them one of the Harry Potter movies. So I could not believe my luck when Martha mentioned that she had with her a copy of the third film. I was thrilled. We had scheduled a movie day for the entire freshman class after their final exam, and I suggested we get the Harry Potter movie approved by the counterparts and show it to the students.

Unfortunately, Ruth overheard our conversation and informed me that the teachers had already chosen *The Chronicles of Narnia*. I suggested making it a double feature and adding *Harry Potter* or, better yet, just swapping them. Ruth said no. *Narnia* had been chosen for its Christian message, she explained. Some teachers did not agree with the message of *Harry Potter*. Besides, she felt that *Harry Potter* would be the first thing the students would be exposed to when their country opened up. I brought it up with Mary, who also told me that my wish was an impossibility.

"Movies are influential. The counterparts might not have a problem with *Harry Potter*, but we do. There's a reason why

Narnia was chosen. He says so," she said, motioning toward the ceiling.

Any new information had to go through two sets of gate-keepers. What I saw as pop culture the missionaries saw as heresy, and so might the counterparts, so whatever information reached the students was doubly censored. But it seemed strange that their Lord did not like Harry Potter but had allowed the story to spread around the world faster than just about any in modern history.

AS LIGHT AS some of those exchanges with the students were, or perhaps because of the joy we shared, I would feel heavier than ever as I put the metal tray away and walked down the cold, dark enclosed walkway to the teachers' dormitory. It felt as though any ray of hope that had shone over us in those moments was being shut off with each step away from them. Upon reaching my room, I would reflect upon my day with the students, going over each detail, writing it down, and would be struck by a gnawing feeling, a disturbing, almost physical sensation that something was deeply wrong.

Being in North Korea was profoundly depressing. There was no other way of putting it. The sealed border was not just at the 38th parallel, but everywhere, in each person's heart, blocking the past and choking off the future. As much as I loved those boys, or because of it, I was becoming convinced that the wall between us was impossible to break down, and not only that, it was permanent. This so saddened me that some frozen dawns, when I woke up to the sound of the boys doing their group exercises, I had to fight not to shut my eyes and go back to sleep.

24

"I FEEL LIKE THE DAYS ARE JUST ABOUT WAITING," A STU-
dent said at dinner. They rarely expressed their feelings, and I
felt exactly as he did, so I said, "Me too."

"Professor Kim Suki feels that way too?" he exclaimed. He
seemed surprised that I commiserated.

I nodded. "What are you waiting for?" I asked.

"To see my mother and father, of course!" he said, breaking
into a big smile.

They were also anxious about their studies. They were to
continue with only English lessons until the arrival of science
and technology teachers. By then, it would be one and a half
years of a break in their studies since they were first brought to
PUST. "I am worried," a student confessed. "I don't know if it
is okay to stop studying my major for that long."

For the last writing assignment of the semester, I told them
to write a letter to anyone. I was giving them a break after a recent five-paragraph essay assignment, which they had found too
difficult, and I was also giving myself a break, since reading and
marking those essays on topics such as banning cell phone use

and cigarette smoking had been so tedious. I had been afraid that another assignment would put them off writing forever, but surprisingly they seemed happy with it. Once I read them, I could see why.

Many wrote to their mothers. They were heartfelt letters. One wrote:

> *Dear mother, the faster the days elapse, the more I miss you. But this takes a toll on my studying so I try to avoid feeling homesick. I look at your picture every night before bed, and I want to make you proud.*

Some wrote that on Sundays, they kept photos of their mothers with them all day for strength as they did their duties. Some talked about their fears of failing to master English and bringing shame to their families. The contents of these letters were similar, but they rang with the same truth. The boys were lonely and scared.

Those who wrote to their friends were uncharacteristically open about their frustrations. "I am fed up," one wrote. "I know you are working at the construction site. I feel bad for complaining about my life but I am fed up with my daily routine. I get up at the same time, eat at the same time, leave our room only to learn English. I get stressed about grades." Another wrote, "I study only English and I am forgetting basic algorithm."

Several talked about essay writing to their friends:

"I am not learning our subject but instead learning a lot of English. Do you know what 'essay' is?"

"One of the most difficult challenges is to pass the writing exam and win over our Reading and Writing teacher Kim Suki with my essay. Essay in English is completely different from writing in Korean. When I first began to write them, I did not think I could finish one because writing an essay was very confusing to me. But the more I learned, the more attractive I felt to essays, and through essays I could change peoples' mind."

"Here there are many good professors, but one in particular, Kim Suki, is very close to me. She taught us essays. I consider writing essays is climbing a peak of mountain everyone is afraid of climbing."

Some wrote to their friends at the construction sites, using the address of the sites: "I am afraid that it is too exhausting for you at the building site on Mansudae Avenue. I think about you, dear friend, all the time."

"In August, you showed me the video in which the buildings were flattened down with a loud explosion. It was a wonderful scene. Now you are building a modern teaching building there. I am sorry I cannot work with you."

"Now that the winter is getting worse, it must be difficult at the construction site, and you may come down with a cold. Remember you are one person to the world but to me you are the world."

In their letters to friends and families, they referred to the last time they had met, which was often more than a year ago. They apologized for not being in touch, referring to events they had missed, such as birthdays. But they never mentioned that they were not allowed to write. Instead, they blamed themselves:

"I thought of you, dear mother, on your birthday. I am sorry I could not write, but you know how I am a lazy boy."

"I am sorry I could not call you on your birthday, my friend, I had too much English homework."

"I am sure you never thought you would not hear from me for three years. I don't know if you are ill or how you are living. You will be surprised to receive this letter from me tomorrow, and I am sorry for not writing, but I was busy with exams."

Some either wrote to their girlfriends or referred to them in their letters. One wrote about her beautiful appearance and how he missed her and longed to see her during the winter vacation. Another wrote to his friend about his girlfriend: "My girlfriend who is very active likes to go bowling. What does your girlfriend, whose nickname is Talkative Sparrow, like? Please send my regards to my fabulous angel."

Another student wrote to his best friend, who had been dating his sister and had just broken up with her. His letter described a romance between two people who had known each other for a long time, ending when the boy broke up with her for something silly and she was very hurt. He told his friend to forgive her so that when he came home for the winter break, he would be able to see the couple smile. I knew that he was an only child and had no sister, so this seemed to be a veiled letter to his ex-girlfriend about their own situation.

The most detailed one was by a student whose spoken English was not as good as the others'. He was quiet and rarely participated in class, so I was surprised when he handed me a very long letter, saying that it was a secret:

> *I was sixteen when I first met you. You were fourteen. I taught you math at your home, and your parents were happy. Then you moved away and I did not know how to find you until you called me one day to tell me that you were taking the exam for the university. I then called you every day to see if you passed. Then I tempted you to come out, and we met often, I walked you home, then you walked me home. The last time we met at the skating rink and had a fight. I am sorry. Next time when I come home,*

I will do what you want. You can teach me Russian. I will teach
you English. Big ship leaves slowly, so wait for me.

He added a postscript—"Professor Kim Suki, she is a real
person"—then wrote down her name.

One wrote to his brother in the army whom he had not seen
in three years. Another wrote to Katie about Sports Day and
how all the students had fun but thought of her well-being. "We
ran together with you in our hearts," he wrote.

Despite their guardedness, what came out in those letters
was astoundingly tender and deeply earnest. "I am so glad at this
chance to write down what is on my mind," several wrote. This
prison-like life was really getting to them. They were cut off
from everyone to whom they could express themselves. These
letters, which they knew would never reach the recipients, were
their only outlet, and although it was in a language that was not
theirs and only for homework that would be graded, they em-
braced the assignment as though the letters were real. And not
one mentioned the Great Leader or the "powerful and prosperous nation."

Then I came upon a troubling letter addressed to me. It was
from Kang Sun-pil, who explained, in great detail, that he had
come by during office hours a few weeks ago to show me his
homework assignment about *kimjang*, and that I had glanced at it
and told him that it was "okay." But when he received his paper
back, he saw that he had gotten only 87 points. He considered
this a betrayal. Part of the letter read:

I felt disappointed and felt as if you are changeable and deceived
me. After that, I lost my temper for several days because of regret.
Of course it is not acceptable to criticize a professor, according to

grades. And I thought it is not appropriate to ignore the respect
and expectation of a student. You think I am rude to you and
criticizing you but I don't want to deceive you and pretend to feel
happy . . . Even though you think I am not a gentleman, I want
to write honestly.

Instead of closing with "sincerely," he wrote, in Korean: *From a student who once respected you.*

Sun-pil, one of the highly ranked students, was nervous that he might lose his place. From an early age, he had been selected for Number One schools. I could almost never read his feelings so I was surprised by his highly emotional letter. Also, he had signed his name in Korean for an English class assignment, which was not allowed. From then on, he stopped meeting my eyes or making any effort in class. Finally, I asked him to come see me during an office hour.

As expected, he came with his buddy, Shin Dong-hyun. He sat there, visibly upset, and the mood was tense. But other students came in with questions and acted as if he weren't there. Suddenly they all seemed to have blocked him out.

"Why don't we wait until you answer all their questions?" he said to me quietly.

Once everyone was gone, and it was just me and him and his buddy, we began to talk, or rather I began to talk. I told him that I understood that he felt betrayed because he thought I was "changeable" but I found his accusation hurtful since I did not intentionally deceive him. He sat quietly without a word. Dong-hyun just stood by the door as though he did not hear us. I could see that Sun-pil was nearly in tears.

"I would like your permission to speak in Korean," he said finally.

Although I was normally not allowed to let them do so, I told him he could. It was the first time any of my students had spoken to me in our shared first language.

"When I met you in the summer, I was so impressed by you. You taught us paragraphs and promised to teach us essays, and I was so glad. Then when you said that you would return, I was afraid to even believe it in case you didn't, and when you really came back for the fall semester, I was overjoyed. So I came to the office hour every day although I didn't really need your help. I wanted to learn from you, and above all, I respected you. I guess I felt disappointed by the way you handled my request for help. You said it was okay, but you didn't really mean okay if you were going to give me a low mark. If you didn't think my paper was okay, why did you say it was okay?"

It was a reasonable question. I apologized for upsetting him and explained that when he flashed his paper before my eyes and asked for my opinion, there were about five other students trying to get my attention. By the word *okay*, I told him, I meant only that his paper was good enough, but that did not mean it couldn't be better, and it was his responsibility to work on it further to improve it. I was not his babysitter, nor was I offering office hours solely to help students raise their grades. Just because I said okay, I did not want him to take that as the definitive answer. I told him that he should have his own opinion. He was a twenty-year-old man who had been at the top of his class all his life. I respected his opinion, his estimation of himself, his ability to claim responsibility. I meant what I said, and as I was speaking, I realized I too was getting emotional. I wanted him to know that he should think for himself, the very quality that was never encouraged in this country.

He nodded, and after a long pause, said exactly what I had wanted him—and all of them—to say all along: "I guess for so long, it has become a habit to just believe everything I hear." Then he told me that this was the first time in his life he had had a conflict with a teacher, and added, "I think perhaps I expressed my feelings to you because I felt that I could and that I cared. I believe that you and I will be closer through this conflict."

I agreed, offering peace: "Yes, that was just a small conflict that came out of our cultural differences."

Then Dong-hyun, who had been quiet throughout, said, "But we never think of you as being different from us. Our circumstances are different. But you are the same as us. We want you to know that we truly think of you as being the same."

25

AT DINNER ONE night, Jun Su-young came to me with a detailed drawing of an appendix. He had heard that another student had asked me a question about anatomical terms in English, and that I had answered that I was not very knowledgeable about human anatomy. So Su-young had spent hours at the library looking up all the relevant terminology in English and had drawn up a chart to show me. It was heartwarming to watch him talk about something that truly engaged him, and I put down my utensils and stopped pretending to eat my bean sprouts and cabbage soup, as proud as a mother watching her son give a talk about some new thing he had learned in school.

Then Ri Dae-sung, next to him, snapped, "This is like a medicine class, not dinner. It is *so* boring, what he is talking about. He is a medicine major, but we are not. It is like a foreign language. Not even English, but some other foreign language. So we can say he is talking to himself." We all cracked up.

It was then that I saw a face I recognized across the room.

It was an American colleague, a foreign correspondent whom I had met for the first time during the 2008 New York Philharmonic coverage. He had been trying to get back into Pyongyang since then and had been courting PUST's President Kim for that purpose. I was suddenly filled with dread, as I knew I could not say hello to him. He saw me as well, but he knew that I was there in the guise of a missionary teacher and was enough of a veteran journalist to look away casually—although his gaze met mine for a moment. I was afraid that someone might notice, so I immediately lowered my eyes. But here, everything was noticed. The students at my table looked behind them to see what had caught my eye. Dae-sung asked, "Do you know that man? Who is he?" I just shrugged. "Maybe a new teacher?" With smiling eyes he replied, "Well, too late! The semester is almost over and we are going home!" The boys burst out laughing. I felt calmer, although my heart was beating rapidly, as though I had been discovered.

Now the boys were talking about going home for the winter break, but Su-young said that he wished he could stay at PUST. He claimed that he was not homesick and preferred being here, to which Dae-sung rolled his eyes and snapped, "Nonsense."

I don't know why that sounded so funny then, but we all found it hilarious. Perhaps it was the way he said it, or the expression on his face, or the fact that our days were so mundane that even the tiniest things amused us. Perhaps it was akin to what a student told me once: that it did not matter what TV drama they watched because it was inevitably funny when as many as sixty of them watched it together. Or perhaps, in that vulnerable moment, I sought refuge with my students. For a moment the outside world, the one to which I really belonged, where I was a writer, had entered that Pyongyang cafeteria, and it was jarring, and I felt disturbed, as though I did not want to be pulled out of this new world, in which I shared private jokes with young North Koreans, all of us together in our isolation.

Then Dae-sung broke the spell and, pointing at Su-young, said, "All Koreans miss their mothers. All students are homesick. But this weird guy here says he is not homesick. So this is like a foreign language again. In this case we can say, he is again talking to himself!" Everyone cracked up again.

Then Su-young looked at me and asked, "Professor, are you coming back to teach in the spring?"

For the past week, they had been talking about this nonstop. We would talk about an eclipse, and they would say that the night before while looking at the moon they wished that Professor Kim Suki would return in the spring. I would ask them what they had done over the weekend, and they would answer that they dreamed Professor Kim Suki told them she was coming back in the spring, which made them so happy. All I could say over and over to the repeated question was that I would try my best, but I could not promise. I was not yet sure if I could stand to come back. So instead I asked what they would do during the winter break.

On December 24, they would pay their respects to Kim Jong-suk since it was her birthday. That was also the day when, in 1991, Kim Jong-il had been given the title of Supreme Commander of the Korean People's Army, so they celebrated that too. It was one of their most important holidays, the others being February 16, Kim Jong-il's birthday, and April 15, Kim Il-sung's birthday, known as the Sun's Day. On all those days, children received gifts from the Party, such as book bags and toys. On January 1, everyone got up early and went to the statues of both Great Leaders to pay their respect.

One student said that he had two parties a year at his house, one on Sun's Day, and the other on New Year's Eve. Last year, twenty of his friends came over, and they built a snowman together and stayed up all night talking and drinking beer. This was the first time any student had admitted consuming alcohol. Another student said that his family held reunions during winter. His extended family was scattered across the country, and on one day of the year, they came together; the location depended on which relative's house was available.

"But we never do it at the ones in Pyongyang, since then everyone needs a special permit to enter there," he added. This was the first time I'd heard a student mention any restrictions on travel.

BACK IN MY room, I felt agitated knowing that my journalist friend was at PUST, most likely housed in the teachers' dormitory, where guests were always put up. But it did not matter. There was no way to communicate. I could not tell him anything that was going on with me, and he could not tell me any of his news. In this system, we simply were not allowed to know each other. He would most likely be here for a few days and leave. He would see what he was allowed to observe, and get out when he was told to leave, and write about the designated sliver that the regime had permitted him to see. It would not be anything close to the truth of this place, and he would know that, but he would be helpless to find out more.

None of that had any bearing on my daily life, and it was strange how quickly I could put the thought out of my mind. His presence was irrelevant because, for the moment, we belonged in different worlds. This realization was alarming. It felt like a taste of how my students viewed me, or of what might have been behind the vacant gazes of Pyongyang citizens. A foreign visitor could never penetrate their world, let alone appease their suffering. No one ever deviated from the script.

The next day, the journalist "accidentally" passed by my office. The door was open, and he held out his notepad, which read: *Is there a place where we could talk?* He did not understand much about PUST, but he knew that anything we said aloud would be recorded. I shook my head and quickly wrote on the pad: *Nowhere, I'm being watched by everyone.* I could not invite him into my office since that would immediately have created suspicion.

Instead, I stood nearer and whispered, "The other teachers are watching."

He mouthed the words, "Unbelievable."

"How long are you here?" I asked.

"Thursday, just a five-day visa," he answered. It was Tuesday.

"Good, that sounds good," I said, standing at my door, looking out into the corridor. No one seemed to be about, although anyone could walk by any second. I had to think quickly. He had already put his notepad back in his bag, but then I noticed that he was coughing. So I took a tissue from my pocket and wrote on it, *Breakfast is 6:30 a.m., but if you get there early, maybe you could sit with some students without the minders looking and talk to them.* I then handed it to him, saying, "You're coughing, do you need tissue?" He took it and said, "Sure, thank you."

This was as far as the conversation could go, so I whispered, "I'm happy to see you."

He nodded and walked away, but seeing him again unsettled me. I suddenly felt anxious and homesick. I wanted to get out of here and return to my civilization. There he and I were, sleeping in the same building, eating in the same cafeteria, and our communication was limited to those few guarded words. Perhaps this was a glimpse of what the older teachers who were born in North Korea felt when they talked about the helplessness of returning and not being able to connect with parents and siblings whom they had not seen in decades. Everything was designed to subjugate you and seize your will. We were controlled by the regime. Even the seasoned foreign correspondent. Even I.

Once he had walked down the corridor and disappeared, I regretted telling him to interview the students. What if he were to get them in trouble? I felt like a traitor to my students, and my mixed loyalties confused me. I wished that I had thought quickly enough to ask him for his room number. I wanted to plead with him to not trap them with any tricky questions, but I could not think of a way to relay a message.

Then I noticed that Ruth's door was open. She was next to me, both in the dormitory and the office. The walls were extremely thin, and she must have heard everything that was said. I spent the next few minutes in paranoid horror.

What had I said? Was it obvious that we were friends?

That sounds good, I had said.

The other teachers are watching.

I'm happy to see you.

I was certain I had whispered, "The other teachers are watching." But Ruth taught Speaking and Listening. Her listening was more acute than others'. Also, I was not sure if I had said, "I'm happy to see you" quietly, or if I had just blurted it out. *I'm happy to see you.* I had never realized that a phrase so little and innocent could haunt me so relentlessly.

Finally I walked into her office. Her nose was buried in her work. I asked her some random question about classes, and she looked up, but from her expression, I could not detect anything at all.

LATER, MUCH LATER, once we had both safely returned from North Korea, the journalist would email me this:

> *I thought the place was horrible. It makes Gitmo look like a des-*
> *tination resort . . . Gitmo is a prison camp for Al Qaeda fighters*
> *and Islamic radicals, yet they have a soccer field and eat much*
> *better than those kids at PUST do. One is a university, the other*
> *is a prison camp. But good luck to any student trying to get off*
> *campus in the middle of the night . . . When I had a cold during*
> *that trip there and President Kim drove me to the campus clinic,*
> *we passed the basketball court, and I saw you and you were wear-*
> *ing headphones, watching the boys play basketball, and I couldn't*
> *talk to you. And all I wanted to do was talk to you because I*
> *knew the pain you were in.*

26

WITH BOTH FINAL exams and Christmas approaching, two things happened that felt like a blessing. First, *Narnia*, the selection for Movie Day, was rejected by the counterparts. My fellow teachers were puzzled by this, since the film had been approved and screened in the spring, but it appeared that the counterparts had become suspicious of their insistence on this particular film.

Then the second thing happened. Surprisingly, *Harry Potter and the Prisoner of Azkaban* was approved for my English lesson. With hardly any time left to find another film and get it approved, the teachers felt that there was really no other option but to show *Harry Potter* to the entire freshman class, for Movie Day, which took place the same day as final exams. The news soon spread around campus.

"Are we really going to see *Harry Potter*?"

"Will we get to see them all, Harry and Hermione and Ron?"

"Will we see Quidditch too?"

One by one, they rushed up to me to ask the same things. The news consumed them. The story of the boy wizard had only been an abstraction for them, and they could not believe that they would actually get to see a movie based on it. For them, the lure was not so much the storyline, of which they knew virtually nothing, but the fact that the rest of the world had seen and loved it, that it was a true blockbuster. This unexpected chance to join the Harry Potter bandwagon made them feel included in a world that had always been denied to them. They wanted to know everything about it, and at each meal I had to explain the Harry Potter phenomenon, which was certainly belated since all seven films had been completed and the child actors were grown up and at college, the same age as my students.

The teachers planned to make popcorn for the occasion. They had brought with them the microwavable kind from China. I told the students, rather prematurely it turned out, that I would bake a chocolate cake. During the summer, Beth had baked her class brownies, and ever since then the students talked about brownies with wonder; one student called it the best thing he had ever tasted. The problem was that not only had I never baked a chocolate cake—or anything—before, but that the cake would have to serve a hundred students.

I looked up recipes on the Internet and quickly learned that the ingredients could not be found in Pyongyang. Some teachers had brought baking powder and vanilla extract; the real problems were butter and cocoa powder. All they sold at the shops was margarine, and the only cocoa available was the instant drink mix. I decided I would simply buy lots of chocolate and melt it down. This would not result in a real chocolate cake, but chocolate-flavored bread seemed better than nothing. There were no ovens except in the school kitchen, and I got permission to use one of them, but it looked nothing like any oven I had ever seen. The task of baking a chocolate cake for a hundred students in North Korea was way more complicated than I had imagined.

The excitement over the upcoming Movie Day topped with a chocolate cake was short-lived. Mary stormed into my office, furious. "I'll never show *that* to any of my students!" she shouted. "What's your motive for wanting to show such filth to our students?" This usually mild-mannered woman was visibly shaking with anger. "What kind of a Christian are you? What would Christians around the world say about our decision to expose our students to such heresy?"

I had not been told that all the other teachers, although not thrilled, had acquiesced to the movie selection, except Mary, the most fundamentalist in her beliefs. Unlike the rest of the missionaries, who had been born into devout Christian families, Korean Chinese Mary was a graduate of YUST and had been indoctrinated as a student. It made me wonder if any of my students would turn out like her if one day North Korea were to open up.

I asked her if she had read any of the Harry Potter books or seen any of the films. It was a naive question. Even though I saw it as a typical story about a little boy who fights bad guys, with some magic thrown in to cater to kids' fascination with the supernatural, for Mary, Harry Potter was the devil incarnate. She repeated that she would never watch such a thing or show it to our students even if she had to single-handedly demand to cancel Movie Day entirely. Then she ran off in search of substitute films.

A few hours later, she called an emergency meeting in her office. She had managed to collect a few random DVDs from other teachers. *Indiana Jones and the Kingdom of the Crystal Skull* was deemed too violent. *Madagascar* was a cartoon, and the students had specifically expressed their wish to see something that was not a cartoon this time. She liked *The Blind Side* because it had good Christian values, but the other teachers felt that there might be love scenes in it that would be inappropriate. The same went for *Titanic*. Finally, Mary suggested *Lord of the Rings*. Martha pointed out that it also had wizards in it and that it was three hours and forty minutes long.

All through the meeting, while the teachers looked at each DVD from Mary's meager collection, my heart beat rapidly. I was afraid one of them would be selected to replace *Harry Potter*. My students were so anxiously anticipating seeing it that I did not have it in my heart to tell them that they would not, in fact, be watching it. Also, this being our final week together, the film seemed like my last chance to expose them to something from the outside world. So I told Mary, firmly, that as their teacher, I absolutely would not break my promise to my students. Mary replied, just as firmly, that she absolutely would not allow it to be shown. The others at the meeting seemed nervous as Mary and I began raising our voices. The tension escalated so much that we were both crying in the end. Finally Beth, the dean of the English department, stepped in, and we came to a compromise. She would immediately send out a group email to gather DVDs from all teachers in order to pick another film for Movie Day and have it approved by the counterparts, but after the final exam, as part of my final lesson on December 19, I would be allowed to show *Harry Potter* to just one of the two classes I taught.

It was a horrible compromise, and yet I knew that to show the film to only twenty-five students was still better than showing it to none. I agonized for hours, and cried, before choosing Class 1, because they were the ones who had first asked about Harry Potter, and because the movie was quite difficult to follow for non–English speakers, and I knew that Class 1 would understand more of it than Class 4.

So this was how *Avatar* came to be chosen for Movie Day, on December 17, instead of *Harry Potter*. The exam started later than the appointed time of 8 a.m. due to an electricity outage. The winter morning was so dreary that, even after we opened all the curtains in the classroom, the students could hardly see their tests in the dim light. We waited for it to become more light outside and, as if by magic, it began snowing and the snow continued all through that last day, as though it could cover up whatever was about to occur in that devastated land. Once the exam was over, the students ran outside to take pictures, and the snow kept falling, and the boys looked happy as children as they fought to sit next to their teachers before the camera.

None of us knew then that it truly was the last day of an era. This was the last day of Kim Jong-il's life, although the news would not break until two days later, December 19.

Later that afternoon, for the showing of *Avatar*, I did manage to bake a very thin loaf of bread with a lukewarm chocolate flavor, and the boys seemed happy with it. One pointedly told me that it was *definitely* not a brownie, but cake was quickly forgotten as they gathered to watch a Hollywood blockbuster with spectacular special effects for the first time in their lives.

27

DURING THE LAST week there, I dreamt of vomiting. I vomited up the images of the silent villages alongside the roads, the gaunt faces outside the van window, the Great Leader slogans and the Great Leader songs and the Great Leader portraits that marked every building, every living creature, every hushed breath like a branding iron. In my dream, I threw up every last bit of my final days into a black plastic bag, which was so heavy that I had to drag it with both hands to dump it into a pit next to the teachers' dormitory. Alone in the Siberian winds, I stood gazing down at the bag that seemed to be breathing, so resilient that it refused to die.

Then I woke up, and it was 5:40 a.m. Outside it was pitch dark, but I knew that the students were awake. By 5:50, they were outside running in rows, shouting *Joguk Tongil*, which means "Reunification of Motherland." It was good for their health, they uniformly claimed at meals, to wake up so early and run in the dark shouting such wishes. My little soldiers were also little robots. In groups, they inevitably mouthed the right answer, which would then be reviewed in weekly Daily Life Unity critiques, but in private, their voices resonated.

Every day is the same.

Every day is about waiting.

I am fed up.

On that Monday morning, December 19, 2011, I showed *Harry Potter* to Class 1. It was an emotional morning, as I knew I was upsetting Class 4. Soon after the movie started, some boys from the other classes, who were all assigned to self-study in nearby classrooms, began peering through the windows. Finally, there was a knock, and I told my class to continue watching the film and walked out to find several students in the hallway.

"We want to see the film too, Teacher," they said. The monitor from Class 4 was also there, demanding to know why their class was not being shown the film when I was also their teacher. I told them that singling out just one group was beyond my jurisdiction; that it upset me more than anything I had ever done in my life; and that if I could have, I would have shown the film to every one of them; but that I was a mere teacher and had no such power.

"Will you please forgive me?" I asked, breaking down in tears.

Finally, one of them said, "We understand, Teacher. We just wanted to see the film too. As you know, we do not have many chances."

Then the monitor from Class 4 said, "Don't worry, Teacher. We understand you. We would like to invite you to our classroom after you finish your film. We have a surprise for you."

The surprise turned out to be songs: "Our Unforgettable Teacher" and the "Song of Suki," a regional folksong they had been vaguely aware of, whose lyrics they had searched out during their August vacation and written down neatly on a piece of paper as a parting gift. They all sang them together, and they asked me one last favor.

"Will you say something to us in Korean?"

The request took me by surprise since they knew that as an English teacher, I was not allowed to speak to them in our mother tongue. But I also understood why. They were afraid that I might not be coming back, and they wanted to share a moment of closeness that went beyond words.

So I thanked them, *Gamsahamnidah* . . .

Then I told them this, in Korean:

"Thank you for letting me be your teacher for as long as time allowed us. Thank you for teaching me so much more than I taught you. As long as I live, I will treasure each of your faces and names, one by one, in my heart, and from very far away I will always think of you, and wish you to grow up into real gentlemen. I want you to remember always that I am proud of each one of you."

Then I bowed the way Koreans do when we say goodbye. I knew that I would not be coming back and I could not stop my tears.

There was still so much I wanted to say, and moreover, I still felt horrible for letting them down, but I thought I could explain better later—my final lunch was reserved for Class 1, and dinner for Class 4.

WHEN I CAME down to the cafeteria at 11:30 a.m., I saw that most of them had finished lunch earlier than usual and were already leaving. A few students from Class 1 waved at me, however, and said, "Professor, please sit here. We will wait for you to finish your meal." One of them then explained that the entire student body had been summoned for a special meeting at noon. I did not ask what the meeting was about since they often had mysterious meetings in the afternoons.

They were still high from *Harry Potter*, which they thought was incredible. They especially loved the scene in which Hermione tells Harry that for Professor Snape's class, she has to finish writing an essay on werewolves. They found it funny that Hermione and Harry didn't like essays either.

But there was not much time to discuss Harry Potter, since they had to go to their meeting and were upset that I was leaving the next morning. One of them said, "We have been too sad for days that you are leaving us, Professor." They asked, yet again, "Professor, are you coming back next semester?" I told them that honestly, I really was not sure if I would be allowed back in their country, but even if I did not make it back, perhaps one day they would have access to the Internet and then we could Skype. They remained silent until finally one of them, who seemed deep in thought, said earnestly, "Perhaps I could become a delegate at the UN. Then I could come to New York and see you again in person!"

They got up for their meeting and were walking away when one of them turned and said, "When will we see you again, Professor? Face to face?" I burst out laughing at their childlike insistence and said, "Come on, gentlemen. I'm not gone yet and will be here for dinner! So see you then!" At that, they broke into smiles and walked off, and none of us had any idea that we would never meet again—*at least not like that.*

IT WAS A bit before noon when I headed back to the teachers' dormitory, stopping briefly by the clinic to visit a student who had fractured his ankle while playing basketball. I had been

checking in on him, since due to exams, his buddy was not
able to stay with him as much as usual. He could not participate in any meetings, and I knew this would upset him. His
face brightened when he saw me, and we talked about what
he would do during the break, but he kept bringing our conversation back to the same question: "So will you come back
next spring, Teacher?" Neither of us was aware that back at the
special meeting in the IT building, the entire student body was
watching the news announcement of Kim Jong-il's death.

It was about twenty minutes later when Martha knocked on
my door and said, "You must come to the meeting right now."
When I opened it she dropped her voice and whispered, pointing at the ceiling, "He's dead."

I ran to the special room where all the teachers were being
given the news, and I learned that the students, upon hearing
of the Great Leader's death, had rushed over in groups to the
Kimilsungism Study Hall. Our liaison informed us that if we
wanted, we could go there to pay our respects as well.

Back in my room, I turned on Chosun Central TV, which
showed the announcement on repeat. The anchor, wearing a
black *hanbok*, sat at her desk in tears, telling the news to the
nation. Kim Jong-il—General Secretary of the Workers' Party,
Chairman of the DPRK National Defense Commission, and
Supreme Commander of the Korean People's Army—had suffered a heart attack on a train, during a field guidance tour.
He had worked day and night and was fatigued both physically
and mentally, all brought on by his overwhelming concern for
building a powerful and prosperous socialist nation, his people's
happiness, Korean unification, and the independence of all the
nations around the world. He died at 8:30 a.m. on December
17 in Juche Year 100.

I looked out the window and saw some students coming

out of the Kimilsungism Study Hall, so I ran outside. When one of the counterparts saw me approach the building, he hesitated only momentarily before escorting me inside. I had never been inside before, and I learned later that no other teacher except for our liaison went there. In that moment, however, all I thought about was my students grieving. The dead man was their father, and the least I could do, I thought, as someone who had taught them for months and loved them, was to show my respect by acknowledging their sorrow.

Inside, I could smell incense burning. On either side of the huge portrait of Kim Jong-il, a few students stood in a row. This was a familiar sight; sons stood like this at Korean wakes to greet visiting mourners who came in and bowed and lit candles. I knew that I was to stand before the portrait for a brief moment of silence. There was no pressure for me to bow, and I did not. I saw no student weeping, but the mood was solemn and funereal. On the way out, I passed a few students, but no one met my eyes. They lowered their faces and walked straight by me. Throughout the afternoon, this was the way. I knew that they were somewhere on campus, but the place felt eerily empty. The few who were walking about never looked up. Even when they did, their eyes did not see me anymore. Dinner was canceled. It was announced that bread would be brought to the students' dormitory instead, and teachers were to eat whatever food they had in their rooms.

There was nothing to be done but finish packing my suitcase and watch TV, on which the anchor announced a ten-day period of mourning and gave details of the funeral that would be held on December 28. Every district capital would hold a memorial service, and all people were instructed to observe three minutes of silence per day. During this time, there would be an artillery salute and mournful horns from naval ships and the flag would be lowered. There would be no merrymaking of any kind, and no foreign tributes would be accepted. Each report ended with a reminder for the people to honor their late Great Leader by joining hands to assist Captain Kim Jong-un in continuing to build the powerful and prosperous nation.

I paced back and forth in my room. Even in reporting death, the messages on TV were circular, the same information and images repeated over and over. My flight was due out the next morning, and for a moment, I worried that it might not leave, since the entire country seemed to be shutting down before my eyes. There was no way for me to reach out to my students, and the night was long. I still had a pile of marked essays that I had meant to give back to them at dinner. But now it appeared that I would not see them again, so tucking the papers under my arm, I took the enclosed walkway to the clinic. It was utterly dark, and I passed no one. The clinic seemed empty as well, but in a dark corner, I saw a curled-up form sobbing on an air mattress. It was my sick student. He barely moved when I called his name, and I said nothing except to put the pile of essays next to his bed, telling him that I was sorry. He did not turn around.

AT 6:30 THE next morning, I ran to the cafeteria. The bus was picking us up at 7 a.m. for the airport, but I wanted to see my students—if they were there—one last time. They were indeed there, but they did not look up. Their eyes were swollen and red, and there was no expression on their faces. It was as though the life had been sucked out of them. I knew that I was no longer welcome among them in their time of mourning, so I took my tray and sat on the other side of the cafeteria, facing them. I looked and looked at each one of my beautiful boys, whom I knew I would not be able to see again. I watched them raise their spoons to their mouths. I watched them pick up their trays, and cast their eyes in my direction with no recognition, as though I no longer existed for them in this world that was now missing their Great Leader. Yet I continued facing them, just in case one of them looked up and noticed that their world had now changed, perhaps for the better.

Acknowledgments

I WOULD LIKE TO THANK THE FOLLOWING INDIVIDUALS AND institutions for their invaluable help and support in the writing of this book: Molly Stern, Rachel Klayman, Domenica Alioto, Suzanne Gluck, John Glusman, the John Simon Guggenheim Memorial Foundation, the Fulbright Scholar Program, *Harper's* magazine, the Open Society Foundation, the MacDowell Colony, and the Corporation of Yaddo.

Author's Note

THIS BOOK IS A REPORTED MEMOIR, BASED ON JOURNALS and notes kept beginning in 2002, when I first visited the DPRK; between 2008 and 2011, when I pursued the story of PUST; and throughout my stay in Pyongyang, from July to December 2011. Whenever possible, I wrote down or typed up events and conversations the day they occurred so that I would be able to reproduce dialogue verbatim. I have relied on some outside sources for verification: maps, photographs, and newspaper articles, both in Korean and English.

With the exception of James Kim, president of PUST, the names, and in many cases the identifying details, of the missionaries, minders, and students have been changed. In particular, I have sometimes blurred the identities of the students in order to protect them from reprisals. I have rendered all missionaries' names as Western, even though some had Korean names, so that they can easily be distinguished from the students.

In a few cases, I have altered the chronology of events. For example, the stories of a few of the field trips in the book are told out of sequence so that the narrative will flow more smoothly. Also, I first saw PUST in 2009, during a brief unveiling ceremony before the school actually opened, but I do not mention that here and drew on those impressions for my account of seeing PUST in 2011. My descriptions of the events themselves are unchanged and are told as accurately as possible.

For transliteration, I have used both the McCune-Reischauer system (used in the U.S. since 1937) and the Revised Romanization system (the official style in South Korea). Since the McCune-Reischauer system is more commonly used in English, many of its spellings are well entrenched. Two examples are my own surname, Kim, which would more accurately be transliterated as Gim, and the word *kimchi*, which should be *gimchi*. But Kim and kimchi are familiar, so I have used those spellings. However, when romanizing words that are less commonly used in English, I have used the Revised Romanization system, which is more accurate. Thus I spell Gwangsan with an initial *G* rather than a *K*.

The styling of place names in the book is also purposely inconsistent, depending on the prevailing style. I have used hyphens for words such as *province, mountain,* and *palace* in combined nouns: Chungcheong-do, for example, for Chungcheong province and Myohyang-san for Myohyang mountain. However, I have omitted the hyphen for Gyeongbokgung (Gyeongbok palace), because that is how it is commonly styled in English.

In Korean, when writing out full names, the last name always comes first, as with Kim Jong-il, Lee Myung-bak, or Kim Suki. In this book, I refer to the minders, the counterparts, and some of the teachers by their last names. With the students, however, I use either their full names with the last name first, as in Park Jun-ho, or their first names only, as in Jun-ho, since that was how I addressed them and how they referred to one another.

I do not pretend that this book offers a complete picture of North Korea, but I believe it offers a rare one. In the course of my career, I have traveled the defectors' common escape routes to China, South Korea, Mongolia, Thailand, and the Laotian border and interviewed more than sixty North Korean defectors as well as defection brokers and leaders of groups that aid defectors. This book, by contrast, seeks to capture a slice of the lives of the elites in the DPRK, the sector of society about which the least information is available, relying on my observations of and interactions with privileged young men aged nineteen and twenty. The sustained contact I had with my students at PUST is extremely unusual, and allowed me to glimpse a world generally closed to journalists and other outsiders. There were several unique circumstances that allowed for a fuller experience: the fact that PUST was in its first year of operation and still disorganized; the impending regime change, which seemed to make my students feel more vulnerable; the boys' youth and innocence; my position as their second foreign teacher ever; and the fact that I was a native speaker of Korean, which gave us a common language.

I have written this book with the knowledge that it will anger the DPRK regime, the president of PUST, and my former colleagues there. Although I am sorry to cause the president and faculty of PUST distress, I feel a greater obligation, both as a writer and as someone deeply concerned about the future of Korea, to tell the stark truth about the DPRK, in hopes that the lives of average North Koreans, including my beloved students, will one day improve.

About the Author

SUKI KIM IS THE AUTHOR OF THE AWARD-WINNING NOVEL *The Interpreter* and the recipient of Guggenheim, Fulbright, and Open Society fellowships. She has been traveling to North Korea as a journalist since 2002, and her essays and articles have appeared in the *New York Times*, *Harper's*, and the *New York Review of Books*. Born and raised in Seoul, she lives in New York.